Praise for *Recovery 2.0*

"Tommy Rosen is a true leader in the world of addiction recovery. In his book, *Recovery 2.0,* he offers transformational guidance for anyone ready and willing to release the chains of addiction. This book is a true service to the world."

— **Gabrielle Bernstein,** *New York Times* best-selling author of *Miracles Now*

"Tommy Rosen has written something extraordinary that is going to change the way people look at addiction and how to approach recovery from it. His rallying cry that we must bring the gifts of yoga and meditation together with the power of the 12 Steps is timely and important. And his emphasis on healthy food choices as part of any complete recovery strategy is cutting edge. As Tommy says, 'Get psyched. Your life is about to change.'"

— **Christopher Kennedy Lawford,** *New York Times* best-selling author of *Symptoms of Withdrawal,* activist, and actor

"*Recovery 2.0* is a must for anyone who has either struggled with addiction or knows someone who has. Tommy has a perspective on recovery that is ahead of the curve. This book will become your go-to so you can learn to thrive beyond addiction. If you want sobriety and fulfillment, this is your book."

— **Mastin Kipp,** founder of TheDailyLove.com

"In a field and subject matter littered with failure, Tommy Rosen and *Recovery 2.0* are paving a new way forward. Whether you or a loved one is struggling with any form of addiction, this book is a must read!"

— **Nick Ortner,** *New York Times* best-selling author of *The Tapping Solution*

"Tommy Rosen is a clear-seeing and compassionate teacher who has done the work himself and mastered the ability to help others do the same."

— **Rolf Gates,** author of *Meditations from the Mat: Daily Reflections on the Path of Yoga*

"Through his own journey into recovery and becoming a global yoga teacher, mentor, and guide, Tommy has made a tremendous contribution to all beings about the nature of addiction, the liberation through embodying the ground of our own being, and discovering the high of our own inner pharmacy. Highly recommended for all on the path to recovering our essential Self."

— **Shiva Rea,** author of *Tending the Heart Fire* and founder of Prana Vinyasa Flow and Global Mala Project

"*Recovery 2.0* is part memoir, part guidebook, and part love letter—written from a deeply caring and experienced friend, Tommy Rosen. Tommy's honest and direct storytelling helps us to understand the power of addiction and encourages us to be open to the varying tools, both traditional and contemporary— including yoga—that can end our addictive behaviors, while also understanding the internalized trauma that is core to both our dis-ease and our healing. I love this book and know that it will serve as a practical and spiritual resource for many on their path to recovery."

— **Seane Corn**, yoga teacher and co-founder Off the Mat, Into the World

"Anyone in search of holistic, sustainable addiction recovery will treasure this book. Birthed though the lived experience of his own addiction and recovery, Tommy Rosen has created an important resource for all affected by the dis-ease of addition."

— **R. Nikki Myers,** founder of Y12SR: The Yoga of 12-Step Recovery

RECOVERY

RECOVERY

2.0

MOVE
BEYOND
ADDICTION AND
UPGRADE
YOUR LIFE

TOMMY ROSEN

HAY
HOUSE

HAY HOUSE, INC.
Carlsbad, California • New York City
London • Sydney • Johannesburg
Vancouver • Hong Kong • New Delhi

Published and distributed in the United States by: Hay House, Inc.: www
.hayhouse.com® • *Published and distributed in Australia by:* Hay House Australia Pty. Ltd.: www.hayhouse.com.au • *Published and distributed in the
United Kingdom by:* Hay House UK, Ltd.: www.hayhouse.co.uk • *Published
and distributed in the Republic of South Africa by:* Hay House SA (Pty), Ltd.:
www.hayhouse.co.za • *Distributed in Canada by:* Raincoast Books: www
.raincoast.com • *Published in India by:* Hay House Publishers India: www
.hayhouse.co.in

Interior design: Riann Bender

"Comes a Time" by Jerry Garcia and Robert Hunter. Copyright © 1976 Ice
Nine Music Publishing Company, Inc. All rights reserved. Administered by
Universal Music Corp. (ASCAP)

Cataloging-in-Publication Data is on file at the Library of Congress

Tradepaper ISBN: 978-1-4019-4448-3

10 9 8 7 6 5 4 3 2 1
1st edition, October 2014

SUSTAINABLE
FORESTRY
INITIATIVE
Certified Chain of Custody
Promoting Sustainable Forestry
www.sfiprogram.org
SFI-01268
SFI label applies to the text stock

Printed in the United States of America

This book is dedicated to my teacher Guruprem Singh Khalsa.
You blessed my life and showed me the way from dark to light.
Were it not for your love and kindness, Recovery 2.0 would not be.
Thank you.

CONTENTS

ACKNOWLEDGMENTS

This book would not have been possible had it not been for the efforts, presence, and love of so many people.

Editorial

I want to thank Jill Mangino, one of the greats, for introducing me to Patty Gift at Hay House. Patty, thank you for giving me a shot.

To Cindy DiTiberio for helping me get a great first draft to Hay House.

To Sally Mason, my editor at Hay House, and Laura Gray for extra support—thank you for your great spirits.

I want to recognize Louise Hay, Reid Tracy, and the posse at Hay House for shaping and distributing words that change people's lives.

Personal

Prayers of gratitude going out to my parents, David and Ellen. Thank you for everything you gave to my life. Thank you for sticking by me. I hope you love this book. I miss you.

To my sisters, Julie and Karen—we came through something extraordinarily challenging and still love each other. I'm so blessed to have you in my life.

Tommy and Barbara, how could I ever thank you enough? With wisdom and love, you kept the light shining and all of us together.

To Peter, Emily, Wendy, Jimmy, Jody, Justin, Drew, and Mike. You have given me more strength and a sense of family than you could imagine.

To Aunt Arlene, Jami, Jimmy, Joby, Allison, Ben, Patty, Hy, Rachel, and Andi. Thank you for your love and support always.

To Neil H. and Rick R., and all my brothers and sisters on the path of recovery. You saved my life. There are no words.

Gratitude to Gabor Maté for his friendship and for writing the foreword to this book.

To Rolf Gates, Nikki Myers, and Noah Levine—thank you for lighting the way for so many to find and embrace yoga and meditation as a part of recovery.

Epic thanks to Robert Hunter, John Perry Barlow, and The Grateful Dead—your contribution to this book came in the form of hope, joy, insight, and love wrapped in musical notes that made my heart and spirit soar.

To Andrew, Bennett, Lea, Tim, Alex, Noel, Win, Cumby, Rudi, Christina, Mark Steve, Kevin, Mike, Susan, Chris, Gabe, Marc, Bowen, Max, Shane, William, Alfie, and all of my brilliant, dear, amazing friends from way back when. No one could possibly understand what we share. Oh my God, thank you.

Special message of gratitude to my pal and expert writer, Max Ludington, who assured me time and time again that I could actually write. Your words have meant so much to me.

To Mastin, for your friendship, support, and love, which arrived daily.

To Scotty, for helping me escape.

To Joe Tolson, Donna Zoll, Robert Jameson, Lou Fabale, Guru Singh, Danielle Schreiber, Jeremy Brook, Dani Scherrer, and a few dozen other gifted healers—thank you for keeping my mind and body together through it all.

And most important, I want to acknowledge my amazing wife, Kia Miller. I could not have sat still long enough to write even a single page without the salve of your love surrounding me as it has been all these years. Thank you for loving me so completely and for always believing in me. I love you.

FOREWORD

At age 21 Tommy Rosen enters the Galleria dell'Accademia in Florence, where stands possibly the greatest sculpture humankind has ever created. Tommy does his best to appear engaged, moved, inspired. In truth, he sees nothing and feels nothing. He is utterly lost in what, later in this powerful volume, he calls the "mental fog" of addiction. All he can think of is himself and all he longs for is an escape from that self—through cigarettes, drugs, or other people. It will be long years until he is able to free himself from the self-perpetuating cycle of addiction and self-loathing. Before he does, he comes near to destroying himself morally and even physically.

And now Tommy has given us what I unreservedly regard as the best book I have ever read on the subject of recovery from addiction.

What does it mean to recover? To recover is to find something, something we had lost sight of but which has always continued to exist despite our confusion, our despondency, despite even our determined efforts to destroy it. "In recovery from addiction," Tommy tells us, "you are recovering your identity so you can live according to your own unique Truth."

Like others before him, but with a uniquely clear vision, Tommy Rosen recounts his own journey from abject defeat to Truth, from despair to transformation, from darkness to wisdom. He does not sentimentalize recovery, nor does he try to warm our hearts or inspire our souls. He just shows the way it is: he tells the full grungy truth about the addicted state and his often painful and meandering path to healing. He is refreshingly candid about the sources of his addiction. Not escaping into the safe haven of genetic causation, he openly—and without blame—confronts the multigenerational pain in his family of origin that led to his own flight from the self. He opens our eyes to the fact that addiction is not primarily a dependence on this or that substance or behavior, nor simply a disease of the brain; it is a dis-ease of mind and soul.

Recovery 2.0 shows that full recovery has to be sought on multiple levels: physical, mental, emotional, spiritual, and even social. Do not read this book if you want an easy fix. Tommy delivers something much more real than that: clarity, profound honesty, and a path to live by.

He astutely summarizes what we may call the universal addiction story that, in one form or another, represents the worldview of every addicted person: "I am not getting what I need in my life and I do not know how to get it. I feel the world has let me down. No one seems to recognize or understand me." In short, my life is unlivable. I cannot live it, only *escape* it.

The addiction story goes hand in hand with what Tommy identifies as the "Frequency of Addiction." The insightful psychiatrist David Hawkins suggested that humans in various emotional states "vibrate" at certain frequencies, with numbers on the lower end of the spectrum being associated with feelings such as apathy and shame and numbers on the higher end with love and peace. Tommy's Frequency of Addiction, which leads people to "have a sense that something is lacking," creates a profound disconnection in them. They lose themselves and their intuition and thus live a life in which they are a "divining rod for difficulty, challenge, and pain." The essential insight here is that the energetic core from which we live will determine how our lives unfold. Consciousness is destiny. Beyond abstinence, Tommy Rosen's book explores and guides a transmutation of consciousness. "I learned the hard way," he writes "that one can recover from severe drug addiction and alcoholism but still live life in the Frequency of Addiction."

A great strength of this book, apart from the lucid, engaging, utterly honest, and self-revealing way it is written, is how clearly it illuminates and casts fresh light on familiar forms of treatment, in particular the 12 Steps. If you thought you knew and understood the 12 Steps, no matter whether you celebrated or critiqued them, I invite you to suspend your opinions until you read through Tommy's refreshingly candid discussion. It is penetrating in the most positive sense. In ways that only the most die-hard cynic could dismiss, he explains daunting concepts such as embracing our powerlessness in order to gain power or, for example, that "God thing" in the 2nd step. Yet Tommy does not see the 12 Steps as a panacea, the movement as flawless, or its teachings as complete. He is, one may say, a grateful but highly objective participant and advocate. "Don't let the 12 Steps become your life," he advises. "Get a life because of the 12 Steps."

As an addiction physician and a close student of addictions, I have had the experience of meeting recovered addicts and actually envying their history of degradation because, post-recovery, they radiate a presence and joy that, I feel, have eluded me. Sometimes I joke that maybe I should become a raging alcoholic so that I can go through recovery and find deep meaning in life. The truth is that, even though they are not presented as such, the 12 Steps can provide a stepping-stone to spiritual awakening. Tommy explains, "If there were no connection between the 12 Steps and addiction and they existed simply as a spiritual path for humanity, I believe many more millions of people would have found and embraced them."

Not all who go through the 12 Steps get the spiritual awakening this process is meant to provide. Even in recovery addicts often "hit bottom," which can lead to relapse. What Tommy so beautifully illustrates is that recovery is not an event but a process with its own ups and downs. What matters, in the end, is not how we fare or feel any one day, but what we are committed to in the long term.

Not surprisingly in a teacher of yoga, Tommy finds that the yogic path is an essential commitment in the long term. In this case, we speak not of the "hot yoga" that has become very popular or the many yoga classes that teach postural techniques, but of the very philosophy of embracing unity with truth. Here, as with the 12 Steps, Tommy is an unfailingly articulate and patient guide.

By means of such practices, and many others suggested in this book, we are taught and encouraged to rely on what Tommy calls the "infinite pharmacy within," the capacity of our nervous system to function freely, for our brain and glandular system to produce the natural body chemicals that induce states of pleasure, joy, and connection.

This book, the culmination of a life that took its author to the depths of despair and self-loathing before showing him the path to his own unique Truth, is now before us to help light our path. We are, in the end, left grateful for Tommy's suffering, for his struggles, for his courage, and for his generosity in articulating and sharing with us the hard-won wisdom he acquired on his journey to grace.

Gabor Maté, M.D.
author of *In the Realm of Hungry Ghosts:*
Close Encounters with Addiction

INTRODUCTION

ALL SOULS ON DECK

Addiction is the greatest social problem of our time. It causes damage, heartbreak, and emotional and physical scarring. It breaks up families and carries self-destruction in its wake. Addiction is responsible for a large part of crime and, consequently, our prison population. It underlies several of our most costly medical epidemics—type 2 diabetes and childhood obesity, to name but two. Addiction has no respect for age, gender, or race. It cuts across every socioeconomic classification.

While you may not be a fall-down drunk, addicted to painkillers, a gambling addict, a chronic pot smoker, anorexic, or addicted to porn, you likely struggle with addiction in other ways such as workaholism, overeating, shopping beyond your means, or engaging addictively with technology such as video games, texting, and Facebook. If you don't believe you suffer from addiction in any way, chances are you know and care about someone who does.

The cost to the individual is intense sadness, existential pain, and in the worst cases, insanity and death. To be caught in addiction of any kind is one of the loneliest experiences you can have. And what's really interesting is that the great majority of people

I've met who struggle with addiction are extraordinary people. Unfortunately, their gifts remain locked away in some space they simply will never access until they recover.

To a large extent, our society's understanding of addiction has been narrow in scope, focusing more on specific addictive behaviors than on addiction as a condition unto itself. We have lacked key perspectives about the causes, nature, and anatomy of addiction, which we will look at in detail in the pages ahead. Our methods of treatment have focused on psychological processes such as talk-based therapies, cognitive behavioral therapy, and group interaction and support, but we have largely missed the critical necessity of mind-body practices such as yoga, meditation, and other healing modalities. We have also missed the undeniable connection between addiction, the food we eat, and other lifestyle choices we make.

As is often the case in our treatment of dis-ease, we have been overly focused on symptoms rather than underlying causes and conditions. When the symptoms go away but the causes and conditions lie untreated, addiction in all its forms will come again like weeds in a garden. There will be the constant threat of relapse *even for those who have recovered from acute addiction.* Thus, addiction is more rampant today than ever before. Everyone is touched by this growing problem. The consequences of unchecked addiction are too great to overlook. We must work together to find a way to bring ourselves and our world back into balance.

There is a solution. Through my 24 years of addiction and 23 years of recovery, through personal experience, and in working with others, the tenets of Recovery 2.0, a holistic program and philosophical movement of recovery, have come clear.

From the Recovery 2.0 perspective, mind-body practices such as yoga and meditation are required if one is to heal from the disease of addiction to the fullest extent possible. In Recovery 2.0, we recognize a direct correlation between our diet and the volume of mental chatter and addictive behaviors we experience. Therefore, we consider our relationship with food to be one of the most important relationships in our recovery. The 12 Steps also play a major role in Recovery 2.0 philosophy, and part of the purpose of this book is to debunk misconceptions about the 12 Steps and share the best practices for navigating them.

You must consistently treat addiction on all planes of existence—physical, mental, emotional, spiritual—or you will miss part of the solution. *You have to go deeper within yourself to heal, all the way down to the soul level.* It is absolutely possible to do so. With proper attitude, direction, inspiration, and love, anyone can. Part of the challenge has been that we have not known how to do it. We have not realized that deeper levels of detoxification and transformation are available and are often necessary to uproot addiction and thrive in recovery.

It really comes down to this: addiction will do everything in its power to dismantle a person's life and then end it. Recovery, therefore, must respond with a powerful and holistic combination of elements designed to free a person from addiction so they can build an extraordinary life.

Addiction has been in my life for as long as I can remember. Early on, I discovered the real gateway drug available to children everywhere: sugar! Fueled by processed foods packed with sugar, I bounced off the walls throughout my childhood, finding epic distraction and addiction around every corner. Pinball, video games, and television were the addictive pastimes of the first 15 years of my life. These always competed with a much healthier obsession with sports, which provided me immense joy and kept me saner than I would have been without it.

My drug addiction began in 1980 when I was 13 years old. My best friend and I bought some marijuana on the street, smoked it, and got high. The resulting sense of relief and excitement was so compelling that from that moment until I had my last cocaine binge and headed to drug rehab at Hazelden in 1989, drugs and alcohol were a regular part of my life and at times completely dominated my experience. The end of my drug use was abject horror by anyone's standards.

But you've heard this story before. You've probably heard and seen the gory details of addiction's destructive power hundreds of times. There is nothing novel about the ravages of alcohol, cocaine, and heroin abuse. The novelty of this tale has more to do with what happened for me in recovery.

Like many people, I took part in what I now refer to as Recovery 1.0, better known as the 12 Steps. I went to meetings, I worked the program, and my life got a lot better. My enthusiasm, health, and energy came back. I started to get into really good shape playing sports, working out, and practicing yoga. My relationships with my family improved slowly yet steadily. I had great friendships and girlfriends and began to have more meaningful work opportunities. The positive effects of 12-Step recovery were being realized in my life, and it felt amazing.

Over time, though, certain behaviors that seemed acceptable in early recovery started to present challenging consequences. I found myself gambling and therefore had a badly skewed relationship with money. I smoked cigarettes, which caused me nothing but inner conflict. My relationships with women became more and more difficult. I carried tremendous tension and stress in my body.

Despite the fact that the 12 Steps had delivered me to a place beyond acute addiction—a miracle in and of itself—I was still mired in the Frequency of Addiction, which turns a person's mind-body system into a magnet for addictive thoughts, addicted people, and addictive behaviors.

This was frustrating and confusing. I had assumed that the 12 Steps were all I needed to handle anything life threw my way. I felt that I had done the necessary work to live the life I was being called to live, but this assessment was terribly wrong. I was headed unwittingly for a true spiritual ass-whooping. I would require additional tools to get deep enough into my body, mind, subconscious, and spirit to move through the stuckness I was feeling and transform myself into the person I needed to be. This was where my Recovery 2.0 journey began.

As you move through this book, you will walk down a path toward a realization of what Recovery 2.0 actually offers. In Part I you will be guided to look at addiction from a fresh perspective, investigate its roots, and follow the thread of addiction as it played out through the first 22 years of my life. In Part II you will investigate the current landscape of recovery and read a brief chronicle of my time in rehab and my entry into the 12 Steps. I will debunk some of the myths and mine some of the most helpful lessons of the 12 Steps so you can use them in your own work in Recovery 1.0. For those of you who have already done these steps, please do not skip this section. You may receive some important new insights before moving on to the "2.0" part of this book. In Part III you will see how I reached my bottom *within* recovery and understand why Recovery 2.0 was necessary in my life and why it might be in yours. In Part IV you will learn about the elements involved in creating your own Recovery 2.0 path, and you'll find a vision for attaining freedom through advanced recovery. And finally, in the appendices of the book you will find powerful tools and excellent resources to help you on your way.

This book may challenge your beliefs about addiction, recovery, and the 12 Steps. But in return, it will offer a vision of life beyond addiction and clarify the elements that will help you realize it. And I hope it will inspire you to go after it with all your heart. Please keep an open mind to these concepts. May they help you to move forward along your path toward contentment, fulfillment, and freedom! That is my wish for you.

PART I

A NEW UNDERSTANDING OF ADDICTION AND ITS ORIGINS

CHAPTER 1

ADDICTIONS AND AGGRAVATIONS

In my lectures, workshops, and retreats, I ask people to raise their hands if they don't think they are struggling with any addiction. Inevitably, several people's hands go up. I then lay out my definition of addiction: *any behavior you continue to do despite the fact that it brings negative consequences into your life.* I see people around the room mulling it over, and there are still a few who feel they are not struggling with addiction in any way. I tell them up front, "Look, you really want to find a way to be a part of this group and reap the immeasurable benefits of being an addict." People laugh and think I'm kidding. I'm actually quite serious. My designation as a person in recovery from addiction has given me endless gifts, not the least of which is a clear-cut pathway to an exceptional life. It has been like hitting the jackpot, though it certainly didn't seem like it at the beginning.

THE BIG SIX ADDICTIONS

Many people, when thinking about the word *addiction,* think about what I call the Big Five—drugs, alcohol, food, people, and money. Recently, the Big Five have become the Big Six, taking into consideration technology addiction. These are the most prominent areas where human beings get tripped up.

Drugs: "Drugs," of course, refers to illicit and prescription drugs and describes one of the biggest businesses in the world. The illegal global drug trade is estimated at $400 billion a year, and prescription drug sales are around $270 billion in the United States alone. We are taking an epic amount of drugs in this country and "despite being the birthplace of the global 'war on drugs' and having some of the harshest drug penalties, the U.S. has the highest marijuana and cocaine use rates in the world."[1]

Alcohol: Then there's alcohol, our society's pressure-relief valve, which is embraced in almost all social situations. Alcohol is so ingrained in our culture that it would be hard to imagine what life would be like without it. Yet each year 80,000 Americans die from some form of alcohol abuse, and alcohol is a factor in 40 percent of violent crimes. It is estimated that there are more than 20 million people in the United States who struggle with alcoholism and need treatment.

Food: When people are addicted to food, they have struggles with emotional eating, bingeing, anorexia, and bulimia. Food addiction is what we call a process addiction. One cannot just give it up like alcohol or drugs. Rather, we are in process with it all the time. Countless people struggle in their relationship with food. Nowadays, America is facing a new epidemic: obesity. And it has spread to our children! Now we have a country filled with obese children. It's a horror. This has led to the related epidemic of type 2 diabetes, which is painful, costly, and preventable.

People: Next in the Big Six is people, which naturally involves relationships, intimacy, and sex. There are three main relationships in life: to self, to others, and to God, Universe, Spirit, or whatever your word is for that (if you happen to have a word). Codependency is one of the most painful forms of addiction. It is my belief that underneath other addictions, we will often find codependency lurking. Nikki Myers, addiction expert and founder of Yoga of 12-Step Recovery (Y12SR), tells us: "Codependency is the disease of the lost self. It compels us to look outside ourselves to another person for fulfillment. It is the most common addiction and often is there beneath the other addictions."[2] Codependency has a lot to do with placing the needs of other people before our own and having difficulty setting healthy boundaries. There is also a strong theme of control in codependent relationships, where one person is consumed by the need to control the behavior of another person who is often afflicted with some other form of addiction.

Then there is sex addiction. Sex addicts use intimacy and their bodies to try and fill the emptiness they find inside. In the last decade, the Internet has added a particular twist to it all by making everything available to almost anyone, anywhere, anytime. It is simply too easy to hook up with someone you do not know and have sex. It is too easy to access Internet pornography. In our world today, if you struggle with sex addiction there is literally no escaping the availability of these things.

Everyone struggles with relationships and sexual issues. It is a part of the human condition, though perhaps addicts struggle more than the norm. People want more sex or a different kind. Some married people want the freedom to be . . . well . . . free. Others wish that their partners were more present with them. Still others are cut off from this part of themselves altogether. Some single people want to remain single and cannot understand why every time they sleep with someone things get so complicated. Other singles long for a deeper, more committed relationship. And then there are those among us who seek relief from the challenges of life through sex and relationships. They experience the release of the sexual act over and over again, but it never seems to be enough to do the trick. They are insatiable and off balance. It all originates with trauma and takes root in a suitable host.

Money: Money-related addictions include gambling, habitually being in debt, shopping, and overspending. A bad relationship with money leads to amazing suffering. I have seen people at my retreats raise their hands and talk about how they simply cannot stop shopping. Purchasing things makes them feel better, gives them a temporary sense of worth, and eases the discomfort they are feeling. Shopping, they will tell you, is how they pass the time. They cite boredom as a cause; it sets in like a plague and quickly becomes too much to bear. "I have to do or buy something," they explain. This is an addiction to having and doing. Must have, must do. A person in this state has a hard time finding peace.

Later on I will share my gambling story with you. For now I will simply tell you that one of the saddest moments of my life came after a long session at a blackjack table. I was sitting next to a man who had gambled with me through the night. I was suffering badly and didn't realize until the morning that his suffering was worse. He looked at me after losing thousands of dollars and said dejectedly, "You know, I've lost my family because of all this. My wife and kids have left me and I can't stop."

Technology: Contained within the very computer I am writing this book on is a universe of possibilities. In terms of knowledge, practically everything is accessible right here at my fingertips. If I want to learn how to build a car from scratch, I can do that. If I want to tune my guitar, instructions are seconds away. If I need quick investment advice or want to know something about a particular company, it's no problem.

The business opportunities that exist because of my computer are infinite. I can organize my financial life with online tools. I can trade stocks, check my bank account, and wire money. I can implement endless marketing, promotions, and sales initiatives 24 hours a day. And as a consumer, I am pleased to report that through my computer I can buy just about anything.

The social possibilities available through this computer are mind boggling. I can send any communication in seconds to anyone with access to an e-mail account, anywhere in the world. In real time, I can share my current experience via text and photos. I can make free telephone calls around the world that sound clearer than landlines. If I'm looking to meet someone and have a date, there are countless places online to do so. Let's say I'm sick but feel the need to go to a 12-Step meeting. The folks at InTheRooms.com have my back. Truly, the ways to engage in virtual relationships of one kind or another are endless.

As a person who struggles with addiction, I have had ample opportunity to observe the shift in my own behavior and that of others regarding the use of technology. Many people cannot remember the last time they went to the bathroom without bringing their cell phones with them. It seems like they are going to be missing something if they just sit on the toilet without a cell phone. Somehow, they feel an overwhelming sense of lack unless it's with them nearly all the time. I used to be this way. The cell phone was getting in the way of my being present for my life, and I had to change because this is unacceptable to me.

Almost everyone I speak to admits to having texted while driving a car. At this point, I turn my phone off and put it out of reach so I do not engage in this terribly dangerous activity. Driving while purposely taking your eyes off the road is absolutely insane. You are moving at high speed in a metal contraption filled with combustible liquid, and you deliberately avert your eyes from the road in order to respond to a text message? Wow! That text message must hold a lot of promise for you. And of course, it does; pulling you out of the relatively boring present moment, it offers you the illusion of endless possibility.

THE FOUR AGGRAVATIONS

After I run through the Big Six during retreats, I ask again if anyone in the room still thinks they are living addiction-free. Usually, a few folks still say they are. "Well let's take a look at the Four Aggravations," I suggest.

The Four Aggravations are negative thinking, self-doubt, procrastination, and resentment. These are *thought addictions*. When I introduce these, a few hands go up in protest. "Those are not addictions. Nobody craves those things." And that's true, but I remind them of my definition of addiction: *any behavior we continue to do despite the fact that it brings negative consequences into our lives.* The Four Aggravations are thought-based behaviors. You may feel that you have no choice in these behaviors, but, of course, that is incorrect, and by choosing to engage in them, you are continuing to engage in activities that do you harm. By my definition, that's addiction.

Negative thinking: Thoughts are more powerful than most people imagine. They affect the way we feel, the way we perceive things in the world, and even the way our lives unfold. Just think of the importance of having a good attitude and a positive outlook on life. Ask any athlete whether they feel it makes a difference to think they are going to win. People who are stuck in negative thinking will inevitably have a harder time in life. First of all, they don't enjoy themselves because they see the shadow parts of everything and miss all the beauty. They often have "bad luck" or are accident-prone. Of course, being accident-prone is no accident. These folks get sick or hurt because negative thinking has that effect. Negative thinking depletes your life force. It is a form of thought addiction that most of us have been caught in at one point or another. Some people are stuck there most of their lives.

Self-doubt: Self-doubt is negative thinking turned toward oneself. A teacher of mine once told me not to complete a negative sentence about myself, even in my head. I had long doubted my ability to find a mission and purpose in this world. I'd tell myself, "I'll never find my thing." I'd tried for so long that it seemed like it would never happen. I had the same destructive thoughts about my relationships. I thought I would never be able to find a loving, working relationship. Do you doubt your ability to love, to be loved, to complete things you've started, or to live a successful life? Self-doubt is a killer of motivation and a self-fulfilling prophecy that makes it hard to complete anything. It is a corrosive and sometimes unconscious dialog that runs counter to everything we would hope for ourselves.

Procrastination: Procrastination was one of my worst addictions as a child. Here's the self-defeating reasoning behind procrastination: "I'm not going to do what I need to do. Instead, I am going to try to distract myself from dreadful feelings, which are now growing inside me *because* I'm not doing what I need to do." When you stop and put procrastination into words, you really see the incredible absurdity of the reasoning. All you have to do is start doing what you have to do. Instead, you try to fix the feeling you have because you are not doing it.

Throughout my childhood, consumed by hyperactivity, which I further exacerbated with an atrocious diet, I'd get home from school on Friday nights with a lot of homework that I would swear to complete quickly. The thinking was to get it out of the way and clear the decks for a great weekend. But it just never happened that way. Most weekends would go by without me breaking into my homework. All the while, I had a nagging, obsessive voice in my head reminding me of the unfinished task at hand. I'd pack the weekend with sports, pinball, social activities, and television. Later on, I'd pack the weekend with partying, drugs, and alcohol. By Sunday evening I was totally overwhelmed to the point where I couldn't think straight. It always felt like it could never get done, so I didn't start. I'd go to school the next day and be behind for the whole week until I got to repeat the experience the next weekend. For me, there was a direct connection between procrastination and my desire to use drugs. I needed strong, mind-altering drugs to help me stop thinking about all the things I needed to get to but wasn't doing.

Resentment: That brings us to resentment. As the old adage goes, resentment is a cup of poison that you pour for someone else but end up drinking yourself. Breaking up the word resentment into two parts, re-sentiment, helps us understand that the word means to feel over and over again. Most people who struggle with addictions are swimming in resentments, though they may not realize the extent of it. The "Big Book" of Alcoholics Anonymous, the seminal text that launched all 12-Step programs, states, "Resentment is the number one offender. It destroys more alcoholics [read: addicts] than anything else." Working through resentments, therefore, is one of the main focuses of the 12 Steps. A person stuck in resentment perceives an injustice of some kind that simply won't go away. One of the people I encountered in my early recovery summed up his experience with it in a few sentences: "I broke up with my girlfriend. She went out with me for six months. I went out with her for two years."

Anything can cause resentment in us. The worst part is that, if left unprocessed, resentful feelings build upon each other and fester over time. There is no science I know of to back up this statement, but I believe that resentment is involved in the development of cancer and other degenerative diseases.

Do you have angry conversations with someone else while you are alone in your car? Do you have a feeling of venomous anger toward a situation or person that you find unacceptable? Maybe you feel resentful toward yourself; that's called remorse. Whatever the case may be, you cannot hope to live a great life without processing the venom of resentment out of your body.

Interestingly, the Four Aggravations are what fuel the Big Six. In almost all cases, if you track addiction back, you will find that the Four Aggravations were there first to varying degrees. Since all human beings are working on finding balance and homeostasis, it makes sense that if we feel these aggravations, we will try to address them. We will reach for things to feel better. If we are not hip to an upgrade to something other than using drugs, alcohol, and other addictive behaviors, we will turn to what is available and easy. And in our world, that's the Big Six.

CHAPTER 2

THE ROOTS OF ADDICTION

Addiction is fueled by an underlying state or condition of dis-ease. Please note that I have hyphenated the word "dis-ease" to bring your attention to the main characteristic of addiction: a lack of ease in your life. In the state of addiction, you lack ease, or, put another way, you are distant from ease. The point of recovery is to close the gap between you and ease.

People speak about drug addiction and alcoholism as the specific problem a person has. "He's an alcoholic. He cannot control his drinking." "She is a heroin addict. She's dependent on drugs." Yet the underlying condition of dis-ease is there first and then the behavior begins in order to address it.

For example, it is not fully accurate to say that my problem was with drugs. Yes, I took a lot of drugs and hurt myself quite badly doing so. Yet for a long time at the beginning of my using, drugs (marijuana in particular) were a solution to a problem that had been there for some time. They were my chosen medicine—my

method of dealing with the underlying lack of ease I was feeling—
and they worked. I felt that I had found a solution.

Nine years later, when I got to rehab, all drugs and alcohol
were removed from my life. Guess what was waiting for me:
my core issues, my condition, my dis-ease. Nine years of self-
medication had not, in fact, cured me. Masked by my "medicine,"
my issues had been patiently biding their time until the day came
when I would have to work them out.

If you struggle with drugs, alcohol, or other addictions, you
certainly did not begin with those problems. You may have been
trying to hide from one of the Four Aggravations. Or you may
have begun with curiosity and a spirit of exploration. Perhaps you
had a lot of fun at first. Later on, problems started to develop and
life began to pile up on you. The Four Aggravations intensified,
and at some point you developed a regular need for your chosen
medicine to "fix" how you were feeling. Enjoying the results that
drugs and alcohol produced, you concluded you had found the
right medicine for you. Ironically, you may have been correct for
a spell, except that no medicine can be considered truly healing if
its effects do not automatically render it obsolete in a reasonable
amount of time. In other words, if you smoke pot because that is
your chosen medicine when you are 15 years old, but then 2 or
4 or 20 years later you are still smoking pot, you might need to
inquire as to the effectiveness of that medicine.

The real question is: where does dis-ease begin? What are its
contributing factors? What leads to a chronic, systemic lack of ease
in your life that would cause you to seek relief from it in addictive
behaviors? To answer these questions, you must understand the
roots of addiction. Your personal history—birthplace, environment, early food choices, and the family circumstances into which
you were born—holds part of the key. In looking back, there you
can find two of the ingredients that will be critical if you are to
succeed and live an amazing life: understanding and compassion.
In the pages that follow we will take a close look at the roots of addiction. First, though, let's quickly address the genetic piece of the
puzzle. While this area of science is quite prevalent in discussions

concerning addiction, you will not benefit from spending much of your time here as a person seeking recovery. It will be much more important for you to understand what the young science of epigenetics is now telling us.

THE GENETIC MISCONCEPTION

Certainly, we are born into situations beyond our control that set the stage for our lives. The laws of karma, for example, led me to my mother's womb. I had no influence upon her beliefs, thoughts, or actions. I experienced her reality through the chemistry in her body. I was encoded with her strengths, challenges, habits, and memories. I had my own DNA, of course, which included my father's input, but while in the womb I was intimately connected to my mother via the amniotic fluid we shared. Amniotic fluid, which surrounds a developing fetus, is even flavored by the food a mother eats. A mother's food habits (and drug and alcohol consumption) will shape the future food preferences of her child.[1] Unfortunately for me, my mother depended on smoking and drinking alcohol to deal with the traumas and stresses in her own life. So as it turned out, my first addictions actually were my mother's addictions. But in my opinion, this has little or nothing to do with my genetic makeup and it has everything to do with the aforementioned environmental influences upon me while in the womb.

Many people look to genetics to account for and explain their addiction. It does seem to run in many families, and this would indicate that the genetic piece of addiction is an important one to consider. As an individual in recovery from addiction, I ask, "Why bother?" If you are genetically predisposed to addiction, you can't do anything about it. No point in worrying. Your time will be better spent doing the things you actually can do to make your life better and move ahead down your path.

Of course, we cannot change the genetic cards we are dealt. We have strengths and weaknesses, predispositions and tendencies.

However, the science of epigenetics is helping us learn that through our choices we can actually affect the expression of those genes, and this means we are not controlled exclusively by our genetic makeup. The work of cellular biologist Bruce Lipton outlines the idea that our perceptions control our biology. We are, to a great degree, the result of the environment around and within us, including our thoughts and beliefs; the food we eat; the media we watch; the toxins we encounter in our air, food, and water; the exercise we do; being in nature; exposure to sunshine; and our friends and family. These are the things that will set us up for health or dis-ease. The big takeaway is that *your genes do not control your life. You are not a victim, not even of your own heredity.* Dr. Lipton is often quoted as saying that this new biology moves you out of victimhood and into mastery. We participate more than we might imagine in the unfolding of our own reality. We have an innate ability to direct the flow of our life, whether in a more positive or a more negative direction. The good news is you are in the driver's seat. The challenging part of it is that you may have some work to do before you become a great driver.

Anyone can become a full-blown addict, regardless of their genetic makeup. Mistreat a human being—expose them to the ravages of trauma, abuse, loneliness, and insecurity—and voilà, you have an addict in the making. All you need now is an addictive substance or behavior that helps the person feel relief from what ails them. Conversely, anyone can avoid the fate of becoming an addict even if they are genetically predisposed for addiction. It will always come back to environmental inputs. Love leads to security, strength, and health. Trauma leads to dis-ease, which leads to looking away aided by some kind of addictive behavior.

So it turns out that when it comes to addiction, environment is the more important factor. And this also explains why addiction runs in families. Different members of a family end up sharing common environments and common traumas, and they can even pass these on from one generation to the next.

Let's look now at some of the inputs that can contribute to the formation of addiction.

14

THE ROLE OF FOOD

Your relationship with food directly influences the way you experience life. The connection goes much deeper than you may realize. Your energy levels, mood, thinking, actions, immunity against dis-ease: all functions of the body and mind are affected by the food (and water) you consume. Therefore, *any attempt to understand addiction that does not include a deep look at your relationship with food will be sadly incomplete.* It doesn't matter whether you are a drug addict, alcoholic, sex addict, compulsive gambler, or emotional food binger; there is an intimate connection between what you eat and how you think, feel, and behave.

Between the ages of two and eight, I had an English live-in nanny named Irene Murphy who took care of me most of each day. Rene, as we called her, had me hooked to the gills on strong black tea with lots of white refined sugar and milk. I began every single morning with a sense of excitement as I drank that tea. Shortly thereafter I felt a slight sense of depression from what I now know was a sugar crash. Though I didn't know it at the time, I was experiencing my first addictions: caffeine and sugar.

In addition to tea at breakfast, I ate mostly sugar cereals, including all the classics—Cap'n Crunch, Frosted Flakes, Honeycomb, Fruity Pebbles. Sometimes when I felt like it, I would even put sugar on top of these cereals! I often had bagels with butter or cream cheese, toasted white bread with butter and cinnamon and sugar, and a ton of grilled cheese sandwiches and pizza. All the milk I drank was pasteurized and came from cows that lived miserable lives on factory farms.

I ate any kind of meat: beef, pork, chicken, fish, as well as processed meats like salami and bologna. This was neither free-range nor grass-fed nor organically raised meat. I loved McDonald's. I ate an ungodly amount of Chicken McNuggets. I loved Chinese food, which, of course, was packed with MSG. I continuously sought out French fries, mashed potatoes, rice, and pasta with bottled spaghetti sauce.

I did eat fruit, because fruit also had what I was looking for: S-U-G-A-R, albeit in a more natural form.

And then there was junk food! I ate a ton of candy and was particularly fond of chocolate. I basically grew up on Coca-Cola. *Coke! It's the real thing.* Well, it was for me, one of my first and most detrimental addictions. I couldn't avoid drinking it whenever I could get my hands on it, and I couldn't stop drinking it once I started. So I had three to six Cokes a day.

If you look at this diet as a whole, you are probably horrified. I look at it and feel sad. Mine was the diet of an addicted child, and while my case may have been extreme, most kids in the United States today are consuming some version of it. What becomes of someone who eats like this?

Considering that nothing I put in my body was actually leading to health, I set myself up with a foundation of malnutrition. I grew up in a weakened condition and was susceptible to illness, allergies, and the dis-ease of addiction. There is a connection between what we take in and the behavior that comes out. Unfortunately, I didn't connect the dots at that point.

Since I was often sick, I took lots of antibiotics. I also struggled with monumental migraine headaches, living in fear of them for much of the first part of my life. I missed a lot of school, could not sit still or concentrate, was anxious and hyperactive. I had huge energy bursts and the tendency to crash because there was nothing in my diet that could sustain my energy throughout a day. I bounced off the walls throughout my childhood from one sugar event to the next.

Right around 14 years old, my peer group started to grow up but I did not. My body simply did not grow until late in my adolescence. I didn't really reach puberty until I was 17 years old and was always small for my age, a fact that I was terribly ashamed of and that caused me immeasurable heartache. There is no doubt in my mind that this was due, in great part, to my diet.

I had no idea that there was a connection between my diet and the health problems of my childhood, and that through very poor food choices I was setting myself up for a whopping problem with addiction as an adult. I now realize that *addiction is an opportunistic dis-ease attracted by weakness.* It will take advantage of a situation that presents itself, and if it can get a foothold, it will.

With this in mind, it is easy to understand how much of a role food plays in the formation of addiction. Later on we will learn that it is also a critically important part of overcoming addiction and thriving in recovery.

THE ENVIRONMENTAL AND CULTURAL CONTEXT FOR ADDICTION

The environmental and cultural context of your childhood has a big influence upon your life and will play a central role in your story of addiction. Growing up in New York City in the 1970s certainly played a major part in mine.

This period in the city's history was intense no matter who you were or where you lived. Anger, violence, and racial separateness were more pronounced than they are now. There was more crime and more corruption—among civic leaders, union leaders, the police, and more. The city's streets were covered with garbage and dog shit, with millions of pieces of chewed gum smeared into the sidewalks everywhere. People littered and spat. There were way too many homeless people around. Unfortunately for these people, the winters were brutally cold and the summers unbearably hot. People died all the time on the street. You'd hear about it and think, *How does something like this happen in a city like New York?* I'd see men and women with swollen legs and infections, mucus and coughs. It was a horror.

Drugs and drug dealers were everywhere, and I do not mean white-collar drug dealers, though they were present as well. I'm talking about dealing in the street. The spots closest to us were at "the Bandshell" in Central Park, up and down 86th and 42nd streets, and the "stores" in Spanish Harlem (a court of last resort for us white kids). The '70s were a time of excess. People let it all hang out. They partied hard. They hit the clubs en masse and made drugs like quaaludes infamous. Addiction was rampant.

I turned 13 in 1980; Ronald Reagan was about to take office and Nancy Reagan of "Just Say No" fame came along with him. But in New York City, you could buy any drug almost anywhere on the street. In addition, if you smoked pot in New York during the early '80s, you probably knew about "The Pope" and 777-CASH. These seven digits would get you to the largest, most successful door-to-door pot-dealing operation in history. It was incredible. You'd call the number. Someone would pick up. "Delivery. How can we help you? What's your address?" In 20 minutes, some dude on a bike would show up at your apartment building with your order: a marijuana bike messenger sent from heaven.

As teenagers, we thought this was the coolest thing imaginable. It was hilarious—the absurdity and convenience of it, the total nonchalance of the messengers, the phone operators, and, I imagine, The Pope as well. He ran this organization for years, putting away something like $50,000 or more a day.* The cops would make an occasional bust, and things would quiet down for a while: the phone number wouldn't work all of a sudden. You'd keep calling back, and eventually they'd pick up: "Delivery. How can we help you?" Incredible.

In those weird years in NYC there were a few notable Upper East Side gangs made up of random characters, thugs really, who simply existed to harass people. They had names like Fat Ali and they would mug you if they got the chance. I was successfully mugged twice, but there were at least five other instances where I got away. You had to know a few rules about how to avoid this fate.

For example, you simply didn't go into Central Park at night. If you went in there, you were asking for trouble. And so it was that one memorable night in 1980, my best friend, Andrew, and I rode our bikes into the park. I had a new ten-speed Metro, and I was so excited to have it. These two Puerto Rican guys, who were about 18 (we were 13), rode up to us on their own bikes. Man, they knew they'd hit the jackpot when they saw us. This guy came right up to me and said, "Yo, homeboy, get off your bike." Andrew took off and got away. I tried, but got thrown off the bike. Then this dude picks up my bike onto his shoulder and rides away with it into the night on his own bike. The whole thing was over inside of a

---

* This was a figure we heard in discussions with the bike messengers or in the media at the time.

minute. They just took off, and I never fought back. I'm not sure what I could have done, but in retrospect I wish I had done something. I came away from that experience feeling powerless and incapable of taking care of myself. When I got home and told my mom what had happened, she got mighty pissed off at me for riding into the park in the first place—and that was all the processing we did around that incident.

Andrew and I, meanwhile, went right to the phone book and looked up Johnny Kuhl's Combat Karate. We intended to learn a thing or two so the next time some guy put my bike up on his shoulder and tried to ride away, I could knock him out with a roundhouse kick to the temple. Whatever qualities or support I needed to follow through with that effort, however, were not available to me at the time. I never made it to a single class.

It felt to us like the whole city was getting high and for good reason. What else could anyone hope for in a city that was bereft of values and was left to people like The Pope, who could drug it into a more manageable state? People didn't feel well. There was a lot of suffering around, and, as we do, people reached for something to feel better. Some very large percentage of the population needed something—cigarettes, marijuana, alcohol, pills, cocaine, or heroin—to cope with what was going down in their world.

All of this made growing up in New York City a mixed bag. On the one hand, you felt that you were privy to "the real world," and there was definitely a sense of pride that went along with being a city kid. At the same time, I really didn't like living there. Yes, there were theaters, movies, the arts, culture, and diversity, but the city and its madness were an outward representation of my own disconnection within.

I'm not blaming New York for creating my addiction. Nor am I suggesting that every person living in New York in the '70s and '80s was an addict, though sometimes it seemed that way. As the brilliant saying goes, *consciousness is contagious*. We tend to "catch" the consciousness of what is around us. We are susceptible to our surroundings and the "vibration" of the people we spend time with. New York City just happened to be a great place for addiction to take root. .

THE POWER OF FAMILY

My life up to about age five is unknown to me except through the recollections of my now deceased parents, David and Ellen; my two older sisters, Julie and Karen; my "nannies"; and my aunt and uncle, Barbara and Tommy.

What I know from their accounts is that when I was born, my home was filled with turmoil. My mother and father were approaching the end of their time together. Part of my infancy was to experience yelling and the anger and sadness they projected onto each other. They were in chronic emotional pain and had no tools to help guide them out. From here at 47 years old, I am filled with compassion for them. They were up against a lot.

My mother, Ellen Rosen (née Ellen Israel), was born in 1940 and grew up in a financially well-to-do family in Stamford, Connecticut. Mom was an exceptional woman in many ways. She was highly educated, amazingly well read, very capable, and funny. Her greatest flaw was low self-esteem, which is ironic because her intellectual capacity was enormous, and beneath a protective icy exterior lay a heart of gold.

Her father, Ace, a shrewd and successful businessman, was the patriarch of our family. Her mother, "Lovey," as we all called her, was more or less absent from my childhood.

Ace was a male chauvinist to the core and liked to be in control of things, a fact that was evident across all areas of his life. He was high in business acumen but lacked a lot when it came to family matters. Whereas in business Ace had put together some incredible deals for which he would become legendary among his peers, his claim to fame as the patriarch of our family was to divorce his wife, Lovey, and marry her sister, Helaine, less than a year later. This caused a 30-year rift in our family. To emphasize the effect of this on my mother's life, try to imagine the following:

As a student in high school, my mother came home one afternoon in 1954 to find that her parents, who had been separated for almost a year, were suddenly divorced. On top of that, she was told that Ace had married her aunt, thus confusing her relationship with her first cousins, who were now her step-siblings. It still makes my head spin trying to figure it all out. Here's the roughest part: The whole matter was never to be discussed. No one could bring it up. No one could express anything about it. No processing of any feelings at all.

Even as a young child, I had already figured out a few things about Ace. He was intimidating and aloof, at least to me. He had a lot of money and because of this he had some kind of power over my mother, and therefore over my sisters and me. Though no one ever said it out loud, we never went to visit Ace out of love or appreciation. It was always obligation. We had to go. It was as if some terrible fate would befall us if we didn't show up. That terrible fate, of course, would be to lose access to Ace's continued financial support or to miss out on the possibility of some future payout.

My mom and Ace never got along. He did everything in his power to exact control over her and she did everything in her power to prevent it. At 18 years old she ran off in defiance of him to marry her first husband. She got pregnant the next year and had my sister, Julie, shortly after her 20th birthday while attending Barnard College as a sophomore. That marriage didn't last long, and suddenly my mother was a single mom at the age of 22.

I have very few memories of my grandmother Lovey. She was not, in my recollection, a particularly warm person, but in comparison to Ace she may as well have been Amma, the hugging saint.

Like my mother after her, Lovey was an epic smoker: three to four packs a day. Chain-smoking—finish one, light another. I recall the day Lovey died from emphysema in 1977. I came into my mom's room and she just flat out burst into tears and held me in her arms. I felt the depth of the loss for her. I felt her desperation. My mother loved and needed her mother very badly. Frankly, her grief and sadness freaked me out. I wanted to fix it, but there was nothing I could do. She had lost her mother and her father was Ace.

My father, David Rosen, was born in 1930 in New York City to first-generation American-born Jews. Dad was a lover of the arts and had great taste. He knew and loved painting, sculpture, theater, and music. He was affectionate and caring, with a great sense

21

of humor. He, like my mother, suffered from dreadfully low self-esteem and emotional challenges that would get in the way of his happiness and tremendous potential.

Truly salt-of-the-earth people, my father's family was markedly different from my mother's. For one thing, they were poor. Life with them contrasted strongly with life on my mom's side of the tracks. What they lacked in funds, though, they made up for in warmth. They hugged, squeezed, and loved the crap out of you whether you liked it or not. There was a Jewish doting ritual that went on every time we showed up to my grandparents' home. First, they spent ten minutes telling us in English interspersed with Yiddish how much we had grown and how beautiful we were. They hugged us and passed us around to each other for more love. They pinched our cheeks and called us *tatala* and *bubele*. It was amazing to be loved like that, albeit a bit over the top. Family was everything to these people. *Everything!*

You could not find two people or families who were more different in the way they lived and understood the world than my parents. Yet in 1962 at a dinner party, Ellen and David did in fact meet, and they fell in love and got married. They would have my sister, Karen, in 1965 and then have me in 1967, but it was not until 1968 when I was one year old that my father decided to tell my mother that he was gay.

This would be a shocking revelation to any spouse in today's world, but in 1968, before the gay rights movement, and for someone with my mother's backstory, this was inconceivable and irreparably devastating. She still had hopes in those days of proving herself to her father, and this new revelation that she had married a "faggot" (Ace's term for my father) was not going to help her sense of self-worth.

I cannot imagine my mother's incomprehension as my father told her that he was gay. What did that mean? Was he sleeping with men? Why did he marry her? Was he bisexual? How could she ever save face with her family and friends? Her shame must have been immense: equal, I imagine, to my father's. He was pretty much ostracized after that. There was really no coming back from it.

This was the situation into which I was born: a lot of tension, sadness, and anger in our home that went on for years. At the same time, I had plenty of great times in my childhood. I went to top schools, had wonderful friendships, went to summer camp, played a lot of sports, went on trips, and had all my material needs met. Both my parents loved and always wanted the best for my sisters and me. Yet just beneath the surface there was always a sense that something was dreadfully wrong. Like an itch you could never scratch, this nagging feeling plagued me throughout my childhood.

THE INHERITANCE OF TRAUMA

There is a reason addicts behave the way they do. Addiction comes from somewhere; it is not random. Addiction has its origins in trauma, often from early childhood or even from prenatal experiences in the womb. Dr. Gabor Maté, the renowned physician and author, tells us that addiction is "rooted in childhood loss and trauma" and is "nothing more than an attempt to self-medicate emotional pain."[2] It doesn't have to be a huge trauma, just something painful, threatening, or confusing that you look away from or are unable to process when it happens, leaving its energy stuck in the body.

What I've come to realize is that *all dis-ease, including addiction, is caused by constipation in one form or another*. This could mean constipated bowels, blood flow, or some kind of stuck energy. Whatever the case may be, when there is blockage there is dis-ease. *Healing begins by removing those blockages.*

The concept of energetic blockages and how they affect us is beautifully illustrated in Peter Levine's amazing work on trauma. Levine offers the possum's behavior as an example of a healthy way to manage traumatic experiences. One of this creature's survival mechanisms is to play dead in order to avoid being killed when predators approach. After it has successfully deterred an aggressor, a powerful biochemical reaction related to fear, instinct, and survival takes place within its body. The possum has built up an enormous amount of emotional energy inside, and to release this, it shakes vigorously. The shaking lasts maybe a minute, and when it ends, the chemistry of fear and trauma exits its body and permits the possum to return to a state of balance. Levine writes, "Animals in the wild instinctively discharge all their compressed energy and seldom develop adverse symptoms. We humans are not as adept in this arena. When we are unable to liberate these powerful forces, we become victims of trauma. The result, sadly, is that many of us become riddled with fear and anxiety and are never fully able to feel at home with ourselves or our world."[3]

As the insightful saying goes, *your biography becomes your biology.* Both of my parents, as you now know, carried a lot emotionally. These emotions in the form of trapped energy were in the tissues of their bodies—in their muscles, joints, and organ systems. They remained unprocessed from the moment they got stuck there as the result of some experience. And they produced the most awful emotional and physical symptoms. They breathed poorly. They moved poorly. They ate poorly. And they felt poorly. You would not necessarily have noticed this level of dis-ease. Certainly, later on, when my dad got very heavy and sick, it was noticeable. Yet even *they* didn't realize what was going on; they had a low level of awareness and sensitivity to their plight. By the time they took notice it was too late. They had missed many signs along the way, and this is how most people live: disconnected from their bodies and their intuitive selves.

I've come to understand that the roots of my addiction *are* the stuck emotional energies that were lodged in my parents' bodies and never got worked out. Instead, these were passed down to the next generation. They were as much my inheritance as my ability to run fast or my brown eyes. I would develop my own version of those stuck emotional energies, and I would have to find a way to work them out (as we all must) in my life.

I cannot say it any more plainly than this: feelings left unprocessed are buried alive! They will act as an energetic blockage to your happiness and health. Later, these energetic blockages will cause a variety of emotional and physical symptoms, which will get more and more serious unless you shift onto a path of healing. This is one piece of the puzzle of healing addiction and dis-ease in general. The challenge is that, as addicts, we have developed a strong reflex to avoid pain, insecurity, discomfort, and sadness. We look away by any means necessary. In the final analysis, addicts of any kind are primarily addicted to looking away.

CHAPTER 3

PERPETUATING ADDICTION

It has been very helpful to me in my recovery to look at addiction as an entity unto itself with specific characteristics and predictabilities. I have sought to understand its personality, its likes and dislikes. We've looked at the roots of addiction and understand more about where it originates. Now let's turn our attention toward the elements that perpetuate it. Why is it so hard to let go of behaviors that are so clearly to our detriment? There must be very powerful forces involved that would cause us to hurt ourselves again and again. And in fact, there are.

THE FREQUENCY OF ADDICTION

Everything in the universe vibrates. Of course, you are no different. Think of your body-mind system as a tuning fork that vibrates at a certain frequency, which is influenced by all inputs from your life: family, friends, education, culture, food choices, media choices, personal habits and lifestyle choices, deeply held beliefs, thoughts, and more. As you change the inputs, your frequency—the way your cells vibrate—will change as well. This is subtle yet very profound.

Addiction carries a frequency all its own. If your mind-body system is attuned to the Frequency of Addiction, you will be under the influence of the energy addiction brings. It will affect the way your entire reality unfolds for you. Your thinking will skew negative and feel quite loud, if not completely overwhelming at times. You will have a sense that something is lacking, and you will be disconnected from your body and intuition. This means that the decisions you make may not be in your best interest. Instead of living a life that attracts harmony and flow, you will be like a divining rod for difficulty, challenge, and pain. You will feel like you are swimming upstream in life. These are the conditions from which anyone would seek refuge. And, oh my God, have I been there!

I will share with you an experience I had in Florence, Italy, when I was 21 years old. Keep in mind that by this point, I had been "seeking my refuge" in drugs, sex, and other distractions for about eight years. I had just finished a semester abroad in Cannes, France, and had come to Italy, where I spent several well-intentioned but disconnected days with my mother. She had returned home, and I would have about 36 hours to myself to explore Florence before heading to meet up with my girlfriend at her home in Thessaloniki, Greece.

Florence is by all accounts a magical city. If you are interested in painting, sculpture, and architecture, you could not hope to be in a better place. I arrived in the morning and checked into a small yet comfortable hotel room. I planned to walk around the city, stopping in museums, churches, and cafés, seeing the sights and eating some great food. What an adventure!

Coming down from my hotel room around 10 A.M., I began to feel a bit uneasy, maybe a little lonely all of a sudden. I asked the concierge how to see Michelangelo's famous statue of David at the Galleria dell'Accademia, and he suggested I take a cab there. On my way out of the hotel, I bought some cigarettes, Marlboro Reds.

They tasted different from the American version, but they served their purpose.

Cigarettes gave me an identity. They helped me portray an image that, suddenly, I very badly needed to portray. The image was something like this: "I am a foreign traveler in this city. I am intriguing, fun, and not afraid. I have it together. If you are a woman, you'll want to go to bed with me. If you are a guy, you'll want to hang out with me. I'm cool. It's cool. It's all good." Cigarettes also served another purpose, which on this day was very important: they helped to pass time.

I arrived at the Galleria dell'Accademia and lit up a smoke outside. I started to think about where I might find some pot in a city where I knew no one. For the past eight years, I had never been far from marijuana, and my semester abroad in Cannes was no different.

Inside the Galleria I navigated to the statue of David. I did everything I could to appear as if I knew what I was looking at, I was moved deeply by it, and I had some kind of preternatural understanding of this piece. But the unavoidable fact was that I couldn't have cared less about this statue. I was consumed by my feeling of dis-ease. *What are people in this hall thinking of me? How do I appear?* I was so cut off from any inspiration that it was painful to try to pretend otherwise. Yet I held what I felt was a look of deep curiosity and knowing as I looked at David.

When the truly disturbing negative thoughts started to come, they stuck to me like flies on molasses. I could not get away from them. *What are you doing here all alone? You can't even enjoy yourself in this amazing place. Everyone else is having a blast. They're loving it. Not you. You're miserable . . . and so alone.*

I had no idea why these horrible thoughts were bombarding me. I was in a beautiful city, but I might as well have been in hell.

Smoke a cigarette, Tommy, I thought. *Good, I'll go outside.*

Heading toward an exit, I passed extraordinary works of art, feeling all the more insignificant. An astonishing wave of worthlessness came over me. It was horrible. I didn't feel as if I belonged anywhere. I started to become inwardly desperate. My breathing became shallow and the chemistry of fear began to flow steadily through me.

I did what I could do to catch anyone's attention, but it was as if I had a visible plague that everyone knew to avoid. I stared at every attractive girl I saw, trying to get her to look at me. Perhaps we would have a conversation, which would lead to a meal and then sex and then I'd be okay. But I wasn't okay. I was having a panic attack.

I headed back to my hotel, went upstairs, stripped down, masturbated, showered, and decided to start the day again. Sitting at the edge of my bed, though, I could feel that the thoughts were not subsiding. With each passing moment I felt more and more like a loser stuck in a hotel room in a beautiful city with no ability to simply have an enjoyable day. What was wrong with me? What was I going to do to occupy myself for the next 36 hours before I headed to Greece?

A few blocks away from the hotel, there was a post office with a bank of phones inside. You could pay at the counter to call anywhere in the world. I thought of calling my girlfriend, but what would I tell her? I had no idea what was happening. But I knew I needed to talk to someone to be relieved of this madness. I started to call everyone back in the U.S. whose number I knew by heart. Maybe it was the time change or just bad luck, but no one was picking up.

Suddenly I remembered that a dear friend of mine was traveling in Europe—Germany, I thought. I called her home in New York to see if there was some way I could get her number in Germany. Her mother picked up, but unfortunately, she didn't have a way to connect with her daughter at that point. I pressed to get any information I could, because by that moment I had made the decision that I would travel to fucking Germany if I had to in order to be with someone I knew.

All in all, I spent about 90 minutes in the post office trying to connect with someone, but I struck out. As I wandered the streets like a schizophrenic, my outward demeanor was relatively calm, but inside I was completely freaking out. I was vibrating with the Frequency of Addiction.

The next thing I thought about was *food!* Yes, I would go and eat a ridiculously expensive dinner somewhere, and I would drink a lot of wine at that meal and I would feel better. I found just the spot and hunkered down at a table to begin what was probably a two-hour solo feast.

There were multiple courses, all very good, and an amazing bottle of red wine, a 1977 Barolo that they decanted for me at my table using a candle as backlighting. This was culture. I felt special, relieved for a moment.

I got drunk but not drunk enough. I rolled out of the restaurant, smoked a cigarette, felt a bit nauseated, and got a cab back to my hotel. It was only six in the evening, but I was done for the day. I stripped down, got into bed, masturbated again, turned on the TV, and eventually fell asleep. My glorious day in Florence had come to an end.

THE UNDERLYING "ISM"

I would not fully understand what happened to me that day for a long time to come. Now I consider it to be one of the most important days of my life because of what it taught me about the conditions that underlie addiction.

In recovery circles, people often use the suffix of the word alcoholism, the "-ism," to describe the irritability and discomfort that plague most addicts. "He's got the -ism," one might say about a person who is struggling with that underlying condition of restlessness. This feeling compels a person to reach for something to feel better. Even if you know you have a problem and want to stop, this sense of dis-ease is incredibly difficult to sit through. If you do not have help to get out of it, you will reach for whatever is around you to shift this dreadful feeling.

I spent my childhood using kinetic activity, television, movies, sports, sports trading cards, pinball, video games, and sugar-filled food to distract me every possible moment. I was always active and never alone. I only knew myself in relation to other people. What people thought of me was what mattered. I had no idea how to look inside and get to know myself. I had never developed the capacity to be alone. That day in Florence at 21 years of age was the first day I had ever been alone in my life.

Long before drugs and alcohol entered the picture, I already had a sense of insecurity and discontent. These feelings are hard to pin down in the moment. Something feels wrong, but you can't point to anything in particular that, if it were fixed, would make you feel better. It's like you have a feeling that you forgot something important and it's nagging you. A friend might console you and ask, "What's the matter?" You'll say, "There's really no problem. Everything's okay." But you know that there is something wrong and it grows in importance with each passing second. It's a kind of madness. It's the "-ism."

By the time I was 21 and had that day in Florence, my sense of discomfort had grown quite a bit. I was fine as long as I had people, girls, drugs, adventures, excitement. I had been successfully avoiding the -ism for so long that I had forgotten I was still vulnerable to it.

Yet the minute I was alone, the -ism came out to mess with me. I could not sit comfortably with myself. Much later on I would realize that the day in Florence was a snapshot of a young man perfectly attuned to the Frequency of Addiction.

THE ADDICTION STORY

There is another extraordinary force that helps perpetuate all addiction. I call it the Addiction Story. This is the story you tell yourself that builds the case for continuing your addictive behavior. Every addict has one, and it must be disproved if one is to move out of addiction. Without knowing it, addicts repeat the Addiction Story to themselves internally, a negative mantra over and over again. Like a twisted shaman, they repeat the words and keep themselves locked into a certain way of being, suspended like a piece of metal equidistant between two identical magnets. This story gains momentum over time; such is the power of storytelling and myth. The Frequency of Addiction supports and is supported by the Addiction Story. One cannot thrive without the other.

The body-mind system's search for balance and homeostasis is constant. The system seeks the middle way. If we move too far in one direction the system will make choices to move us back. However, when we find ourselves in the Frequency of Addiction, this natural move toward homeostasis is overridden. To be stuck in our Addiction Story is no different from being possessed by a demon who has taken control of the system. System override! The demon does not have your best interests in mind—it just wants to feed itself. It uses all manner of tricks and tools to continue to force the system to support its agenda. It co-opts your mind and puts it to good use by creating the most vivid, splendid, and realistic story, one so intricately woven that you will die to uphold it. Thus the machinery of denial is constructed. Denial—the constant vigilance to not know what you know. It takes an unbelievable amount of energy to keep it up. What an astonishing dis-ease addiction is!

The demon does not take over quickly. It's not like in *The Exorcist,* where one day you are a child of light and the next day you are full-blown possessed. Rather, it is gradual. The invitation for the demon to come is made long before it arrives in full force, and once it is there, the addict's recitation of the Addiction Story grows in volume and power. As Samuel Johnson is said to have written, "The chains of habit are too light to be felt until they are too strong to be broken."*

Once I found marijuana, I began to create my Addiction Story, gathering up evidence to convince myself (and everyone else) that my story was true. My story's basic premise was that marijuana was a necessary ingredient for me to succeed and enjoy my time in this world. With each enjoyable escapade or warm connection I made with a fellow pot smoker, or a girl I hooked up with who smoked pot, I added to the body of evidence. *This is cool. This is for me. I choose to live with this substance as a central part of my life.* So, if

---

* Samuel Johnson, the lexicographer and man of letters, penned something similar to this in 1748.

that was the choice I made for years and years, what was going on beneath that choice? What was actually there beneath the illusory tale known as the Addiction Story? At the deepest level, the real story went something like this:

I am not getting what I need in my life and I do not know how to get it. I feel the world has let me down. No one seems to recognize or understand me. I feel confused, insecure, angry, and sad, like a victim of circumstances beyond my control. I do not trust that the earth and its inhabitants are ever going to provide what I need in this life. Therefore, I am going to take what I need by whatever means necessary. I am building a world that makes sense to me. In this world, marijuana (substitute any drug or addictive behavior here) is king. It brings me a sense of ease, joy, and laughter. It makes me feel cool and different, and it gives me a sense of myself that I love. It has given me a community of peers who get me, and the ability to attract girls. I have found something that genuinely makes me feel better and I don't want it to be taken away *ever!* I will do whatever I can to maintain my story that this is the correct path for me because if I don't, the truth is that I have no idea how to get through life without it. I am not enough. I feel powerless in this world. My heart is broken.

Given this story and all the intricacies of its tenets, it is not hard to see why it is so difficult to break through the armor-plated walls of denial. Behind every addiction is a story. And addicts are the best of storytellers. It is damn near impossible to disprove a story to someone who still wants or needs it to be true. That was certainly the case for me.

Without any knowledge of a better way, without the capacity for honest self-reflection to review my actions and their consequences for my life, having shut out all outside information (unless it directly supported my story), I started to get further and further away from myself and the things I cared most about. My

Addiction Story became at once more bolstered and more desperate. It was so critically important to my ego not to let go of the story.

If you've ever been stuck in a dysfunctional long-term relationship, you can understand the idea of sticking with something despite the fact that it is not working. You focus on the parts of it that still work or, if those are gone, you reminisce about them and hope they will return. You explain away the parts of the relationship that do not work because you remember how things were in the beginning. "Well, things aren't so bad," you tell yourself. Perhaps you peer into the future and imagine yourself (a little older) without your "partner" and all you can see is loneliness and sadness. Thus, trapped in fear, you come to the unhealthy conclusion that everything is just fine the way it is, and what could you have been thinking was so bad in the first place? You look away from Truth and stay stuck a little longer.

CHAPTER 4

"FORMATIVE" YEARS

Often when I speak to people about drug addiction, they are expecting a diatribe about the horrors of advanced addiction much like what we see in movies or on TV. So it is surprising for them to hear me share stories about what it was like before it got that bad. I share about the times when it was good, when life was flowing and some of the most memorable times of my teenage years were taking place. These were my formative years, and drugs had a profound and lasting influence on my personal development. It wasn't all good or all bad. I had great times and I had painful times. The main point is that my relationship with drugs changed over time and ultimately became unsustainable and life-threatening. In looking back, we can see where the momentum got started and learn a lot about the way addiction unfolded in my life.

ALCOHOL

I grew up on East 70th Street in Manhattan in an upscale apartment building. In the living room was a liquor cabinet that was always well stocked. Mom's drink was Dewar's Scotch whiskey and water. While Mom drank regularly, she was more of a good-time party girl than what one thinks of as a hard-core, raging alcoholic. She could tie one on and loved it, but it was rare that I remember seeing her truly fucked up.

There was, however, one night where she came home a bit drunker than on other nights. She came into my room to put me to bed. I was about ten years old, and I smelled cigarettes and alcohol on her breath, which was nothing new. But she was slurring her words. I realized she was a bit out of control and trying hard to conceal it.

I said, "Mommy, are you drunk?"

She slurred back, "I'm just a little tipsy. That's all."

The most amazing fear came over me. I wasn't safe. My mom was not really there. If something were to happen, she would not be able to protect us. It unnerved me. She kissed me good night and left the room. As was my habit, I pulled the covers over my head in such a way that they covered my eyes but I could still breathe. For a long while now, I had been having these terrible visions of a black knight coming to cut off my head. I knew it was going to happen. I just didn't want to see it coming. As long as I kept my head under the covers, I would be able to die without having to see it coming. Occasionally, I would be so frightened that I would bound out of bed, run to Rene's room, and stay there until the fear passed. Rene, my nanny, was tough, but loving, and very consistent. I could always count on her.

That liquor cabinet stayed full throughout my childhood and it carried no particular weight in my mind. It was a part of my mom's life. It was synonymous with fun, parties, and being social, but also with weirdness and fear. I didn't hit it up until I was 13 years old, hanging, as always, with my best friend, Andrew.

Andrew and I had known each other since we were five years old, but our friendship really began in earnest when we started comparing notes about our parents and childhoods. Suddenly, I had someone to talk to who also carried heavy feelings about the way things had been at home. We shared honestly and deeply with each other from the get-go, and what formed between us was a powerful, lifelong bond. Andrew was my running partner through the brightest and darkest moments of my childhood. And naturally, he was there the first time I drank alcohol.

On the evening before Mother's Day in 1980, Andrew and I grabbed a bottle of Smirnoff vodka and sat in my bedroom opposite each other with a glass between us and a quarter in our hands. The game was simple. You had to bounce the quarter into the glass, and if you made it the other person would drink a shot. The idea was to go quickly, of course. We were 13 but probably looked like we were 10. Light and thin, we raced our way through that bottle and opened another one within about 30 minutes. We got a bit through that bottle when the alcohol hit our bloodstreams with a vengeance. All of a sudden everything was spinning. The nausea was astonishing. Actually, it was something beyond nausea. It was a united effort from the 30 trillion cells in my body to be rid of the poisonous intruder that was now threatening my life. We had poisoned ourselves. Realizing that I was in trouble, I got up and lurched toward the bathroom.

The next thing I remember, it was morning. My pounding head was slung over the edge of my toilet, and there was vomit everywhere. My gut was burning and painfully empty. My mouth was caked and dry. I stood up, looked in the mirror. I was alive, but in rough shape. As I leaned down to drink some water from the faucet, it all came back to me in a flash. "Andrew!" I exited the bathroom and walked into my bedroom. There was Andrew lying on his back in the middle of the floor. The entire room *was* vomit. It was as if Andrew had actually tried to cover the whole space with it. He was unconscious but breathing. "Andrew, get up. We're in serious trouble." Andrew opened his eyes, thank God, and then threw up over his right shoulder.

There were four main directives in my life as a teenager—*connect with people, have adventures, feel better, and find freedom.* This first dance with alcohol may have qualified as a form of adventure with a friend, but as far as feeling better and finding freedom went, the experience was a failure. I never liked the feeling of being drunk. I drank beer here and there through college. Later, when I was using cocaine, I'd drink alcohol out of necessity to calm my nerves. In 1988, I spent a semester abroad in France and took a shine to drinking red wine. I liked the warm feeling it created over my whole being. That was the only positive feeling I ever got from drinking alcohol, and I imagine it is what other alcoholics are looking for in their bottles.

Reflecting back on that debacle, my first exploration with changing my consciousness, I honestly wasn't trying to obliterate myself. I just didn't know better. The point for me was to have an experience. I truly wanted to feel something. Feeling drunk took me out of feeling altogether. That was not interesting to me. Alcohol was not my ticket, but I was not done searching for a better way.

MARIJUANA

On a cool autumn day while hanging out with Andrew, I smoked pot before going into a bodega to play pinball and video games. About a half hour later, as I walked into the street, I felt the feeling of being high for the first time. There was a sense of release in my body and mind. It felt like I was having the first deep breaths I had ever taken in my life. A tension I had always carried was gone. It was like a vacation from it all, time out of time.

Marijuana really changed things—I had needed a change, and here it was. It immediately dawned on me that I could do this anytime I wanted to. I had the power to transport myself to another viewpoint and change the way the world appeared. God, it was amazing. I felt powerful. Andrew and I ran around for the rest of the afternoon and then proceeded to eat a lot of pizza, candy, and basically anything we could get our hands on. Next, I went home and experienced the first in a long line of very rude awakenings that would get increasingly more intense the older I got. *I didn't like being in my home.* I guess I had always known this on some level, but I saw it clearly in juxtaposition to the way I felt while high. My mom was unhappy. Her discomfort was hard to be around. I felt powerless to help her or do anything about it. My sister Karen and I did not get along. We were at each other's throats in one way or another for most of our childhood and adolescence. My older sister, Julie, was off to college by this point. Consequently, what I did at home, *all* I did at home, was distract myself in every way I could from what was right in front of me: tension, anger, pain, and sadness.

Marijuana was an improvement from the drugs I had been doing: Doritos, Coca-Cola, candy, junk food, pinball, and lots of American midafternoon to late-evening television. It took care of the symptoms of anxiety. Marijuana, it turns out, calms the hyperactive brain. When I smoked it, my emotions shifted immediately. My anger went away. I could access pleasant feelings, which seemed inaccessible without it. Marijuana served the powerful need I had to calm down and feel better. Up to that point in my life, I knew of no other thing that could accomplish this so well.

Here I had found something that would make me feel "easy" for short periods of time. What I didn't know then was that there were long-term consequences attached to those periods of ease. As time went by, the ease came at a greater and greater cost. But in the beginning, that feeling was so compelling and the antics so fun that it worked beautifully, even magically. That was a big part of the reason why I had such a difficult time letting it go.

I had been lectured many times about how dangerous marijuana was. I heard it was a "gateway drug" that would lead to other drugs. I heard it could make you crazy and drive you to do things you wouldn't normally do. However, compared to my personal experience, the warnings of society, parents, and teachers about the dangers of marijuana meant nothing. I was actually smoking pot. I had direct experience, and you know what my experience said to me? "Tommy, you have hit the jackpot here!" I was not going crazy. I was enjoying myself in a way I had not known possible. It was such an amazing relief. I could enter this world at will. There were realizations, good times, and laughter. I embraced it fully. How could anyone talk me out of it?

I had fallen in love with a substance. Even though people said it was harmful, I thought it was amazing. And as is the case for everyone, *personal experience trumps all other information.* Once you experience something directly, you know it. The people warning against it were just speaking from a place of fear about something they knew very little about. It was clear to me that they knew very little because if they knew what I knew, they would be smoking alongside me.

There was, though, one immediate problem with getting high. It meant doing something that my parents were passionately against. Though my mother may have partied with it at some point, smoking marijuana was absolutely forbidden in my house. The need to hide it from her was stressful and created a lot of paranoia. Yet the situation with my father was more worrisome. There was a unique and very powerful bond between us. He was the affectionate, humorous, warmer antidote to Mom's bitterness and sadness. We had a love between us that was ineffable. Consequently, to do anything that distanced us from each other presented me with an existential dilemma. He was adamantly against drug use and expressed his opinions regularly: smoking pot or doing any drugs was unacceptable to him. This posed a serious problem. It put me in direct opposition to my father. I could live with my mother's disapproval, but the fact that marijuana put a rift between my dad and me was a severe consequence.

ADDICTIVE THINKING

Relatively early on in my pot-smoking days, I tried to quit because of the guilt I was feeling. I couldn't stand that there was dishonesty, a philosophical rift, between my father and me. Either I was going to have to give up being honest with him, which felt like an impossible-to-bear fall from grace, or give up smoking pot. I gathered together all my drug paraphernalia—several pipes, bongs, rolling papers, lighters, and a little bit of pot—and threw it all down the incinerator of our apartment building. I had resolve and knew that it was over for me. I felt a great relief . . . for about eight hours, until the old feeling of discontentment and boredom—the -ism—set in. My resolve left me so quickly and completely that it was as if it had never been there at all. The impossible-to-bear fall from grace was inevitable. Luckily, I had "logic" to help me create the Addiction Story I mentioned earlier:

marijuana was a necessary ingredient if I was going to succeed in this world.

Once it was pretty open that I was smoking pot regularly, both my parents would plead with me: "When are you going to stop smoking pot?" I'd tell them the truth—"I'll stop when I feel like it." There was a deeper truth to that, though. I was never going to want to stop, and I knew it. I was still getting something from it, I knew of no substitute for the feeling it produced, and there weren't enough consequences to want to let go of it.

In addition to the issues my pot smoking created between my parents and me, there were also some aspects of my relationship with it that worked in opposition to my own spirit. For one thing, it prevented me from getting things done. While it did "free me up" for humorous antics, unusual reflection, and leisure time, it seemed to get in the way of things like academics, reading, sports, and any activity that required focus. It messed with my motivation to go hiking, bike riding, or to the gym. Completing tasks, even simple ones, became almost impossible. It was absurd how incapable I was of actually doing anything. This was a constant through my high-school years and got somewhat worse when I got to the University of Colorado. I'd have a full day of classes and plan to get to the gym, eat some good food, and hang out with friends. Instead, I'd smoke pot and the rest of the day was reduced to, well, let's just hang out, play some Frisbee or hacky-sack, play video games, listen to the Dead, socialize, and look at the beautiful mountains of Boulder, Colorado. Now, as I write this, I'm thinking how fun this day may sound to you. But it isn't fun if that is all your life has become. Your spirit is asking you to do something different, to create, to express yourself as only you can, but you don't seem to be able to summon the focus and motivation. Your spirit gets squelched, and your ability to manifest much of anything is severely diminished.

I earnestly tried to stop smoking pot a hundred times or so in my 11-year relationship with it. On one such occasion, I summoned all my strength and resolve to quit for 30 days. I remember waking up on day 22 and feeling so proud of myself. I knew I was going to make it to 30. A bizarre thought entered my head: *Since you already know you can make it to 30 days, you don't need to actually make it to 30 days.* If that's not addictive thinking, I don't know what is. I think I made it to noon that day before I pulled a bunch of bong hits and was off to the races, smoking pot on a daily basis once again. When I departed for rehab in 1989, a friend said to me, "You're not going to give up smoking pot—just the cocaine, right?" My response? "No rehab in the world could get me to give up smoking pot!"

Through a decade of using drugs, the pattern was always the same. I'd get so excited about getting high and really go after it. Eventually, I'd feel an inner desire to stop for real. I'd get however far I would get and then be undermined by addictive thinking.

Addictive thinking comes to those stuck in the Frequency of Addiction. It's as if you have a powerful magnet attached to your head that brings a constant barrage of destructive thoughts. *It is the thinking that precedes the action, so if you think addictively, addictive actions will follow.* I lacked the capacity to resist that thinking. It dominated me as it dominates every addict. We can delude ourselves, but if we try to go toe to toe with addictive thinking we are going to lose almost every time. To underline this point, despite the fact that I am 23 years sober, I still realize that if that kind of thinking gets a hold of me, I, too, am capable of relapsing into behaviors that can crush my spirit and life. The fact for me today is that the dis-eased thinking doesn't come. I am spared one day at a time. People who do not struggle with addiction simply cannot understand this.

A BIG EGO AND LOW SELF-ESTEEM

As I mentioned, a major consequence that came with smoking pot was that it got in the way of playing sports.

As a child, my love of sports, both watching and playing, was significant. Thank God for the physical activity that sports gave me. I always had a connection with my body. I loved moving, running, and athletics. These things have always been central to my life. Even during the nonathletic periods when I was using cocaine and heroin, I thought about sports, athletics, and working out often. Athletic endeavors haunted me while I was a drug addict.

I was a talented athlete as a child and had always dreamed of becoming a professional baseball player. It was all I really wanted to do. Unfortunately, there was no Little League in New York City in the 1970s. There were sports teams once you got to high school, but our elementary schools did not have leagues. To fill the gap, a group of guys started a private league, which organized baseball, basketball, and football games on Saturdays. I cherished those days. When the leagues were not in session, I would wake up and head out to Central Park by myself. It was maybe 9 A.M. and I knew no one would show up there till 11 or 12, but I'd sit there with my baseball glove and ball and wait. I always played with kids older than I was, because I could handle myself well. My father had taught me not to be ashamed to ask the older boys if I could play with them. "Just ask them!" So, when someone showed up, I'd go right up to them and say, "You need an extra person? Want to throw the ball around?"

Sports allowed my self-esteem to blossom. One of the most memorable moments of my childhood came when I caught a fly ball for the first time. I had been trying for a while but could not quite get it. Maybe I was eight years old. I caught the ball and told a counselor about it. Well, from that moment forward to this day, one of my greatest pleasures has been to chase down a fly ball in left field. I have memories of playing in high-school games where I caught balls that simply should not have been caught. I knew I was great at this. The joy that went along with it is ineffable.

At Horace Mann School in Riverdale, New York, I was on the junior varsity baseball team in ninth grade. The next year I would try out for the varsity team. Of course I would make the team as a sophomore. This was the thing I had put all my energy and passion into, and it was the only thing I thought I could be exceptional at. Baseball was my way up and out of the feeling that I was not really capable of much.

Varsity baseball tryouts took place in February. The truth was that the coach was looking for a catcher and a few big hitters; I would not fit the bill. A few days later they posted the varsity team on the board. Not only had I not made the team, but they had chosen a freshman to fill the catcher position. He was a solid player, but more important, he had size and strength, two things I lacked. While I did have great agility, I had not developed real strength yet to back it up.

Not being chosen for the team was a gut shot, a huge disappointment. I could not understand how a freshman was chosen over me. It did not matter that he was a catcher and that was the position that needed to be filled on the team. It did not matter that I was prepubescent and could not hit for power. All I could see was injustice. A mistake had been made. I had been wronged.

A more mature version of myself might have used this moment as a rallying point of inspiration. Instead, I used it as a rallying point to escape the terrible feeling of lowness I had in myself. One of my classmates, Greg, was there by my side, feeling a lot of disappointment as well. We blew off school immediately and headed to my house to get good and wasted. Our method? Vodka-Jell-O shots, Whip-Its (small canisters of nitrous oxide), and pot! Not the most glamorous trifecta, but it did the trick.

Soon thereafter, I began smoking pot quite a bit. My priorities were shifting. I hung out with other kids who smoked pot and embraced the counterculture that went with that. I had always been a confident kid, athletic. I believed in myself a great deal, but I was also badly driven by ego, emotionally wounded, and caught up in appearances. What others thought of me carried too much weight. I had not yet developed the inner resources that it took to feel okay about myself. There were also strong psychological forces working on me that were rooted in my family history.

A big ego mixed with low self-esteem is a painful and dangerous combination, one of the classic psychological setups for and symptoms of addiction. On the one hand, you have a false sense of reality as seen through the lens of ego. You feel deserving, even entitled. Your perception does not extend beyond your own skin, so you take everything personally: this is called narcissism. Most teenagers have this to some extent. Perhaps I had it to a greater extent. On the other hand, you feel so shitty about yourself that any disappointment can totally wreck you. And by the way, let's define "disappointment" as what results when the world deals you up a reality that is different from the way your ego sees things. Such was the case that day. I decided to blame the world for my pain rather than accept that I had learning and growing to do. I didn't have the strength to accept disappointment and failure, whether perceived or real. My impulse at the time was to point out the world's injustices, arrive at a verdict of "Fuck you" as fast as possible, and then take the appropriate next right action: get good and wasted.

While I had always been very popular in school, it was around the time I didn't make the varsity team that I felt my identity shift in a big way. I was no longer at the top of my class in athletics because most folks had gotten bigger and stronger than me. I was catching a lot of shit for being small. Many of my oldest friends made fun of me. I was ashamed to the point where I could not get undressed in the locker room at school and chose instead to shower at home after sports. I wanted to wrestle, but the wrestlers were forced to shower at school after practice, so I decided not to go out for the team because I simply could not endure the humiliation. I did my best to play it off like I didn't care, but things had shifted for me at Horace Mann.

HIGH TIMES AT BOARDING SCHOOL

I transferred to The Taft School in September of 1983 as a junior. The transition was difficult. My size continued to be a challenge. People thought I was a freshman, which brought a lot of social issues. The kids at school who smoked pot—and there were a good number of them—stood out to me in **bold print**. One day I was feeling particularly out of place, a bit lonely and insecure. I went to the phone to call my pal, Andrew, and requested that he send me some pot. It came in a small, well-constructed package a few days later.

Armed with new confidence, I approached two of the "bold print" guys and said, "You want to get stoned?"

Somewhat surprised, they said, "You smoke pot, Rosen? We had no idea, dude. Yeah, let's do it."

These guys had never paid me five seconds of attention. Now we would become friends because of this common interest. Instant community! Marijuana delivered once again. I had found an identity at Taft and I would wear it until I graduated (barely) two years later.

Frankly, it was a tremendous amount of fun interspersed with incredible paranoia due to the constant worry of being caught. There was a prevailing feeling at Taft that if you got kicked out of school, you faced eternal damnation. Not in the religious sense, but more in the realistic sense. Nothing would ever be okay again. Consequently, kids adopted amazingly clever techniques for getting high without getting caught. I made it all the way to the month of graduation, nearly two years. I was in a room with two of my friends pulling bong hits. Right before my friend Bill took a hit, I said out loud, "Even with all the close calls and stress, we really are not going to get caught doing this." At that moment, a knock came on the door and a teacher entered, catching us red-handed. "You know," I said, "I could be wrong."

We were all suspended for a week and then allowed to return to school and graduate. If we were caught again doing anything illegal, we'd be thrown out. There were only three weeks left until graduation, but I smoked pot immediately upon my return to Taft after the suspension. Part of it was a "Fuck you" to The Man. Part of it was about playing the role of the undaunted and ridiculously daring (read: stupid) teenager. And, of course, part of it was that I just didn't want to let it go.

A NIGHT (AND 12 YEARS) WITH THE GRATEFUL DEAD

During that first year at Taft, at Andrew's behest, I got a pass to leave boarding school and hopped on a bus to the Hartford Civic Center, where that evening a band called the Grateful Dead was going to perform.

I got to downtown Hartford around 6 P.M. The energy outside the Civic Center was picking up; you could feel that something was about to happen. I met Andrew, who had an epic grin on his face, just outside the arena. He handed me a hit of LSD. This was the second time I'd taken it. I was up for this adventure, but nervous. I realized that when the dust settled at the end of this night, I was going to have to get back to Taft. I also had a powerful memory of my first LSD experience, which was both positive and nearly psychotic. Andrew assured me that as soon as the music began all would be well in the world. We took the acid and headed inside.

That night Andrew and I ran around the Hartford Civic Center laughing and experiencing the Grateful Dead. I had never heard music like this before, but my first experience was not just focused on music. There was an unspoken collective *thing* going on in this space. Everyone, it seemed, was on drugs, so we had that in common. Our bodies all moved to this music, so a kind of unified undulation was happening. The LSD seemed to give me unlimited energy. Boundless. There was power in that and I loved it. Andrew and I connected more deeply. I was the newcomer to this scene. He knew a lot of people and introduced me to everyone. There were hugs and laughter and even tears as people were profoundly moved by what was going on. At one point during the concert the Dead performed a rare song called "Saint Stephen." What ensued then will go down as the largest explosion of energy I've ever felt at an event in my life. I had no idea what was happening. All of a sudden Andrew started jumping up and down in the air, face contorting with pleasure, and the whole arena erupted. I just started laughing. There was nothing else to do. Everyone's face read, "I'm having an orgasm right this minute." It was contagious. If you've ever been around someone who is laughing really hard, you know that you start laughing, too. This was like that times a billion.

An hour or so later the show ended. I remember being with Andrew and a whole bunch of new friends, some of whom are dear friends to this day. We smoked pot and cigarettes, drank beer, and just hung out. It was the coolest feeling. There was no immediate responsibility. We were hanging simply to hang with each other. It was a state of just being and enjoying life. I had never done that before. There seemed always to be such pressure on me. Somehow the combination of elements that evening made it possible to slow down enough to enjoy a moment. I can't express to you how important it was for me to experience that.

I returned with a friend to Taft the next day. I had gone to a concert, taken acid there, and had a great time. Now I was back at boarding school, and I could continue on with life as it had been. *Wrong!* Nothing would ever be the same for me. There had been a permanent shift overnight. I . . . was . . . a . . . Deadhead! All I wanted to do was devour everything that had to do with the band. I wanted to hear more music, pore over the lyrics, look at the books, and learn the history of this phenomenon. I had been longing for something different, and boy, had I found it.

I would find other Deadheads at Taft, so I knew that even when things got difficult, there was relief to be had. There was now a place I could go to be with my *chosen kin*. Who knew when or where it would happen? *But* it would happen. I'd be with the Dead sometime soon again. My spirit came alive with the thought of it.

I spent as much time as I possibly could in the Grateful Dead scene from that point forward. On a regular basis I had about as much fun as one could have. I had lots of friends with whom I was on an adventure, traveling across huge swaths of the United States. I started to connect with some really amazing girls. While I was following the Dead on tour, there was relative simplicity to it all. We traveled to the next show. We took drugs and we danced hard. We ate whenever we wanted to. We hung out. We crashed in some hotel room or at a local college or at someone's parents' home. I started to feel a sense of genuine love for myself. Wow, I fit in somewhere! And the people I was with on Dead tour were funny, educated, brilliant, driven, but all in this off-the-wall, zany kind of way. Many of these friends attended Ivy League schools, for example, and like me, they couldn't get enough of the Grateful Dead. We'd see these maniacs at Dead shows at set-break huddling together in some seating section of an arena, lit up on LSD and writing their English midterm papers. We had amazing discussions and deep connections and a ton of raucous laughter. We knew we were living outside the norm of society and we took pride in that. I was discovering the beauty within and around me. I was also escaping the suffocation of my immediate family's anxiety and fears.

CHASING THE HIGH AND LOSING BEGINNER'S MIND

There were many exceptional Dead shows, but there were three shows in particular that impacted me on a level profound enough that the addict part of me could not leave it at that. These nights were so monumental that I would end up chasing after them at future concerts (and in other venues) for years to come. It was complete joy, like when I found marijuana for the first time. I wanted to experience this feeling over and over. Most of the Deadheads around me were in the same boat, so we egged each other on. On the one hand, we had love and understanding; on the other hand, we had addiction and understanding.

There were times when the Dead would come out and have a shitty night. I would get frustrated—really frustrated—with their song selection or the way they decided to arrange their tunes. The fact was, I was coming there for a profound spiritual experience, and if they didn't deliver, I'd get really pissed off. Every now and then I'd catch myself and realize how out of the present moment I was. I was not trying to have an experience; I was trying to re-create an experience. That is exactly what an addict seeks to do. Having felt profound pleasure, I sought to replicate it again and again. Some nights I was more in the moment than others, but I was aware even then that something had changed. My first experiences with the Dead were fresh and new. I had no idea what to expect, no idea what was coming. I had then what Zen Buddhists would call "beginner's mind." Later, I lost that altogether and became attached to a memory in the past.

The present moment is elusive for most addicts—not that we are trying to find it. We'd be happy being anywhere at all as long as we can avoid facing "the now." Our addiction begins the second we start looking away and our Addiction Story is built through the continuation of that habit. We look away because we imagine, correctly or incorrectly, that it will hurt to look. We imagine that the most horrible things will happen if we dig into the original hurts, but ironically, it is only by looking directly at the pain that we can begin to understand it, process it, and heal it. Interestingly, the Grateful Dead were singing songs about the human condition, weakness, addiction, strength, love, and pain. There is so much love and pain in that music. Maybe that is what drew us all there in the first place—there was this mass therapy thing going on. They sang to us *about* us in the strangest, most hauntingly beautiful melodies. During the best moments, there was literally nowhere else on the planet we would have chosen to be. During the worst moments, I was just stuck inside my own mind with the "-ism" messing with me as usual.

BREAKING MY HEART AND BURYING MY SHADOW

After my childhood on the Upper East Side and my attendance at private schools, the world of the Grateful Dead offered something entirely different. It was as if the Grateful Dead world had been constructed for me and others like me, people who craved a kind of freedom that was not available in the world we had grown up in. I have known and heard about many people who are similar to me but who never find their own version of the Grateful Dead. These people often try to kill themselves because they are not graced with a vision beyond their confinement. My parents felt that the Grateful Dead universe was somehow responsible for my addiction. Actually, I think the Grateful Dead saved my life.

However, where there is light, there is also shadow, and I learned a lot about addiction from the Grateful Dead scene. I came to know the difference between kids who were experiencing freedom and relief and kids who were existing so as not to feel much of anything or to avoid something dreadful. Like me, so many had lost or had never found a sense of identity. The drugs and the determination to keep things going as they were, the attachment to having things be a particular way, the need for the show to go on and to remain at a distance from the things that were plaguing us—all these things became a part of our agenda. This was the shadow side of it.

In the summer of 1985, I went out on tour with the Grateful Dead to a run of shows. This particular run was the high point of my time with them. I experienced what I would call perfect moments when everything seemed to click. I was in the zone the whole time. I had been gone for about ten days when I made the mistake of calling my mom to check in. She was beyond livid. I had not thought to call before then. Frankly, it hadn't even oc-curred to me to do so. I had just graduated from high school and would be attending the University of Colorado after the summer. I was 18 and free, or so I imagined. At the moment I called we were about to head into a show at Merriweather Post Pavilion in Mary-land. My mother demanded that I come home immediately. That was a moment of truth. Somehow, my mom still held sway over me—I could not blow her off altogether. As my friends headed into the concert, I boarded an Amtrak train for New York City.

My mother met me at the door when I got home. I was dressed in full hippie regalia, patchouli and all. She announced that she was heading out with some friends for the evening and left. The next thing I knew, I was sitting *alone* in the apartment in New York City where I had grown up. I shook my head in utter disbe-lief, went into my bathroom, and stared at myself in the mirror, saying, "This will never happen again! This will never, ever hap-pen again." Anger consumed me.

It's a very difficult thing to go so quickly from love to hate. In that moment I hated my mother. I hated myself as well for not having had the "strength" to stay out on the road. It was all so confusing. I had experienced no anger for the previous two weeks and in no time at all I was consumed by it. Who wants to be told what to do? No one. Who wants to feel controlled? No one. My issues with my mother were more complex than that. I knew she had had a rough time in her life and I felt bad about it. When she was struggling I really wanted to help. I never wanted to hurt or make things worse. Part of the pain was to realize that there was nothing I could do about her suffering. She was so miserable sometimes that I did not want to be around it. When she tried to control me, my gut reaction was to get away or lash out directly at her. So it was that on many occasions when I could not stand it any longer, I would look directly at her and say, "Fuck you. Fuck off. Get the fuck out of my life. I cannot stand you and there is nothing you can fucking do to control me. You're miserable. I'm not. So fuck off."

The hangover from these bouts of anger was immense—remorse, guilt, sadness. I was acutely aware that men had mistreated Mom for most of her life. My intention had been to fix it all but I was making it worse. It broke my heart to realize this. My next move was to simply get far away. If I felt trapped in her pain, the frustration grew until I lost my temper. One day I'd be on Dead tour in a world of possibility, space, love, and acceptance. The next day I'd be screaming violently into my mother's face. I am not a violent person but these moments were exactly that. I recognized even then that this behavior was unacceptable *to me*. I couldn't get my mind around the two extremes. If most of my friends in the Dead scene had witnessed me yelling at my mother, they would have been shocked, too. I was so angry and didn't know where to turn. I would head to more Dead shows, try to hang around positive people, and come to some manner of acceptance that there was a part of me that I was not proud of and for which there was no solution. I'd bury it alive.

CROSSING THE LINE FROM LOVE TO ADDICTION

Behaviors become addictions when they are used continuously to avoid something. I did not want to look at the problem—actually, I could not imagine how to begin to look at the problem. Though I recognized that something was wrong with me, my main thought was "go with what seems to be working." That meant to distance myself from home as much as possible.

The more drugs I took, the more my anger and other issues were pushed down inside me. The drugs acted as a suppressant, which would take care of the symptoms but never touch the core dis-ease. I was still reaching some ecstatic places through drugs and dancing, but it cost me. The original hurts never got dealt with, so all subsequent hurts got piled on top. It gets to the point where you are feeling emotions that no longer correspond to what is actually happening in the present moment. This is deep-seated resentment, and it is a killer. Without being able to work it out, the pressure of the need to feel better from it will overwhelm you and cause you to go deeper into darkness than you may have thought was possible. Grateful Dead lyricist Robert Hunter wrote, "Day to day, just letting it ride. You get so far away from how it feels inside. You can't let go 'cause you're afraid to fall, but the day may come when you can't feel at all."[1] That lyric always cut right to the heart of the matter for me.

CHAPTER 5

THE PROGRESSION

My beliefs about drugs developed quickly and I separated them into two categories: good and bad. Good drugs were "natural" and came from the earth: marijuana and psilocybin mushrooms, for example. LSD, other psychedelic drugs, and Ecstasy counted as well because they provided powerful, mystical, and mostly positive experiences. Bad drugs were all powders, such as cocaine, methamphetamine, and heroin, and all prescription medications, such as Valium. Through seven years of drug use, I stuck to the good drugs and preached against all the others. I built a whole world around marijuana; I bought it, sold it, grew it, smoked it, and ate it. As you know, it was a big part of my identity. And that was perhaps the thing I missed most—an identity. Who was I? What was I here to do? Marijuana became more than just a medicine. For a while it was my vocation, my avocation, my course of study, my friend. It was a reason to be.

The bad drugs did not fit anywhere in my Addiction Story at the time. It was *unthinkable* to me to ever do cocaine. I used to watch people do it in my first year in college. They were usually behind a closed door at some party. There was this air of secrecy about it. At first I thought that it was because it was such an expensive drug that people who had it didn't want to share it with the whole party. There was some truth to that. Later on, I would come to understand that there was also a certain amount of control, weirdness, and shame that went along with using it. Cocaine was at the next level. It was a harder, more serious drug. It was highly physically addictive and tended to make people want more of it whether they were full-blown addicts or not.

I always preached against the use of this drug. I was the kid who everyone knew would never do cocaine. One night in my sophomore year of college, a friend of mine approached and said, "Tommy, I'm going to hang out with these two girls, and we have a bunch of cocaine. Want to come along?" Before I could think, the word *yes* came out of my mouth. We snorted lines and drank some beers and flirted together till midnight, when we ran out of cocaine. I knew where my friend had gotten it. Without telling anyone, I went into the other room to make a phone call to get more. It was so natural to me. "Oh, we've run out of cocaine. It's midnight. We'll get some more of it and continue this romp."

My friend came in and said, "Dude, what are you doing?"

I said, "I'm getting more coke."

He said, "Dude, you're jonesing." I had never heard that word before. *Jonesing?* Yes, the feeling of wanting more. I was jonesing.

That night was the first night I ever partied with cocaine. It grabbed me by the balls immediately. The feeling it produced was quick and strong. It lifted me up, made me feel good. There was a psychosexual element to it. It was sexy. The girls felt sexy. I felt sexy. I was turned on by the whole experience. For the rest of the night we snorted cocaine until there was no more cocaine to be had. At the end of the night, we went our separate ways. I was hopped up out of my skull and couldn't sleep for many hours. The thoughts I experienced during that time were predominantly negative and hard to take.

What made it all right for me to say yes to cocaine that night versus any other? I had been around it for years and turned it down. Suddenly, I was all over it. I wasn't in a depression—I felt fine, actually. For some reason, the ethics I had, which included not doing cocaine, were thrown out the window.

This speaks to the progressive nature of the dis-ease of addiction. Remember that my core issues were still alive and festering within me. I had not yet begun to face the original traumas of my life. On the one hand, I was carrying a lot of anger toward my parents, while on the other hand, I was living as this peace-loving Deadhead. The Frequency of Addiction was alive and well within me. The -ism was getting more intense. I needed stronger methods of looking away from the present moment and my life in general. I'd been looking away from things for a long time by then, and somehow I needed more of something. The addition of potential sex to the whole situation was compelling because sex was another behavior I sought as much as possible.

The greatest testimony I can make to the progressive nature of the dis-ease of addiction is that I tried cocaine and then later started to smoke it. Once you start *smoking cocaine* you have exited the realm of experimentation. You are truly no longer involved in recreational drug use, and you actually are aware of this. Your addiction really gets to flex its muscle in this venue. This is the "big leagues." You have arrived on the psychotic shores of that rarified thing known as drug-induced insanity.

By late 1988 my addiction had entered a new category marked by the addition of crack cocaine to the roster of activities I was involved in. I had been doing a lot of coke for the past year or two, and somewhere in there, it was suggested to me that I take a hit of freebase cocaine (crack).

People who smoke crack together are stoic and precise in their communication. At first, as the initial preparation of coke is being cooked, the participants—never more than three or four—may exchange mischievous smiles or amazingly cynical jokes, but inevitably the verbal communication trails off until finally the only things uttered are those things that have to be uttered to allow the "partying" to continue. There really are no pleasantries because nothing about the whole experience is too pleasant. There is, of course, the walloping initial high produced by taking a big hit, and everyone looks on as if they're watching you have an orgasm, because in some sick, shadowy way you are. Then everyone else wants to have the same experience over and over again, even though it lasts a short amount of time, is horribly vacuous, and, in the end, leaves you devoid of life force, crying like a man who realizes he has lost everything, because for that night, at least, you have. And eventually you will lose everything for good.

There is a lot of ritual that goes along with smoking crack. You have to prepare it with various chemicals and flame, so there is a regimented alchemical element to it, except in this case rather than turning lead into gold you are turning your life into shit. The dark arts to be sure.

The comedown after a night of smoking crack has to rank up there with the worst experiences one can have on the planet Earth. Unable to sleep, feeling physically awful, dehydrated, malnourished, and filled with self-hatred and remorse, you spend hours at the mercy of the most insane barrage of negative thoughts. Everything wrong in your life attacks you at the level of mind. You are acutely aware of the ways you've fucked up and how this very evening was yet another example of the fuckup that you are.

Occasionally, a girl would "party" with you and there would be some kind of mechanical sex act at the end of the night, but this could only happen after the coke ran out because, at this level of addiction, cocaine even takes precedence over sex. I got to experience that fact one night when a beautiful girl was trying to get me to let go of the partying to have sex with her. Under any other circumstances I would have been thrilled, but I couldn't break away from the magnetic power of crack. She ended up sleeping alone in my bed as I partied into the next day. As she walked out of my house at 8 A.M., we were still at it. She looked absolutely disgusted and pissed off as she caught my eye on her way out. I just took another hit.

I had lost confidence in myself and started to become that guy who everyone knows is out of control. Many of my closest friends whom I had partied with for years were not willing to go to this next level with me. Consequently, the people I spent the most time with were those who had the sickness at the same level as I did. Though this was a smaller number of people, there were still plenty of people around me who were willing and who needed to go to this depth.

I was living with two dear friends of mine and they gave me an ultimatum: stop doing cocaine or you have to move out. I swore to them that I would. Shortly thereafter, I spent about four hours in and out of our house's guest bathroom smoking freebase. I'd be in there "doing my thing" and then emerge exclaiming that my stomach was hurting and go back in about 90 seconds later. This absurd charade continued well beyond the point when my roommates went to bed. The next day they had to ask me to leave.

People had mostly lost faith in me and for good reason. I was not to be counted on. My drug use had increased to the point where I could no longer tell the difference between true and false. I lied all the time.

"Tommy, did you hit classes today?"

"Oh, yeah. Of course."

"Well, I was there and didn't see you."

"That's weird, 'cause I saw you," I'd tell them.

I now partied five to six days a week, stopping only for long, fitful sleeps. I was enrolled in school but only attending the occasional class. I smoked pot in the daytime and drank and did coke in the evenings. What I must have looked like rolling into class the few times I made it! I lost a lot of weight, had colds and coughs. My life force was dwindling.

A friend of mine booked a reggae artist named Shinehead to come perform in Boulder. I helped promote the show by putting up posters all over town. Shinehead had just released an anti-cocaine album called *Gimme No Crack,* and there I was hanging posters all over town that said exactly that. The irony was not lost on me. On one occasion, friends of mine saw me putting up the poster and yelled out, "You ought to take that advice, Rosen." I was so embarrassed and ashamed of myself.

I called my father in Los Angeles and told him that I was having trouble with life and . . . well . . . drugs. I wanted to take a break from it all. He wanted me to come live with him for as long as it took to get my shit together. So I took a leave of absence from the University of Colorado and headed to Los Angeles.

I spent the next 12 weeks taking amazing care of myself. I ate and slept well. I saw a therapist three times a week and a gym trainer five times a week. I started to look better and get my energy back. My body rebounded quickly. My dad and I mostly got along during this time, with a few manageable scrapes. I was grateful for the help and he was grateful to see me coming alive again. We were on the same page about one thing: I was never going to do cocaine again. Man, I was over it. I smoked pot a few times during those 90 days in LA, but that was all the "partying" I did. Surely, I would smoke pot when I got back to Boulder, but only here and there. I felt like I was in control of myself again for the first time in years.

At the end of April, I announced to my therapist that I wanted to head back to Boulder to finish school. Both he and my father begged me not to go back. I would get into trouble again, they said, but I held my ground and made plans to return to Boulder within the week to enroll in summer school and get back on track. I knew I was going to be okay.

I had a friend named Henry; we all called him Hank. We had done a lot of partying together, but he had heard about my hiatus and was inspired by it. Hank had a girl, Shelly, and they had a son. He suggested we all move in together. I told him I was serious about staying away from cocaine and all "hard drugs." He assured me he was serious, too, and so we found a house together. Hank, Shelley, and Hank, Jr., would have the upstairs, and I would have the downstairs.

The morning after we moved in together, I came home from attending to some school business to find Hank freebasing cocaine over the stove in the kitchen. He was in the middle of taking a hit when I walked by the kitchen door. I smelled that smell and observed the whole scene.

All I could utter was, "Uh-oh!"

Hank looked at me with a sick grin on his face and said, "Uh-oh is right."

In that moment, I could not remember why I was supposed to avoid smoking crack. I lost all clarity on this point. I now know that people who struggle with addiction have felt this exact feeling time and time again. The Big Book refers to it as a "mental fog that sets in" preventing us from protecting ourselves against our addiction.[1] It was as if my memory of the previous 90 days, all the therapy, all the gym sessions, all the resolve I thought I'd created, had been wiped out. This is one aspect of the powerlessness that people in 12-Step programs speak about.

Over the course of the next 90 days, Hank and I did an astounding amount of drugs together. He knew how to cook cocaine, and I had wanted him to teach me. The day he caved in to my incessant requests to learn to cook, all he said was, "You're going to regret this." He was right.

Things got further and further out of control. One time I woke up in the middle of the night with Hank on top of me trying to choke me to death. He was screaming, "You're ruining my family! You're killing my family!" I threw him off me, and he sort of came to and ran out of the house. The next day we were doing drugs again without any mention of what had happened.

Believe it or not, I was actually going to see a therapist once a week during this time. Each week I'd be in her office weeping my eyes out about my life. She would plead with me to go to a Cocaine Anonymous meeting, but despite my desperation, I refused to go. "That's not for me. I'm not one of those people. Never. I'll never go." I'd leave her office and wander back into my oblivion.

I knew I had a problem, but I did not understand what the problem was. I had no knowledge of addiction. I had no idea that it was a dis-ease, that it was fatal, and that I was dying from it. I could not bring myself to believe that this was impossible to handle on my own. Of *course* I would pull it back together. I had always managed to get by. I'd find a way again. But I had to admit that I was tired of it all. Nothing was making sense any longer. Yet I couldn't stop. What would that look like? What would my life become? Who was I without drugs and alcohol? Who would ever hang out with me if I didn't have drugs to share? These were the kinds of things I was thinking underneath it all.

My final three-day run came in the middle of July 1989. I had convinced a drug dealer to front me a half ounce of cocaine. If you are not aware, that is a fair amount of cocaine. I had every intention of selling part of it, paying the dealer back, and then doing the rest of it with a couple of friends. Unfortunately, we started to smoke it before we sold any of it, and you probably know how this ended up. In less than a day we smoked all 14 grams of cocaine, and I now owed this dealer $1,000. There was a bigger problem, though: we had run out of cocaine. Hank and I had no intention of stopping. I had to go back to the drug dealer to get more. The second the idea was planted in my head, it was a done deal. I was going to have to convince him that even though I had no money to pay him for the first half ounce, I needed him to front me a second half ounce. After being up all night smoking cocaine and cigarettes, I was looking pretty ragged. I am sure that in my life to that point I never paid as much attention to the details of my appearance as I did in preparation to dupe this dealer out of another $1,000 worth of cocaine. I took a shower, washed thoroughly. I flossed my teeth, not something I had been doing much of lately. I Q-tipped my ears. I put on some cologne. It was ridiculous, but this had to work. I was driven like a wild animal. I could not come down. Like a good corner man in a boxing match, Hank was there helping me get myself together. He'd keep saying, "What are you gonna say when you get there? What will you say? How will you say it? Don't be nervous. Just be cool."

I drove myself over to the dealer's house and laid it out for him. "I've sold the first half ounce. The dude is coming with 'bank' tomorrow. I've got another guy that wants to buy a second half ounce. That I can pay you for later tonight." He looked at me, and I looked at him.

It was a long moment. All he said was, "You sure?"

I said, "Yes. I'm sure."

And that was it. I returned home to Hank, who was waiting, expectant, and then joyous upon seeing my victorious gait. For the next 18 hours or so, we descended to a level of drug-addled depravity that I'd never been to before. I couldn't stop smoking this drug. *Just couldn't stop.* We went through torches, BIC lighters, and then matches. We stopped talking to each other for hours. Breathing had become a chore, let alone speaking. The mental psychosis of using that much cocaine had set in. We continued to cook it and smoke it. I vaguely remember that Shelley and Hank, Jr., were upstairs for at least a large part of this binge. That's a really hard thought for me even now, 25 years later.

Finally, I reached a point where I couldn't do it anymore. My muscles were going into painful spasms. My lungs were killing me, and my eyes were red and swollen with irritation. The pain in all of my joints was excruciating. I hadn't eaten in two days, and I was completely dehydrated. I had never done this much coke before, but I knew the comedown from it was going to be more than I could bear. I called a friend of mine knowing that she had sleeping pills. I begged her to come over to give me those pills. I expressed the absolute urgency of it. "I'm in trouble," I told her. She reluctantly agreed, and in about 30 minutes, she showed up at our house. She walked in and took a look at the whole scene, and I got a glimpse of my reality through her eyes. With a mix of disgust, anger, and sincere concern she said, "You are really fucked up, Tommy, and in a lot of trouble. Only take one of these. You're fucked up!" She threw me a bottle of pills and left. My shame was all consuming, but it didn't matter. I opened the bottle and took two pills right away. By this point, Hank was upstairs. I headed into my bedroom and sat up in bed with a few pillows supporting me. All of a sudden I was seeing bursts of colored paint in front of my eyes—blue, yellow, red. A warmth came over me as I drifted out of consciousness.

When my eyes finally opened again, I was still sitting up in bed exactly as I had been when I'd passed out 30 hours before. I had been "sleeping" for an entire day plus six hours. I couldn't move for a long time as my legs had had little to no blood flow for as long as I had been sleeping. I was massaging them, but couldn't feel them at all. I rolled off the bed onto the floor and lay there. My room was in squalor. It was disgusting. There was no one home—Hank and family must have gone somewhere. There was no one to call. No friends. No girl. I owed a drug dealer $2,000 but did not have a penny. My life was in shambles.

I will never know how I survived that night. At the very least, I should have had severe nerve damage in my hips and legs. Yet slowly the feeling in my legs returned. The only thing I could think to do was to call my father. He was the person to whom I was most deeply connected on the planet. I had always relied upon him when I got into trouble. He would console me and I would be okay. I told him how bad things were, how I had no girlfriend or friends to speak of. How this had happened and that had happened. I told him everything I could—except for the truth.

Then he simply stated, "You're on drugs again. I know you're on drugs! Aren't you?"

I said, "Yes, Dad, I am."

He said bluntly that this time I was going to have to go to rehab. I then bluntly replied that I would not go. There was a silence on the phone that lasted about ten seconds. Then I realized my dad had started to cry. All of my arrogance and stubbornness fell away as I glimpsed the effect I'd had on him. "Dad, please stop crying, I'll go. I'll go."

The next day, I sat down with Hank and told him that I was going to rehab. He put his hand on my shoulder and said, "I'm glad you're going . . . because you've really got a problem." I thought he was joking, and I kept waiting for him to smile. But he wasn't joking—that smile never came. It turned out to be a bigger moment than I realized at the time. Over the next 24 years, I would get sober; find recovery; rebuild my relationship with myself, my family, and my friends; get married; find great meaning and purpose in the work that I do; and learn how to show up in this world one day at a time without the use of drugs in my life.

During that time, Hank struggled with drug abuse and homelessness, spent time in prison, lost his family and relationships, and ended up taking his own life just as I was launching Recovery 2.0. I am filled with sadness that he was never able to embrace a life of recovery. The light in this man was very bright. Addiction ruined his life and then killed him. He was trying to do what we are all trying to do: feel better, find connection, and have a life of meaning. Losing him, like every loss to this disease, is a tragedy.

Addiction is a mysterious thing. You never know what it will take to break its force field and allow a person to change course and survive. My recovery was initiated upon the tears of my father. I do not know why I was given this gift and why Hank wasn't.

The next day, I flew to my father's home in Los Angeles. He had insisted on seeing me first. Four days later, I went off to rehab to begin my life anew. The nightmare of acute addiction was coming to an end.

PART II

RECOVERY 1.0: EXPLORING THE 12 STEPS

CHAPTER 6

THE BEGINNING
OF THE PATH
OF RECOVERY

When a person who struggles with addiction reaches a bottom, it means they are ready for a change. They probably have no idea how to move forward, but they can no longer go on living the way they have. A profound surrender takes place, marked by humility and willingness to receive outside help. For families who have been praying for a loved one to reach this point, it is truly a miracle when it arrives, because until that moment, the situation may have seemed hopeless. Suddenly, a small window of possibility presents itself. So what do you do when this happens? Where do you start?

If you are seeking help with addiction, there are only a few main ways to access recovery in our world today. You can undergo a therapeutic process of some kind with a therapist, one-on-one or in a group setting. You can go to an addiction treatment center. Or you can attend and work through a recovery program like those based on the 12 Steps. It's also worth mentioning that some people seem to have a sudden spiritual experience that shakes them free of addiction without any of the aforementioned processes. This is very rare, and I have no idea how to create such an experience, for myself or for you.

THE LANDSCAPE OF RECOVERY TODAY

Therapy: A Great Start and a Complement

Therapy can be an amazing thing. I know a few people who have managed to recover from addiction with the help of top-notch therapists, but in almost all cases, these folks ended up in 12-Step programs at the suggestion of their therapists. Therapy is an excellent complement to 12-Step recovery and it can be a launching pad for it. Cognitive behavioral therapy, dialectical behavior therapy, somatic therapy, and spiritual psychology are just a few of the countless modalities that complement 12-Step work well. There are many things we all need to work out if we are to be happy, joyous, and free. Having a skilled therapist in your corner is an asset. If you are fortunate enough to be able to afford therapy or have someone else pay for it, take advantage of it. I have personally worked with therapists of every kind and have found that some form of spiritual psychology has helped me the most. You will have to decide for yourself.

If you are dealing with mental disorders or imbalances such as depression, bipolar disorder, obsessive compulsive disorder, or schizophrenia and require medication, you will need to seek an excellent psychiatrist to work with. I have lost friends to dual diagnosis issues, people who had addiction *and* suffered from other disorders. If you are one of these people, you have to be very careful—I want to be clear on this point. If you need medication to have a fighting chance at being sober and healthy, please consult with your physician and get your needs met. You can always work with your support team   doctor, sponsor, spouse, and so on—to find a way off medications later, if and when that opportunity presents itself. For some people, though, medication may be necessary for the long term. Others will be able to get off medication sooner with a conscious, well-thought-out plan of approach. There is no one method to this. In the early going, do everything in your power to stack the odds in your favor for a successful recovery from addiction. Remember, if that fails, you're going to have *much* bigger problems to deal with.

Inpatient Addiction Treatment: Get It if You Can

If you can afford it yourself or have great insurance or a well-off family member, go to a reputable treatment center. You will be in a safe environment, learning what has happened in your life and why. You will get the benefit of counselors and peers who understand addiction firsthand. You will put time between you and your addiction and will be able to build a strategy for continuing care when you return to your life. Obviously, not all treatment centers are the same. Some are better than others, and you will want to do some research and talk to people who have been through it. In a moment you will hear about my time at Hazelden, which was the turning point of my life.

12-Step Programs and Fellowships: Highly Recommended

12-Step fellowships offer the most widespread solution for people seeking recovery from addiction. Meetings are accessible and totally free. There is power in numbers. In 12-Step programs people support each other through the challenges of recovery. Since there are meetings every day in most locations, one can take advantage of this regularity and get into a routine. The ongoing nature of the programs allows for "continuing care." This is very important in early recovery. In the next chapters, we will cover the 12 Steps in detail.

FINDING ADDITIONAL HELP AND GUIDANCE

Navigating through the landscape of recovery can be very difficult, even overwhelming. Which rehab facility is best for this or that situation? Do you need extra medical support? Does insurance cover this? If you don't go the rehab route, how do you find the right therapist? What about continuing care? These and another thousand questions will inevitably come up. Because this process is so personal and specific to each individual, you may want to consider hiring a recovery case manager, if you have the funds to do so. There are many qualified and excellent people doing this work. They will help you navigate the challenges of the recovery landscape and make sense of a complicated situation.

IS THAT ALL THERE IS?

You might be thinking, *There must be something else I can do to change my life and let go of this addictive behavior I'm stuck in. I thought Recovery 2.0 was all about holistic recovery! All you're doing is suggesting rehab, therapy, and the 12 Steps. What about yoga and meditation?*

People often ask me if I think they can get sober by taking up a yoga practice. The answer is "It depends." I believe there are two main things a person in acute addiction needs to recover: a spiritual awakening (a profound shift in understanding of the world and their place in it) and a community to support them on the path toward this awakening. I also believe that daily accountability and structure are critical. You have to be vigilant. Otherwise, you are a sitting duck for your mind, which will prey upon you if you are stuck in the Frequency of Addiction, as we have seen. If you live in a spiritual yoga community that supports you on the path of recovery (read: ashram), and members of that community are there for you when temptations arise (and they will), and especially if you have a teacher who has taken a personal interest in you and is guiding you along, then yes, in my opinion, you might have a shot. However, if you were thinking about hitting some yoga classes at a local studio in your town or city and hoping that would do the trick, I would not wager on your success.

Yoga and meditation, as we will come to see, are outstanding tools for reaching your fullest potential. First, though, for people in acute addiction, I advocate Recovery 1.0, and, for me, that meant rehab, therapy, and the 12 Steps.

HITTING THE JACKPOT

When I arrived at Hazelden in July 1989, I was acutely aware that all my thoughts, words, and actions up to that point in my life had led me to this place. This was the result of the sum total of my activities. I felt like I had failed at life. The idea of going to rehab someday had entered my mind in the previous several years. Several friends had "disappeared" from my party scene and later I'd find out that they had gone to rehab. So, in the back of my mind, I held this belief that if things got really bad, I could always default to that. The thing I had feared for all those years was that my life would fall apart, that I would be exposed and have to face myself. Well, here I was at rehab. Everything had fallen apart.

Strangely, there is an interesting feeling of freedom that goes along with the idea that the worst has happened. Suddenly, there is nothing to fear. Certainly, I felt terrible about myself, but there was no longer a need to keep up appearances. If anyone had ever had a doubt that I was a fuckup, at least now it was out in the open.

What I could not realize in that moment was that *I had hit the jackpot.* To be an addict on this planet is a hell I wouldn't wish on anyone, but to find a path of recovery from addiction is an experience I would wish for everyone.

At Hazelden I was about to get an opportunity to review my entire life. Where had things gotten so off track? I would learn to be honest and find out what to do about the fact that I had not been truthful for so long. I would get to review my family history, my drug history, my relationship/sexual history, and my financial history. Every cranny of my existence would be put under a microscope. Counselors and peers would help me to look at my life and make sense of it.

While at Hazelden I would get turned on to the 12 Steps and would actually do Steps 1 through 5 during my stay. These Steps would provide me with a way out of acute addiction. They ended up saving my life and giving it great meaning. They are with me to this day.

I had a personal counselor at Hazelden named Pat Mitchell. She used to call me "curly top" because of my curly hair, which is now long gone. She had been through a lot in her life, though I never learned any of the details. She had a kind of wisdom that a person only gets from the experience of hardship. She was super loving, kind, and warm, but she was no pushover. God, I needed someone like that.

I met with Pat privately in her office twice a week. In one of our sessions she asked me to tell her about Rene, my beloved English nanny who had basically raised me from about age three to age eight. Some four years after Rene left our home, my mom told me that Rene had called her to tell her that she was sick; she had brain cancer and was heading back to England to settle her affairs. After not seeing her for four years, I ran into Rene "randomly" the very next week in the middle of New York City. I knew she was dying, but she did not know that I knew. I had an opportunity to tell her how much she had meant to me. I really let her know how special she was. As I recounted this story to Pat, my heart cracked open and the tears began. So much grief poured out of me. I could not pull it back together. I kept crying and crying for about a half hour. They were the only tears I would shed at Hazelden, but the depth of the release and healing was enough to open me up to Grace and begin my recovery in earnest. I looked up to Pat Mitchell in a way that is hard to explain. There was trust and love that felt unconditional. She was an angel in my life.

When I arrived at rehab my attitude was poor—it was still going to be me against them. I was running the show. A few weeks later, especially after I broke down in Pat's office, I started to soften and open up to the possibility of change. I had found some humility and was able to put my long-held opinions about everything to the side. It appeared to me that these people actually were on my side and had my best interests in mind. I started to embrace the idea that I was going to let go of all drugs and alcohol, even my beloved marijuana. I also started to take suggestions and do what was asked of me. I learned many profound lessons in rehab that have stayed with me to this day. They are lessons that have stood the test of time and deserve mention here.

THE SIMPLE ACT OF BED MAKING

On day one, I learned how to make my own bed. I had made a bed before but never like this. Here, you had to pay attention. It was done in a specific way. It took me three tries before I could meet the house manager's specifications. At first, the lesson was lost on me. Sure, make your bed. Take care of your things. Keep yourself in order. I had only made my bed before because I was forced to—I didn't care whether it was made or not. Nothing would make me do it except the consequences that outside forces like my mom or one of our nannies or housekeepers placed upon me. Rehab seemed no different, except here you were not allowed to eat breakfast until you completed this simple task, so there was ample incentive to actually get it right. Over my 50 days at Hazelden, it was the first thing I did each day, and 24 years later, I make my bed almost every day and still feel a little uncomfortable when I don't.

At some point, my perspective shifted from tending to responsibilities because of potential consequences to doing things because I actually wanted to. *This is the beginning of the development of an identity of one's own.* My attitude at the beginning of those 50 days was rebellious and contemptuous. "This sucks, but I have to do it or I don't get to eat." My attitude at the end was "I can't explain it and I certainly won't admit it, but I feel good when I make my bed . . . and I'm good at doing it. Shit, I might not be good at anything else today, but I am going to be good at this." Big shift!

On some deep level, I began to grasp the idea that a seemingly mundane act such as making my bed could have an effect on the rest of my day. It was a calming, centering starting point. There is simplicity in making your bed, and simplicity is among the greatest gifts you can cultivate in your life. Making my bed when I first get up slows me down for a moment and gives me shelter from the acceleration of thought that takes place each morning. Once your thinking gets momentum, you're off to the races, and simple acts, which require you to slow down and pay attention, are often pushed to the side. Making your bed is one small step out of your head and into your heart. It is a great, simple example of acting one's way out of bad thinking. Prayers, for me, also happen around my bed. As I am making my bed, I seem to drop into a pleasant conversation with my Higher Power.

MANIPULATION AND SUFFERING

While in rehab, I also had to learn to let go of my manipulative ways. This was put to the test when one of my oldest friends arrived at Hazelden a few weeks after me. Andrew had introduced me to my dear friend Bennett when we were about 15 years old. Bennett had grown up around the corner from me in New York. He, too, was a Deadhead, a true champion of the cause. Bennett was at once hyper-intelligent, handsome, brazen, abrasive, and purely over the top. He lived as many of us did: beyond rules, beyond reproach. You couldn't faze him through authoritarian, parental intimidation—he simply didn't care. Consequently, he was the last person your parents would ever want you to bring home. The first time my mom met Bennett, she threw us both out of the house, utterly disgusted by what she feared her son was becoming.

Bennett's parents also had issues with him. On a regular basis the shit would hit the fan in his home and they would kick him out. He would walk over to my house and throw a coin up to my second-story bedroom window to let me know he was downstairs. I'd call down to the doorman so he'd let Bennett in without ringing us up and alerting my mom to his presence. Bennett would come in, and we would sit for hours listening to the Dead and smoking pot in my bathroom as my poor mom sat in a state of semi-awareness of what was happening under her roof.

Bennett and I became very close. He, Andrew, a few other core members of our posse, and I traveled around seeing the Dead, partied a lot, and ended up spending our adolescent years together. We also came through hardcore drug addiction. Now most of us are in recovery. It would be difficult to explain all that we have come through together.

I got sober a few weeks before Bennett decided to. "Tom," he said plainly on the phone one day, "I may be joining you there at Hazelden before you know it." My heart leapt at the idea. I was so lonely. To have a friend from my past with me through this difficult experience would be amazing—but there was an issue. There were two parts to the rehab facility. One of them was co-ed and the other, where I was, was men only. People from the two different sides were not allowed to speak with each other. If they put Bennett on the other side, it would be torture for us. Still, they might decide to keep us apart if they believed putting us together would be disruptive to our recovery or their process in any way.

For half a day I shifted into manipulation mode. How could I control the situation without telling anyone so that Bennett would end up on my side of the facility? What tale could I weave? There was suddenly huge pressure on me; I wanted something again, and very badly. What would I have to do to get it? What wouldn't I do? This was a familiar mode, and I recognized it even at two weeks sober. "I'm stressed. Whoa. I feel stressed about this. The cause of the stress has to do with my attachment to a particular outcome, namely, that my friend be placed on my side of the rehab center. I'm trying to *make this happen* and it feels very uncomfortable." By this point in my recovery, I had heard about the importance of rigorous honesty. This, above all things, is a cornerstone of recovery. I had heard principles such as "Turn your will over" and "Take life on life's terms." Here was my first opportunity to practice the principle of honesty in a situation where my default would have been to lie and manipulate.

I went to speak with my counselors and told them the whole truth. I even mentioned how much I wanted Bennett, if he actually came to Hazelden, to be on this side. After telling them the truth, I felt a lot better, though I was still attached to the outcome. Four days later while I was doing chores outside, a van pulled up and Bennett got out. Carrying a banjo in one hand and a guitar in the other, sporting dark sunglasses and a small backpack, Bennett approached me looking like death just slightly warmed over. Not even stopping as he headed inside to begin his recovery, he stoically said, "Hello." My counselor came over to let me know that Bennett and I would both be on the same side.

I have found that the truth has set me free. When I drop into manipulation mode, it has not generally served me in my life. If I am willing to forsake my own principles in order to bring about an outcome to which I've become attached, it signifies that I am on the road of commotion. My suffering will be forthcoming. Learning to tell the truth is a necessary component of recovery. I had been dishonest for a long time. At Hazelden, I began to learn how to be honest and to see how this would have immediate benefits, such as the peace of mind that comes from developing the ability to let things go.

LAUGH AS IF YOUR LIFE DEPENDED ON IT

I have laughed a lot in my life. Sometimes, the laughter has been so complete that tears have streamed down my face. But there has not been a time when laughter was so necessary and so epic as between Bennett and me during the three weeks our time overlapped at Hazelden. The sheer joy of it! In the daytime, we attended group therapy, meetings, individual counseling sessions, and meals. Then, at night, Bennett and I would sit awake out at the nurse's station. If you couldn't sleep, they'd let you come out and sit there as long as you wanted. We smoked cigarettes and talked . . . about everything. We covered all the bases well into the wee hours and eventually made our way to our beds and collapsed in elated exhaustion. Bennett was an incredible gift for me at Hazelden. We came together under what many would deem the worst of circumstances and taught each other the importance and power of laughing from the depth of our guts. Those fits of laughter were a salve for my broken heart.

RECOVERING WITH MY PARENTS

My mother and father both came to Hazelden for "family week," which was basically an opportunity for family members to learn about the dis-ease of addiction and to understand their part in it. My sisters sat this one out. We were so distant from each other and had experienced so much hurt that I can understand why they would not have come. My parents, unwilling to face each other, would not come to family week together, so they came during separate weeks, which kept me in rehab a bit longer.

Each of them would spend seven days at "parent rehab," after which they would see me for the first time. We would have a long meeting during which I would recount the story of my life, including all my drug history. The idea was to tell the truth and get free of the past to whatever extent was possible.

I will never forget the day my mother came to visit me at Hazelden. She was waiting for me in the front area and when I came around the corner to see her, she had the biggest smile on her face. I almost didn't recognize her. She was beaming so much love toward me. When was the last time I had seen that or felt that? It had been a long time. In that instant, a bridge was built between us. Though we still had our challenges ahead, I was reminded of the fact that my mom would do anything for me. Somewhere along the way, I had forgotten that. Whenever I think of her now, that smile when I was in rehab is always the first image that comes to mind.

My father's visit was slightly less memorable for me. I do recall a lot of tears on both our parts as I recounted my life history, but it was the aftermath of Hazelden and the different effects it had on my parents that has always stayed with me.

Dad was deeply moved by the common experiences he shared with other parents he met at Hazelden. He really connected with a part of himself through them. It was beautiful. His spirit was lifted for a while, but it was not sustainable. He stated plainly that "the God thing" was a hurdle for him. And since he felt that the God thing was required, he came to the conclusion that he could not progress forward this way. It's strange: Dad did believe in the beauty and magic of life. He cried many tears in realization of the connectedness of all things, but in the end, he could not connect with and open himself up to a power that he could not directly perceive. He did not have that ability. When he needed it most, he couldn't access it.

It's unfortunate, but my dad had no methods for healing and thus no effective plan for getting better. He rarely exercised, nor did he have any method of stress relief. Having never connected with his body, he did not develop a sense of the innate healing forces within him. So he put responsibility for his health and well-being into the hands of others. When he finally made the connection between what he ate and how he felt, it was too late because he was mired in food addiction. His unresolved trauma remained as such until the day he died. In the latter part of his life, he underwent at least four major operations including two kidney transplants, arterial bypass surgery in his leg, and quadruple bypass heart surgery. In short, he lived in a perfect storm that would trap him and torture him for 15 years until his death.

By the time I went to Hazelden, my mom had already been making positive changes in an attempt to get healthy. She let go of drinking, a huge feat, given that she had no program of support, and amazingly, she quit smoking, too, after receiving a cancer diagnosis and undergoing a hysterectomy. She figured that since she wouldn't be able to smoke for a couple of weeks surrounding her surgery, she might as well quit. Unfortunately, though, as someone who had been smoking three packs a day for more than 20 years, she had a lot of stuffed emotions to deal with. Plus she had faced immense challenges on the home front, not the least of which was that her son had become a drug addict and her daughters had issues of their own. So even with these enormous lifestyle changes, the years ahead would not be easy. She desperately needed recovery and support. Consequently, by the time Mom went through family week at Hazelden, she went for it like a drowning person reaching for a life preserver. She got it completely.

For the next two years up until her death in 1991, she never missed her weekly Families Anonymous meeting. I tell people that my mother was on a steep ascent out of the darkness of her life into the light of her own shining spirit. It crushes me that she did not have more years, but I am happy that she was solid and in recovery before she had to move on.

Shortly after Mom died way too young at 51, her friends at her Families Anonymous meeting erected a tree with a plaque bearing a dedication in her honor at the corner of 70th Street and Lexington Avenue in New York City. It is for me the most significant landmark in the city where I was born. My belief is that she has had a hand in the unfolding of my life since she left her body in 1991—a nod here, a wink there. I just feel a presence, a memory. It's like a warm, fragrant wind that lifts me up and holds me.

Dad would never have the awakening that my mom experienced, and we had a rough time with each other in the last decade of his life. He was brilliant, funny, and warm, but his dis-ease later robbed him of these qualities. Even with his challenges, though, one of my father's greatest hopes was for my happiness. He was a champion of my cause. Through the most complex difficulties—both his and mine—he never, ever gave up on me. And just like my mom, I believe that my dad, in some form, has had a big hand in the successes of my life since his death in 2003.

Looking back at my parents' lives, I am struck by the realization that there was no way out for them. My life now is a continuation of their effort to heal. My healing counts for me, but in a strange way it also counts as part of their healing. It makes no difference that they have passed on from their physical form. *My recovery is their recovery.* My addiction and consequent healing were made possible in part by their suffering and through efforts of theirs that I am not able to express in words. I feel that they want me to succeed so badly that the energy of that prayer has affected the outcome of my life. In turn, I feel that the outcome of my recovery affects their lives retroactively, even though their lives are over. Such is the power of healing and recovery. A family can be healed in the present moment in ways that affect the unfolding of time forward as well as back into the past. This is not science; it's a feeling. It makes sense to me the way Higher Power or God makes sense to me. I choose to believe this and it has served me. Use it if it feels right to you.

On the day of my departure from Hazelden, I was not sure what was going to happen. It was clear that I needed a one-day-at-a-time approach to living if I was going to get through in one piece. I had come a long way in 50 days, perhaps as far as a person could come in such a short amount of time. My thought upon leaving was that the experience I had just undergone was a gift that everyone should experience at the age of 22 before they go out into the world to live their life. The tools I learned there are with me to this day—it was an invaluable experience. I may not have attended Yale University as most of the men in my family have done. Yet not one of them has been so fortunate as to attend Hazelden as I have.

CHAPTER 7

WHAT YOU REALLY NEED TO KNOW ABOUT THE 12 STEPS

I am an advocate of the 12 Steps because they worked for me in my life and I've seen them work for countless others. The 12 Steps work, but they require a few ingredients and understandings in order for them to work well. Let's take a look at them and see if we can better understand what is useful, what can be let go of, and what can be added in order to make these powerful teachings even more effective for the addicts of the world who turn to them for help.

Everything that follows here comes from the opinions I've formed based on my direct experience with the Steps and various fellowships over the past 25 years. My hope is that what I share here will inspire you to reap the benefits the 12 Steps have to offer while helping you avoid some of the pitfalls. Many people have misunderstandings about this wonderful spiritual path that I would like to shed light on here. Whether you have experience with the 12-Step universe or not, this chapter will help you better understand both the program and the fellowship, give you practical advice that will help prepare you, and, hopefully, inspire you to give the 12 Steps a try (or a second, or a third . . .).

THE 12 STEPS: YES, AND . . .

Usually, you hear from one of two camps about the 12 Steps. In one group you have the people who cannot entertain a conversation where the 12 Steps and the fellowships that surrounded them are brought under scrutiny. If you suggest that the 12 Steps can be improved upon, they see this as nothing short of blasphemy. These are the fundamentalist attendees of 12-Step programs. Their experience with the Steps and fellowship has been profoundly positive, yet they have latched onto the program with the hooks of dogma and it has caused them to shut their minds to any discourse that calls for an investigation into and evolution of the process that saved them. They take an extreme position. However, among the ranks of 12-Step fellowship you have every possible perspective about the 12 Steps. It would be incorrect to conclude that all the voices inside 12-Step programs are extreme. Unfortunately, extreme voices are often the ones that are heard the most.

In the other camp you have a different kind of extremism: folks who argue against the efficacy of the 12 Steps for a variety of reasons. Some of them feel that the 12 Steps "let them down" because they or their loved ones have not been able to heal from their dis-ease. Others may have had negative experiences with members of a 12-Step fellowship that severely colored their opinions. Still others may have had no interaction with the 12 Steps, but citing the relatively low success rates of 12-Step programs, they get upset and decide to pick apart something they do not fully understand.

There are also those people who strive to apply scientific metrics to the process of 12-Step recovery. They want peer-reviewed science. Unfortunately, we are talking about a process that proclaims itself to be spiritual in nature and has infinite variations from one person to the next. The process of getting sober through 12-Step recovery does not lend itself well to scientific metrics. Of course, we must try to understand what works and what doesn't; we want to grasp and implement best practices. However, we have to accept that trying to apply scientific metrics to a spiritual process with endless variables is inherently problematic.

Thus, very few people seem to be providing a levelheaded perspective on the 12 Steps, a system that is obviously of great importance to us all. The 12 Steps are too effective to overlook, but not effective enough to place them beyond the possibility for improvement. Since addiction is a very painful and costly dis-ease, wouldn't it make sense to try to understand and build upon a system of healing that is working to a considerable extent? One group refuses the possibility of improvement and the other group wants to throw the baby out with the bathwater.

I'm interested in helping you understand what the 12 Steps are and what they aren't. I am not extreme in my position; I have considered both sides of the coin. I credit the 12 Steps with saving my life, but I also see where the program can be made much more successful. Ironically, the people in both of the aforementioned groups will likely disapprove of what I have to say here. They will want me to take an extreme position—or take no position at all, especially publicly. I feel compelled to express what my actual experience has been and then share what I have learned by watching others fail and succeed, and by taking into consideration many viewpoints—extreme and otherwise.

THE CREATION OF THE 12 STEPS

In 1935, Bill Wilson, the man who established Alcoholics Anonymous, found himself in a hospital room for the third time, having somehow survived yet another day of alcoholic torture that most folks could not conjure in their worst nightmares. He was utterly beaten down, frightened of everything, and certain that there was no way out of his problem. When he was released from the hospital, despite what he knew he would drink again as he always had before. With each new episode he felt that much worse that God had decided to keep him around for another day. His wife, friends, business associates, and everybody else he knew felt the frustration of powerlessness, sadness, anger, and betrayal.

Unfortunately, there was no known solution to the problems of alcoholism and drug addiction at that time. Alcoholics and addicts usually ended up in jails, hospitals, and insane asylums after being utterly ostracized by friend and foe. With little or no success, doctors, religious leaders, psychologists, gurus, and shamans had tried for centuries to deal with these people who just could not stop destroying their lives. To be an active alcoholic at any point in history was a terrible fate, but to have been one before Bill Wilson had his spiritual awakening in 1935 meant you were basically without hope.

Though no one could have known it at the time, that day of awakening was a turning point for the human race. Just as happened with Buddha's revelations under the Bodhi Tree, Jesus's Sermon on the Mount, Moses and the Ten Commandments, and Mohammed's Revelations, humankind was about to have a massive Divine download, which would pass through the least likely of places, the heart of a lifelong raging alcoholic named Bill Wilson. (To all the religious folks out there who might take offense at the comparison of Bill Wilson to these iconic religious saints, please don't. The comparison seeks only to relate the significance of the information transmitted through this person and the resulting effect it had on multitudes of people, in this case the world's alcoholics and addicts.)

For on that day, Bill Wilson was struck "awake" and a magical idea flooded into his thoughts that would positively affect the lives of millions of people who had previously had little hope of recovery. The seed ideas, the core of his enlightenment, were these: if I connect with and put my faith in a power greater than myself, and if I can speak to another alcoholic and share my experience, strength, and hope with him, I will be able to recover from this hopelessness known as alcoholism.

Bill Wilson and a doctor friend of his known as "Dr. Bob" went on to develop the 12-Step program of Alcoholics Anonymous and out of this basic framework more than 200 other programs have sprung forth over the last 75 years, including Al-Anon and Narcotics, Codependents, Adult Children of Alcoholics, Gambling, Overeaters, Sex and Love, Debtors, Marijuana, and Cocaine Anonymous, to name but a few. To date, millions of people have overcome addiction and turned their lives around by embracing the 12 Steps.

THE 12 STEPS AS A SPIRITUAL TEACHING

You need to know that the 12 Steps contain very powerful and transformative teachings. When I use the word *teachings* to describe what lies within the 12 Steps, I mean that the process of going through the 12 Steps leads to the Truth, meaning spiritual Truth with a capital "T." Any doctrine that leads you to the Truth is a teaching. For people who diligently and wholeheartedly do the work contained within the 12 Steps, transformation and healing are likely. But even doctrines with the power to take you to the Truth can be misinterpreted and lead you away from it. Any doctrine can be interpreted in a variety of ways. Just look at any major religion and the factions of followers with differing opinions. It is the same within the 12-Step universe. There is no "one way" to approach the 12 Steps, no "one way" to deepen spiritual understanding. There is no standardized approach. This, in and of itself, is an important teaching and one of the keys to penetrating the 12 Steps.

Looking at the 12 Steps as a teaching is important. Usually, we only attribute this high status to a doctrine that is quite ancient, and the 12 Steps are only 75 years old. In that short span of years, 12-Step programs have grown to be the most widely used method of overcoming addiction of all kinds—from alcoholism to narcotics to overeating and many others. Untold numbers of people have used the 12 Steps to recover from acute addiction. Its impact is immeasurable, and when it came into being, it was nothing short of revolutionary.

WHAT'S THE POINT OF THE 12 STEPS?

The actual purpose of the 12 Steps is to facilitate a spiritual awakening in the person who follows them, whereby one's thinking and perspective on the world shift considerably. While it is not usually a sudden experience like it was for Bill Wilson, after a while a person who has worked the Steps can reflect that they have changed to such an extent that they no longer identify with the person they once were. It is as if they have been given a new vision of the world altogether, and in this new vision they have meaning and purpose and a workable approach to the challenges of being a human being. *And,* of course, they no longer desire to drink or use drugs or engage in their addiction of choice.

Establishing this spiritual connection, awakening to Truth, and being of service to others are the core tenets of the 12 Steps, which are accessible to anyone. Since alcoholism and addiction are nonpartisan, nondiscriminating dis-eases, everyone is susceptible to them. Therefore, by design, the 12 Steps have to be accessible and effective for all.

If there were no connection between the 12 Steps and addiction and they existed simply as a spiritual path for humanity, I believe many more millions of people would have found and embraced them. The fact that these Steps were originally intended to help alcoholics and, later, addicts has definitively limited their appeal. I know only two non-addict persons who have gone through the Steps simply to experience their benefits. I am sure there must be others, but probably very few. As stated, countless addicts and alcoholics the world over have gone through these Steps and recovered from what they previously felt was a hopeless state of mind and body.

THE POWER OF 12-STEP MEETINGS

A big part of the reason the 12 Steps are effective has to do with the amazing fellowships that have gathered around them. Meetings are free. Anyone is welcome as long as they have a desire to get better from their addiction. A sponsor will spend time with you and take you through the work of the 12 Steps for free. People in 12-Step fellowship really want you to recover from addiction. They have been through a lot and can speak from direct experience about things you will likely need help with.

The magical alchemy of 12-Step meetings has seriously upgraded my thinking and perspectives on the world. To connect with people in this way is one of the greatest blessings I have known. I have never encountered a group of people who were so willing to honestly communicate their feelings and regularly make themselves vulnerable than at meetings. Of course, I have found some meetings more helpful and enjoyable than others. I have been to plenty of meetings that I did not enjoy. There was even one time in the past 25 years that I left a meeting because it so completely put me off. However, there is almost always something that is shared in words or through someone's presence that has made it important and valuable for me to attend. Just the simple process of holding space for one another so that we can speak our truth creates the possibility for change. It is an act of symbiotic, cooperative engagement aimed at supporting the move from a thought-based to an awareness-based way of life.

THERE ARE INFINITE APPROACHES

The beauty of the 12 Steps is that, if genuinely approached with an open mind and with the help of a caring sponsor, they will serve their purpose of lifting a person up out of addiction. There are an infinite number of approaches to the 12 Steps that will work. Some ingredients are required—honesty, willingness, open-mindedness, and a desire to learn and grow—but as long as these are in place, the Steps allow for a lot of interpretation, and these interpretations are played out every day as sponsor and sponsee sit opposite each other to go through the work involved in the Steps.

Think of the 12 Steps as one doctrine of a spiritual path of recovery from addiction. As happens with all religions and spiritual paths, a congregation gathers around the doctrine. In this case, the congregation is varied, both in terms of the backgrounds of its constituency and the individual approaches to it. In Judaism, there are the Orthodox who have their beliefs about life and what it means to be Jewish, there are Conservative Jews with different ideas, and there are Reform Jews with still other ideas: three groups, three different approaches to Judaism. Within each group are subgroups—sects, factions, families, and individuals—whose ideas vary one from the next. Yet they all consider themselves Jewish. They have access in most cases to the same doctrine and texts. All of them, from the most orthodox to the most reformed, have their own unique paths through their religion. How do they navigate? They navigate according to their teachers. The same is basically true for 12-Step programs.

WHAT IS A SPONSOR AND HOW DO YOU GET ONE?

In the 12 Steps our teachers take the form of sponsors, friends in recovery, and others whom we hear from at meetings. A sponsor is a person who has agreed to guide us through the 12 Steps; we navigate the Steps primarily the way we have been taught by our sponsors. Normally, we choose our own sponsor by approaching someone who "has what we want." This basically means we see in another person a level of experience, intelligence, and success with the 12 Steps that we desire to have as well. In more spiritual terms we might say that they carry a certain vibration or consciousness that draws us to them.

We ask such a person if they would be willing to take us through the Steps. They will be interested in our level of commitment. If we are "willing to go to any length" to defeat our addiction, they will usually agree to take us on. (Please note that occasionally a person is simply unable to take on a sponsee because they are too busy or are leaving town, for example. This should not deter you from asking the next person you connect with. Also, if you decide you have made the wrong choice, you can always stop working with one sponsor and start working with another.)

Your approach to the 12 Steps, therefore, will usually take the shape of your sponsor's. If the sponsor is an orthodox 12-Step person, you will get an orthodox education in the 12 Steps. If the sponsor is conservative or reformed (meaning less "religious") in approach, that will be the experience that is passed to you. There are ultra-orthodox approaches, extremely reformed approaches, and everything in between in 12-Step society. There is no one way that is correct for all: *different people need different things at different times.* This is another very important teaching. I caution you to beware of those persons who insist that there is only one way and that it will always be the same throughout time. This leads, in my opinion, to great challenges. We must be willing to evolve and allow our program of recovery to evolve along with us.

As you may have surmised, I have a very reformed approach to the 12 Steps. Certain people are going to be drawn to me for help. Others would not be able to benefit from what I have to offer and will be drawn to other people. Thank God we are all here with our unique personalities and approaches to 12-Step recovery, because collectively, we can help almost everyone who comes to recovery with sincerity.

WHICH "A" IS RIGHT FOR ME?

The right group for you is the one where you feel most at home! Typically speaking, people who have struggled with alcohol end up in Alcoholics Anonymous. Others who have struggled more with narcotics might resonate more with Narcotics Anonymous. If you've been a cocaine or marijuana addict and want to connect with people who have this same addiction path, you might try Cocaine Anonymous or Marijuana Anonymous. People with relationship issues focused around other addicts and alcoholics will find great support in Al-Anon. Those who struggle with codependency can avail themselves of Codependents Anonymous. Overeaters Anonymous helps people with food-related addictions such as bingeing, bulimia, anorexia, and emotional eating. People who have grown up in an alcoholic or otherwise dysfunctional family can find healing through Adult Children of Alcoholics. Gamblers Anonymous supports recovering gambling addicts, Debtors Anonymous helps those who suffer from money problems and compulsive debt. It is an amazing thing that all of these groups exist.

When I got out of rehab, I was told that I had to attend a meeting every day. While drinking was present throughout my using, drugs were a much bigger problem. My counselors told me, though, that I should try both of the two main fellowships and stick with what felt the best. The important thing is to find one program and stick to it for a while so you can begin to heal within a community of people who can get to know you and support you.

Once you get to your first meeting, you are connecting with the main treatment in the world for alcoholism and addiction of every kind. No matter how you may have suffered, I believe you are in the right place and healing is now possible. It may help you to know that everyone has a hard time with change. It's one of those things that most of us struggle with, especially when we are presented with concepts that challenge our long-held prejudices and beliefs.

DON'T LET "THE GOD THING" GET IN THE WAY

There is a great misunderstanding about the 12 Steps: that you have to believe in God in order for them to work. This was insurmountable for my dad, as I mentioned before. But one of the most incredible things about the 12 Steps is that it can be a spiritual path, not pertaining to any particular vision of God; a nontheistic path, not pertaining to any vision of God at all; or a religious one for those who desire it to be. The 12-Step doctrine is so flexible that it gives us the choice of what we want to conceive of as a Higher Power. Its roots certainly lean in the Judeo-Christian direction, which at first can be off-putting for those among us who have had negative experiences concerning God and religion. Yet just beneath the surface of the words of the Steps is a vast space offering an invitation to anyone who is called to grow beyond addiction and develop themselves into the vision their heart holds for them. Imagine a group of people who are glued together by the terrible hardship of a shared, deadly dis-ease; they've all survived because of a life-saving solution. Think how amazing it is that each person has had their own conception of the thing from which they have drawn the added power they've needed to overcome their dis-ease. It's the most accessible form of spirituality I've encountered, though it certainly may not seem so at first. *No matter who you are, whether you believe in God or not, there will be a way for you to conceive of a power that is greater than you alone. That is all that is needed to step out of the darkness of addiction and into the light of recovery.*

This is part of what has made the 12 Steps so universally available and successful for those who have understood and been able to accept these ideas. It is a terrible shame when I hear people say that they could not accept the 12 Steps because of "the God thing." I urge them to look at the 12 Steps as an opportunity to come into contact with the more spiritual parts of themselves. If the word *spiritual* is problematic, I then explain that by spiritual I simply mean "more subtle." With the 12 Steps, as with all spiritual paths, we are coming into contact with matters that are subtler than what can be perceived through the physical senses. Do you believe that there are things going on in the universe that you cannot perceive directly with your senses? Perhaps *that* is the concept a person would have to be open to if they are to benefit from the 12 Steps.

Most people easily agree that they cannot perceive everything in the universe, that there are things that go beyond their understanding. But the hardest thing for people to imagine is that something beyond their perception might actually be interested in their well-being. It just makes no rational sense, and so a person concludes, "I do not believe in a power greater than myself and that I could tap into this power to draw from it and heal." Yet our whole existence is based upon our heartbeat and our breath, which lie beyond our control. We cannot explain why the heart beats or from where the breath originates. What animates us? No one can say. It is all a gift. Some might say a gift from God. Others might say there is no God. But we are alive, and there are mysteries we cannot perceive with our senses. So many of us have recovered from addiction and alcoholism based on the idea that some kind of power is greater than we are as individuals. That is enough for me. And that's just the point: it can be enough for you, too, if only you can stay open to the idea, not the idea of a God, but rather of a source of power you can tap into that is greater than your individual power. That is all you need. I can't explain how it works because I don't know. I can only tell you it works.

REMAIN OPEN-MINDED AND MORE WILL BE REVEALED

Arriving at rehab in the late afternoon, I was thrust into my first group meeting, which ended with everyone standing and reciting the Lord's Prayer. I had heard it before but had certainly never recited it in my life . . . and I was not about to now. I raised my hand then and there. "Uh, this is not for me," I proclaimed. The whole room exploded in laughter.

I had been carrying an astonishing resentment toward organized religion. It was simply all bad in my opinion. I condemned the violence, war, hypocrisy, separatism, and authoritarianism that it had produced over the centuries. Of course, we all condemn these things. The unfortunate part for me was that I had shut out everything having to do with it. I thought anyone who spoke of God was lost. That was as far as I had gotten with it. Hearing the antiquated words of the Lord's Prayer reflected all of this horror for me. I couldn't get past it. That closed-mindedness, while understandable, is a killer for people who have struggled with acute addiction.

People came up to me after that meeting and told me that they appreciated my honesty and that it would serve me well. I kept hearing that what counted were open-mindedness and willingness. Nothing more. If I had these, people told me, "More will be revealed."

No one tried to get me to believe anything. I was simply asked to reflect upon my personal beliefs and my direct experience with addiction. After six weeks, when I left rehab, I had begun a relationship with "the powers that be." I felt a new willingness to consider possibilities I had previously shut out. This willingness, it turned out, was more than enough to get on a path toward healing my broken heart and life. I did not believe in God per se, but that didn't matter. *I was open to receiving whatever revelation might come.* I would not have to believe something that did not make sense to me. I only had to stay open to what life was showing me. I had to be willing to look at it, feel it, and see how it sat within.

In actuality, I was a deeply spiritual person, though terribly cut off from it all at the end of my addiction. I have to thank the Grateful Dead for providing me with an experience that first allowed me to touch something greater than myself. Though I was not aware of it at the time, those extraordinary moments with that extraordinary band gave me proof that something more was going on when I needed it the most.

The spiritual idea that "more will be revealed" to the open-minded and willing has turned out to be true in my life. In my early years of recovery, I worked with a brilliant therapist named Joe Tolson, who turned me on to a concept that allowed me to open up to new ideas. "Tommy, if you have a problem with organized religion, separate the doctrine from the congregation! Go back and study the words in the doctrines and see where that gets you." So I started to read different interpretations of the Bible, both the Old and New Testaments. I discovered the amazing work of Emmet Fox, whose interpretation of Jesus's Sermon on the Mount was nothing short of life changing. I learned of Thomas Merton, whose poetry about God thrilled me even though I had no definable personal belief in God. I also got way into Buddhist and other Eastern philosophies. Finding the work of renowned Sufi poet Jelaladdin Rumi will go down as one of the great discoveries of my life. Rumi spoke about devotion to the Divine in a way that absolutely melted my heart wide open. I began to see that despite my negative feelings toward organized religion, there might still be a place for someone like me to search for meaning and a Higher Power among the words and poetry of these spiritual masters.

If you are a religious person, the 12 Steps will give you an opportunity to connect more deeply with yourself, your community, and the God of your understanding. If you are not religious, are agnostic or atheist, or have had negative feelings around religion as I have, the 12 Steps will provide you with an access point to deeper parts of yourself and a sense of connection with all. That has been my direct experience, and it has been an amazing, wild journey these past 25 years.

WORKING THE PROGRAM VERSUS WORKING THE FELLOWSHIP

Here's a reenactment of a conversation I have had maybe 100 times in the past 24 years.

Person: "I notice you are not drinking. Uh, is there a particular reason?"
Me: "I had a problem with alcohol and so now I leave it alone."
Person: "You just decided not to drink anymore?"
Me: "Actually I work the 12 Steps."
Person: "Yeah, I tried the 12 Steps, but they didn't work for me."
Me: "Oh. What was your experience?"
Person: "Well, you know, I went to a whole bunch of meetings . . ."
Me: "Did you work the program? I mean did you go through the 12 Steps with a sponsor?"
Person: "No, it just wasn't working. So I blew it off."
Me: "What wasn't working?"
Person: "The 12 Steps."
Me: "I thought you said you never went through them."
Person: "Well, I went to lots of meetings. You know. You can tell when something is right for you or not."

People who attend 12-Step meetings fall into two main categories: those who "work the program," following the 12 Steps as outlined in their fellowship's version of the Big Book, and those who don't. In the latter group, you have people who have gotten sober simply by attending meetings. I know some of them well. These are what you might call the ultra-reformed participants of the congregation. Their approach to the program is based on community and fellowship rather than on self-study with 12-Step work—that's why I call it working the fellowship. I am not standing in their shoes and so cannot say how their approach is working. However, most of the people I have encountered who struggle with acute addiction have needed devotion to some kind of spiritual path in order to find peace and contentment in their lives and stick with their recovery.

Those who work the 12 Steps seem to be the ones in 12-Step meeting rooms who have achieved the most freedom, are most enjoying life, and have the most to offer. The promises and miracles we experience and hear about in meetings are by no means limited to this group, but they are much more frequently realized than by those who just attend meetings. I know from experience that this was true for me. I tried it both ways.

In the first year of my recovery after Hazelden, I attended many meetings. I was not working the Steps and had no sponsor. I showed up; I did my meetings; I left. The lifestyle and community of recovery were not yet a part of my life except for the hour each day I spent in a meeting. My approach to my recovery lacked the level of devotion I had felt when I was in rehab. Gradually, I went to fewer and fewer meetings. Eventually I stopped. Shortly after I had attained one year sober, despite everything I had been through and all that I had learned in rehab, I relapsed. I was standing on a porch at a party shortly after graduating from college and two guys were smoking pot out of a ridiculous six-foot bong. They offered it to me. I looked over my left shoulder. Then I looked over my right shoulder. No one I knew was there. "Sure. I'd love one." This set into motion a year-long relapse.

The point here is that I was floating through life. I had neither principles to live by nor the discipline to apply them if I could identify them. *What was I devoted to? Well, I did not know.* I had learned so much in rehab in 50 days, but unlike in the movies, the progress I had made there did not have a "happily ever after" sheen. Something more was required. I had thought I would never use drugs again. What had happened?

I had not established a community of support or a foundation of principles and ethics that held enough weight for me to stay sober. In all honesty, after rehab, I did not take the 12 Steps seriously. You might say I was between worlds. On the one hand, I had no desire to go back to living as an active addict. But I had not developed a life of meaning within recovery that would compel me forward. I floated in the limbo of non-commitment and indecision. This is a dangerous land to be in for people who struggle with addiction. If you don't have a plan in early recovery, then you definitely have a plan . . . a plan to leave recovery!

DON'T QUIT BEFORE THE MIRACLE HAPPENS

One of the great slogans of 12-Step programs is "Don't quit before the miracle happens." I've described how profound rehab was for me. I've told you about the efficacy of the 12 Steps and how I credit them with saving my life. I came into the program kicking and screaming. Everything was a problem. I became a two-year-old again. Every other word out of my mouth was "Why?" I refused to believe most of what I was being told. There had to be a better way than embracing the ideas in these 12 Steps. So much about it rubbed me the wrong way. And you know what? Some of it still does. Thank God I didn't have to agree with everything to change my thinking and my life. At first, I *did* have to do most of what others suggested. Later on, I would be able to build a program based upon the new consciousness I had found.

The early going was rough. I never knew if I was going to make it through the day. I did have a desire to be sober—I wanted that more than I wanted to use drugs—*but* I also wanted to use drugs.

One of the great challenges all newcomers have to face is the mistaken idea that how they are thinking today is how they will be thinking in the future. If your thinking were to remain the same, what would be the point of recovery? You imagine yourself in six months just as miserable or stuck as you are right now. It's hard work to transform yourself, and doubt can crop up at any moment. You need to be around people who have been where you are and have undergone a shift in consciousness to where they—and you—want to be. One of the reasons 12-Step meetings are so helpful is that they put you around other people who have achieved this. So I'd go to meetings and hear from people who had been around for a while. They talked about how it used to be, often describing my experience to a tee. They shared how things had miraculously changed for them. Thus I had a tiny hint of faith that the same thing could happen for me. But when?

THE FINAL SOBERING THOUGHT

On June 23, 1991, I walked into a 12-Step meeting in New York City. I raised my hand for the third day in a row proclaiming that I had just one day sober.

A guy walked up to me and asked, "Hey, man. What's your problem?" I literally stuttered, unable to give any answer.

"That's right," he said. "You have no idea what your problem is. I've seen you in here these last three days and you still have just one day sober. So, what's your deal?"

He paused a moment and then continued, "You see, you're an addict. You've got a disease called addiction. It has a treatment, but you're not applying the treatment. You're out there in the world with untreated addiction. That's your problem."

This was not new information for me, but the way he put it, his clarity, and his conviction struck me to my core. Before I could say much, he plainly stated, "I'm your sponsor now. We are going to hit a meeting together every day." Normally, you ask someone to be your sponsor, not the other way around, but this guy was pretty clear on the fact that he was going to be my sponsor. He didn't even ask me if I was okay with that. It just was.

On each of the next 60 days, I went to a meeting with Neil. A few times, I decided not to go and Neil came to my house to get me anyway. After two months and 60 meetings, I moved to San Francisco as I had been planning to do, found another sponsor that first week, and began to work through the 12 Steps in earnest. I have stayed sober from the day I met Neil until this moment more than 23 years later. Wherever Neil is, I hope he realizes that he saved my life.

When people ask me what my bottom was before I got sober this last time, I tell it like this: I had a home, friends, money, a girlfriend, and all the trappings of a decent life. Yet I could not shake the hard thought that I would never be able to find out what I could have become if I had been able to put down drugs and alcohol. I could not live with that any longer. That was the final sobering thought that resulted in my recovery to this day.

CHAPTER 8

UNLOCKING
THE 12 STEPS

I have used the 12 Steps as the foundation for my 23 years of continuous recovery. This foundation has allowed me the freedom to pursue my heart's desires and to build a life of meaning and purpose. These ideas have worked for me. And I believe they can work for you, too.

There are great and true teachings contained within the 12 Steps. They can help you build a connection with the more subtle aspects of yourself. They can help you heal your relationships, your heart, and your life. They can escort you from the darkness of addiction into the light of recovery. They can work in anyone's life, as all true teachings can. And yet they are far from a perfect system, and there are a few things you will need to know to navigate these Steps in a manner that is correct for you and to find what you are looking for.

To this day, when I read the 12 Steps displayed on a wall at a meeting, their language is, at best, intimidating. Yet I know they contain power and provide direction to people like me who have suffered badly around addiction. Therefore, I have sought to create something that would help anyone access these Steps no matter where they are on the path.

In this chapter, we'll explore each of the 12 Steps and I'll share the insights that have helped me in working through them. To me, keys are needed to decipher, penetrate, and receive the gifts the 12 Steps have to offer. If you struggle with addiction and have tried these Steps but failed to realize a transformation, you may be wondering what keeps you from moving forward and healing. You are not alone. I, too, struggled in the early months of my recovery. I just did not see how I would ever feel better. I remember thinking that there had to be another way, but deep down I knew there was not. I had exhausted myself trying to get it right, to feel good in this body, calm in this mind, and at ease in the world. I'm not saying the 12 Steps are the only solution; I am saying they were the only solution that was immediately available and accessible to me. I knew they would work even though I had periods of great doubt. I looked around me and connected with people who had obviously changed from who they had been into who they were now. They would describe the obsession of addiction and how everything in life had become overwhelming. Then they would describe what it was like to have space and time. They were able to relax. They were free of the constant self-centered fears and the thinking that went along with them. I wanted that so badly, and I would soon have it.

Before you start, you will need to make sure you are willing to approach these Steps with an open mind. If you have that, you will be well on your way. You must have a desire to live your life to the fullest, to live a life you love. You have to know that the party, the real party, is just beginning. This is not about giving up things you love. This is about gaining the thing you have always wanted for real. If you are not there yet, then the directive is to keep looking for it, keep your chin up, and don't give up.

If you have never worked the Steps, I hope this chapter inspires you to do so. If you are already working the Steps, may these ideas serve to further assist you. And if you have already worked through the Steps, perhaps even several times, may there be something refreshing and helpful here. For the person who has worked the 12 Steps and has still not seen recovery, happiness, and contentment, may you open your mind to the possibility that something in here will shift the way you think and see the world.

Read this chapter through the lens of self-reflection. Get excited by the idea that there is a way to move beyond the suffering and pain of addiction. Do not be daunted by any concept that is not readily accessible to you. Instead, know that when you get to each of these Steps, you will be ready. This is the starting point. Understanding these Steps will give you greater access to them. You are moving out of the darkness.

Please note: This is not a how-to section or a replacement for 12-Step work with a sponsor. This is meant to light a fire within you that compels you to seek out a sponsor and work the Steps in the appropriate way for you with the guidance of someone who has gone through them successfully.

Please also note: I have changed the wording of the original 12 Steps of Alcoholics Anonymous by replacing the word *alcohol* with *addiction* and also by removing any gender references to God. I have made these changes so these Steps will be more universal and inclusive of all.

Step 1: We admitted we were powerless over our addiction— that our lives had become unmanageable.

In Step 1, we face two concepts—powerlessness and unmanageability. To admit that you are powerless over anything is probably not your first reflex, especially if it is your own behavior over which you seem to be powerless. As mystifying as we might be to outsiders, addicts who do not yet have an understanding of the dis-ease of addiction are equally dumbfounded by themselves.

The powerlessness here is experienced by people who cannot stop themselves from taking their drug of choice and, once they have done so, cannot seem to stop wanting and taking more. This is the phenomenon that most "normal" people cannot understand.

Habits are nothing more than a chain reaction between the mind, the glandular system, and the nervous system. Looking at it from the perspective of the alcoholic, it might go like this: For whatever reason, be it external stimuli like seeing someone drink a glass of wine or internal stimuli like experiencing a memory of a euphoric feeling produced by drinking alcohol, the mind directs its energy toward the impression. The individual's endocrine system is triggered by the vision or memory of the experience of alcohol and sends chemicals into the bloodstream, working with the nervous system to provoke a reaction to the stimuli. This all happens in a nanosecond and takes place over and over again, reinforcing itself until the individual has a very hard time breaking this chain reaction in order to bring about a different reaction. This is the land of addiction.

This powerlessness, therefore, extends to an addict's thoughts, not just actions. The person stuck in addiction is overpowered by the thinking that would lead them to a drink, a drug, or an addictive behavior. Once that thinking begins, it is very difficult to prevent the thought from becoming manifest in reality. The addict thinks the thought and then takes action to make the thought real. In this dark way, addicts are exceptionally creative people. They may be set against the behavior, but eventually the thought will wear them down and they arrive at the two words that permit the action: "Fuck it."

It is a wonderful thing to admit the places where we are powerless in our lives. We gain strength from this kind of humility. When it comes to addiction, it is literally a lifesaver to be able to look in the mirror and say to ourselves, "This thing has me licked. It is bigger than me and I will need help if I am to move beyond it." Before we can admit this, there is not much point in continuing. If we believe, and are as insistent as most addicts are, that we can handle the problem on our own, we are not likely open to the idea of embracing a new spiritual path linking us with a power greater than ourselves. We would have neither desire nor incentive to pursue a change in course. We simply have to concede that we do not have this in hand. We've looked at the addiction story and how important it is to an addict to keep it going. Some people need to get good and beat up before they can concede this. Fortunately, not everyone has to go to such dreadful depths to change. I have seen some people get it much earlier in their self-destruction than others.

It is simple when seen through the lens of recovery. We have a condition of dis-ease in the body-mind system. We are disconnected from our heart, meaning out of alignment with our calling. This means we are uncomfortable with life. We are uncomfortable in our own skin. We are in the habit of treating our discomfort with an addictive substance or behavior. The side effects of our self-medication have greater and greater consequences. We eventually come to the point where we cannot continue living as we are but do not have another vision for how we could live. At that precise moment, a door opens and permits grace to happen. Grace can mean "God's grace" if you are religious or simply "opportunity" if you are not. I described that moment for me, when I was on the phone with my father and he started crying.

The unmanageability, of course, is born out of powerlessness. Anyone who has experienced acute addiction can relate to the feeling that life has piled up in such a way that it feels like there is no way through it all. There is stress, there is never enough time, and it feels like you cannot take a deep breath. The details are varied among us, but the result is the same. Addicts often feel as if life is crushing them.

The Key to Step 1:

The 1st Step is the most important one of all, and for so many, this is where the internal struggle begins. Admitting one's powerlessness is hard enough on the ego, but it also hits on a deep fear that most people hold: the fear of change. One senses that "the party is over." By really admitting your powerlessness over this behavior, you are taking a big step toward letting it go. Perhaps you are terrified of letting it go even though you know it has been detrimental to your well-being. Here is a question I have been asked by almost everyone who starts down this path:

"Tommy, is there some way you know of whereby I can drink a little or maybe smoke some pot from time to time?"

My answer is always the same. "You are asking the wrong question." What you really want to know is "How can I be happy and free?" Since you equate drinking, smoking pot, or other addictive behaviors with happiness, you simply don't want to let them go. And yet, when you take a look at your history, it is probably easy for you to see that your "habit" with this thing has not brought you happiness, but rather a lot of pain and suffering. How strange that you would like to find a way to continue something that has been so painful!

Such is the way it is for most people because to change means to venture into the unknown. Many of us would prefer to live in misery we can count on than to move into unknown possibility. You just have to let go of trying to keep things the way they were. That is the trick. Venture into the unknown and you will find that what you had feared for so long was just an illusion keeping you stuck.

Thus, the 1st Step requires tremendous faith. You have been stuck in really bad thinking that has been killing you slowly. Do not listen to your thoughts any longer. Rather, with humility and willingness as your guides, allow others to help you onto the shores of safety where your healing can begin. It's important that you learn where you are powerless—over your addiction. Also learn where you are powerful—in your surrender and in your ability to do a few things that will help you on your recovery journey. Begin to see what you can change and what you cannot. Walk the path of recovery to move out of unmanageability. Do the first thing first. Bring all your presence to doing one thing at a time. In the early going, your recovery must take priority in your life. Embrace it now. Make it the most important thing in your universe, if only for this one day. And then wake up tomorrow and do it again.

Step 2: Came to believe that a power greater than ourselves could restore us to sanity.

By the time a person arrives for the first time on the unknown shores of recovery, they usually have no trouble identifying with powerlessness over their addiction. A sponsor need only draw their attention to the stark facts of their own experience. Arriving here at Step 2, though, we come face-to-face with a few ideas that may be challenging for a person to readily accept. Here, we are introduced to new language—a power greater than ourselves—and also to the idea that we need to be "restored to sanity," which implies we have been insane.

People do not like to believe themselves insane, yet how could hardcore addiction be described in any other way? The root of the word sanity is *sanus,* which means healthy. To be insane indicates a lack of mental health. When people regularly engage in behavior that is damaging to their body, mind, and well-being, we can see the insanity of that.

One strange twist of addictive thinking is that it causes us to repeat "experiments" over and over, which bear the same rotten fruit each time. In my case, doing cocaine always resulted in misery at the end. There was never a moment when I got it right and was able to end the evening on a positive note. It was always a horror show. Yet each time I began to do cocaine anew, I told myself that somehow it would be different. "Tonight I will just do a few lines of cocaine. Then I will stop, do some homework, and lie down to sleep, and all will be well in the world." If you got the same result from doing something 99 times, it would be insane to think that the 100th time you would get a different result.

When it comes to attaching to our thoughts, all human beings are addicts. We all have a thinking problem. Buddha reached enlightenment through meditation, which freed him from identification with his thoughts. He became awake by seeing beyond the madness of the mind and realizing what is. We attach over and over again to our thoughts, bringing pain and suffering into our lives. By attaching to thoughts, I simply mean that we hang on to them and assign them value as if they were real. If you are diabetic and have a thought about devouring a whole chocolate cake, there is nothing threatening about that if you are trained to realize that it is just a thought and you need not react to it in any particular way. You might say to yourself, *How interesting that I think a thought such as this. I'll let it go.*

But addicts—who have a weakened nervous system, an imbalanced endocrine system, and trauma stuck in the body—are sitting ducks for thinking such as this. Part of the recovery process is to learn how to detach from their thoughts, develop intuitive capabilities, and live in the flow. This becomes possible within present-time awareness, which is practiced through meditation.

It states in the Big Book on page 45 that "lack of power was our dilemma."[1] If we have a problem that is bigger than us, we simply have to find a greater source of power. Now, coming to believe that a power greater than ourselves could restore us to sanity requires that we identify and believe that there is a power greater than ourselves. If you believe in God, it is likely you are clear that God is a power greater than you. In your vision of God, God must have the power to help you, which means that God *could* restore you to sanity if God so desired. Take this at face value: the God of your understanding wants the absolute best for you. I tell my students and sponsees regularly that the Universe may not be interested in your personal comfort, but it is definitely interested in your personal growth.

If you do not believe in God, do not let that deter you from moving ahead down this path. Here is one way to approach this step: One of my sponsees has a hard time with "the God thing." While urging him to remain open-minded to whatever life shows him, I ask him the following question: "Are you and I, when we work together toward a common goal, more powerful than either of us is in working toward that goal by ourselves?" The answer, of course, is yes: our powers together when aligned toward a common goal are greater than our powers alone. As a team, and by extension as a community, we are more powerful than we are as individuals. By working together in this way, we have already tapped into a power greater than ourselves, *and* we have not even had to mention the "G" word.

"Coming to believe" is another way of saying that our beliefs are about to change. This suggests there may have been something in our beliefs that has held us back and that is now going to change so that other things can become possible.

The Key to Step 2:
Step 2 presents a few issues for people who have challenges around God and religion, as I did. Right here, we are being confronted with the idea of a "power greater than ourselves," which

at first consideration sounds a lot like I am being required to believe in God. I'm also being accused of being insane and my ego doesn't necessarily like that, though it's hard to deny when I look back at my behavior. Actually, we are only being asked to become more aware of what is really going on around us. To help with this awakening, I suggest you keep a journal of all the strange, unexplainable things that happen in your life. I like to refer to this as your "weirdness" journal.

Make yourself a keen observer of your life and, keeping a small notebook with you, write down anything strange that takes place. Notice, in particular, any coincidences. It could be anything, big or small. For example, one sponsee of mine had been thinking a lot about his mother, whose name happened to be Laura. He had been meaning to call her for a few days. One afternoon he was walking down the street and noticed the word "Laura" written as graffiti on the side of a building. He called her that instant. When she picked up, she told him that she had just been thinking of him and was about to call. He wrote this story down in his weirdness journal.

One time I was heading to Costa Rica to co-lead a yoga retreat with my wife, Kia. I threw my back out just as I was getting on the plane to fly down there. It was a painful spasm in my mid-back, which was going to drastically impact the way I could contribute on the retreat. I was so pissed off—at myself, at the whole situation, at God.

When we got there, I hobbled by myself down the beach from our retreat center to a small, magical town called Playa Guiones. The whole way I was literally yelling at God: "What the fuck? This is what it's gonna be? Really? Really? I'm trying to be of service and now I can't fucking move. How about a little help here? What am I supposed to do? Why don't you show me something? How about that? Actually show me something. You think you can handle that?" I really came unglued. My rant lasted for the whole 40-minute walk.

When I got to town I went to a local grill. I sat at the counter next to the only other person in the joint. He was just finishing his meal. We struck up a short conversation and then, as he got up to go, he put his hand gingerly onto his lower back and said, "I'm going to see this amazing guy here who works on bad backs. He's supposed to be a miracle worker."

Life always continues to show me that my case is being considered. I cannot explain this in linear terms. I cannot prove it with science. It just makes absolute perfect sense to me that there is a "consciousness" that pervades everything, and it is aware of all of its parts, including me, including you.

These synchronicities happen all the time, if only you take notice of them. You can always say, "That was quite a coincidence," and leave it at that, but what a shame to miss all the magic that life constantly presents. My willingness to see life as purposeful, as more than just coincidence, has been a key to my lasting recovery and my appreciation of the way life seems to work. The interconnectivity of everything is constantly being shown: that has been my experience. Of course, when you are in a state of disconnection, like being caught in addiction, this is not necessarily visible to you. Take your weirdness journal seriously. Become aware of what is really happening around you. You do not need to conclude anything. Just notice, watch, and begin to see the signs. Eventually, you will be shown everything you need to see.

In Step 2, I also encourage you to begin to address your body's needs. Step 2 informs us that we have been way out of alignment to the point of being insane. Through yoga and other physical practices, you can detoxify and strengthen your body and bring yourself back into balance. In doing so, you can begin to develop a relationship with the subtler parts of yourself. Through yoga, you can connect inwardly with the breath and the flow of your life force. Breathing consciously, after a time, you will be restored to sanity.

Step 3: Made a decision to turn our will and our lives over to the care of God as we understood God.

Step 3 marks the end of the first part of the Steps. We have admitted our powerlessness over our addiction. We have come to believe that a Higher Power could restore us to sanity. Now, we are about to make a big decision that will shift the way we see ourselves in the world.

The root of the word decision is *decise,* which means to cut away. If you are the type of person who has a hard time making decisions, part of the reason might be that you are unwilling to let go of something. For when we make a decision, we are cutting away something so that something else can take its place. Here in Step 3 we are cutting away the part of our ego that would have us continue to live a life of disconnection based upon our own "self-will." We have been doing that for some time and it hasn't played out well. Aligning with the will of a power greater than ourselves means that we are going to realize the Truth about our own misalignment. Most of us have looked at ourselves as doers. We "make things happen." Yet how can we really take full credit for anything? Everything is a co-creation with forces and powers beyond our full perception and understanding. The universe is moving without my help, and I believe it is wise to learn about how that movement happens and align with it rather than struggle to "make things happen" on my own. So Step 3 is really just a realization that we are open to and recognize the collaboration taking place in this life.

Here in Step 3 we are making a decision to look at the universe as it presents itself and to get into the flow of it all. We are walking through a mystical archway. Once through it, we begin to "take life on life's terms," which is another one of my favorite 12-Step sayings. Throughout the day, I like to pray even though I don't know exactly what I'm praying to. Since I believe that there is a part of the Divine in everything, myself included, I feel that the Divine part of me sends a signal to the Infinite Divine, expressing and receiving the vibration and intention of my prayer. This only means that my prayer is being "received" on some level by something greater than myself, which one might call "the Divine," "Great Spirit," "Higher Power," or simply God.

Here is my current favorite prayer, which we recite after all Recovery 2.0 classes, retreats, and workshops: "God, put me in the places you want me to be, with the people you want me to be with, doing the things you want me to do. Thank you for the joys and challenges of my life. Amen."

It's a great prayer to take "self-will" out of the equation. As I go through my day, I am constantly reminded of my prayer. Whomever I encounter, I know that I was supposed to encounter them and that there is a purpose for the encounter, if only to just be there. One of my sponsees might say, "Well, what if you ended up in a crack house? Would that be the Divine will for you?" The way you can tell if something is Divine will versus self-will is through intuition. Building intuition is one of the foci of Kundalini Yoga and a very important thing to work on throughout life; we will get to that in Part IV. I know that ending up in a crack house is a result of self-will because in my heart I feel terribly misaligned about the very thought of being there. I am clear in my heart that my Higher Power would not have me be in a crack house today—that would not be taking life on life's terms. Not for me. Not at this point. When I practice this prayer, I have the feeling that I am in the right place at the right time most of the time.

For the agnostics and atheists who may choose their recovery community as a power greater than themselves, Step 3 will work well for you. In this case, "turning your will over" may mean simply running your thinking and decision-making process by the group or trusted individuals within the group so that you can benefit from a group conscience rather than being limited to your own. This affords the opportunity of hearing other perspectives. Eventually, you may develop your own intuition, but even then, it is a great practice to seek advice from wise folks who care about you.

Walking through the Step 3 archway does not mean we are enlightened, but it does mean we are willing to look at our lives and the world in a new way. We are not alone. We are in a constantly unfolding co-creation. We do not have to feel like we are swimming upstream. When we do feel that way, we check our alignment and our level of acceptance of what is.

The Key to Step 3:

Many of us have been taught that we should be able to manage our lives by ourselves, yet everything in the world is a collaborative effort. In fact, part of being human is to come up against challenges that we cannot overcome on our own. We will all face situations that require more power than we have access to, and we are ill advised to face problems that are bigger than we are alone.

With Step 3, you are waking up to a Truth. Everything you do is a co-creation, a grand collaboration in a dance with all things. It is presented to you as if you actually have a choice in the matter, but you do not. You can do this the easy way or the wrong way. It helps to begin to see that you are inseparable from your Higher Power and that you are also connected to all beings. To walk through life without this understanding leads to the improper use of personal will, which in turn leads to commotion, pain, and suffering. Cut away the misunderstanding that you are alone and allow for the realization that your case is being considered, even if you do not understand the force or power or consciousness that is doing the considering. This leads to devotion, progress, and bliss. Choose to practice yoga and other health-promoting activities. Cut away the habit of thinking about it. This will help you release your mental and physical blocks and build your intuitive capacities. Be open to developing the ability to perceive things that you have not yet been able to. Be open to having a spiritual experience!

Step 4: Made a searching and fearless moral inventory of ourselves.

To have resentment is to feel negativity toward someone or something over and over again. It feels like venom in the body and keeps us stuck in a painful past. Resentment is low vibration. It triggers us and attunes us to the Frequency of Addiction. It's as if our mind is in a groove playing a really bad song again and again. In the Big Book, resentment is referred to as "the number one offender. It destroys more alcoholics than anything else."[2] That's a big statement, but it is time tested. Think how you feel when you are caught in resentment; it actually *hurts*.

In my opinion, the 12-Step method of looking back to analyze and understand our lives is genius. Rather than just write a history of our life detailing where we have missed the mark, the authors of the 12 Steps instruct us to look back at our lives through the lens of resentment. We write down our resentments toward people, places, and things. Whom have we resented? What caused the resentment? What aspect of our lives did this affect? And most importantly, what was our side of the street in the resentment? This process is laid out in great detail in the Big Book and is one of the most transformative things I have ever done.[3]

On page 62 of the Big Book it states, "Sometimes they hurt us, seemingly without provocation, but we invariably find that at some time in the past we have made decisions based on self which later placed us in a position to be hurt." From the first time I read that until the present moment, I am struck by the importance and clarity of the communication. Some part of me is always involved in my resentments. Seeing this clearly has been humbling but also empowering. It is humbling to look at my own shortcomings in situations where I believe others have acted wrongly. They may, in fact, have behaved poorly, but if I blame others, since I have no control over them, I have no power to be in the solution. My solution in that case is based upon someone else. I need them to apologize. I need them to recognize me. I need them to make the effort or I won't be free. From that place, I am destined to remain stuck. *But the moment I claim the resentment as mine, I can do something about it.* Since I am the problem and I do have control over my own actions and reactions, I can be part of the solution. I need to work on forgiveness. I need to communicate an apology to this person. I can make the effort and be free. If the problem is not mine, then there is no solution. So, the 4th Step helps us to see what we have held on to and why.

After we have written down all our resentments and examined them, we then have a look at the way *fear* has played a part in our lives. We will come to see that our resentments are connected with fear. For example, I carried a lot of resentment toward my mother. Part of my frustration had to do with her nearly constant sadness. I was not angry because she was sad; I was angry because I felt powerless to do anything about it. I resented her because of my own powerlessness. I could not take away her sadness, nor was it my fault. It was just sadness, but I had a lot of fears tied in with it all. In connection with this resentment, my fears were these:

- Fear of not being enough (I can't seem to help my mom.)

- Fear of loneliness (Her loneliness is painful. I hope I don't end up like that.)

- Fear of being stuck in unpleasant emotions (My mom is stuck. Will I be, too?)

Usually resentments have a lot more to do with fear than we realize. So we make a fear list and put them all down in black and white. For most of us, this is a long list. Here are some juicy ones: fear of being alone, fear of economic insecurity, fear of not being enough, fear of ridicule, fear of commitment, fear of authority figures, fear of failure, fear of success, fear of responsibility, and fear of rejection, to name but a few.

What we notice is that our disconnected lives, which have been run on self-will, have been dominated by fears of all kinds. These fears caused us to act and react in ways that brought us pain and suffering.

Yet the footing upon which we stand now is different. We "made a decision" in Step 3 to turn our will and lives over to the care of God as we understand God. We have to exercise the muscle of faith. We have had these fears and now we will be letting them go. It may not happen right away, but we are on the right road. The faith required is that we will only be presented with situations that we can handle. Whatever circumstances arise in our lives, we will have the ability to get through them. We will never be dropped. Everything that happens is for us to learn and grow. We have to have faith to accept this statement. Without faith, fears creep back in and can become paralyzing.

Finally, we also review our sexual history in the 4th Step, always trying to understand where we have been selfish, hurtful, and dishonest. The idea is to develop a healthy and sane sex and relationship life that is in alignment with our heart. Everyone seems to struggle in this area. There is a lot of confusion, insecurity, shame, and jealousy around sex. We are instructed to stay out of judgment of others and to focus on what makes sense for us. We cannot hurt others or allow ourselves to be hurt, so we must set out to understand the ways we have been misaligned and set a vision for our own personal ideal regarding our relationships and sex life.

The Key to Step 4:

We must turn our gaze inward and with humility, honesty, and thoroughness look at what lies within us. We will clearly see that resentment has fueled the disturbances of our mind and has kept us stuck in the past. Here in Step 4, we learn to stop up the massive energy leaks that it causes. The mind cannot fully calm itself or become present until this work is done. Come to terms with the past and release yourself from its grip. This is one of the greatest gifts you can give yourself.

The 4th Step is where we learn the practice of claiming our history as our own rather than blaming someone else for it. The power we seek will come from owning it all. A wise man once told me, "Tommy, your life is one hundred percent yours. You are responsible for everything in it." Sometimes, though, it's incredibly difficult to see and claim your part in something that has been painful for you to experience. Write it down. Write it down. Write it down. You are moving toward freedom.

People spend way too much time on Step 4 because it is uncomfortable to look at resentments and to own their part in them. It can become absurd. I have heard stories of people working their 4th Step for more than a year. This simply means that they have *not* been working it for more than a year. Since this is usually an uncomfortable process, one of the keys is to get it done as soon as humanly possible. I try to get sponsees to get through it in two weeks, four at the outside.

I also caution them that if they start to feel depressed or become morbid in their reflections, they need to stop the process and get into a mind-body practice such as yoga. This will quickly shift their energy and bring them back to a more positive place. Every foray onto the yoga mat or meditation cushion is a fact-finding mission about what is happening in your body and mind. It is the perfect complement to 4th Step work. If you pay attention, you will learn all you need to know about where you are. See where you are, claim it all, and don't blame. Just lean into it. Yogi Bhajan, who brought the practice of Kundalini Yoga to the Western world, used to say, "There is a way through every block." Such is the promise of the 4th Step.

Step 5: Admitted to God, to ourselves, and to another human being the exact nature of our wrongs.

In Step 5, we take everything we have just done in Step 4 and read it to our sponsor or another trusted person. To only admit our faults to ourselves will deprive us of several important benefits. Another person will help us see things we have missed and help us to move beyond shame, guilt, and the illusion of being separate from other people. The 5th Step is humbling and therefore worthwhile. We have to humble ourselves to another human being for the process to be as thorough and powerful as it needs to be.

Hopefully, when you do this step, you will not have held anything back, and thus you will have no secrets. The old adage says it all: you are only as sick as your secrets. After this Step, someone on the planet has listened to your story and knows everything you have been through.

My own 5th Steps have been fruitful and liberating. I did my first one in rehab and ended up laughing so hard with a pastor there that both he and I were crying from it. There were serious parts, too, of course.

Interestingly, my second 5th Step was a bigger deal, perhaps because I was out of the safety of the rehab environment and was doing this "for myself." I got through it with flying colors. This just means that I told the truth and did my best. I have never been struck "enlightened," but I always felt lighter in completing this Step.

As a sponsor, it is an honor to get to listen to someone's 5th Step: to be asked to hear someone's innermost secrets. Over the years, I've heard some amazing stories, which have illuminated the power of addiction and where it can take us. I've come to understand a lot about the human race in general. I've heard about every twist and turn of human behavior—violence, sexuality, weirdness, everything. Through all of it, I have never heard anything in someone's 5th Step that shocked me. It is all so human. I see what we are capable of when things get way off track as they do in addiction. I also see the miracle of transformation: addicts who have been so far down in the darkness being lifted up into the light of recovery to have extraordinary lives.

I believe everyone should do Steps 4 and 5 at least once in their life, preferably many times. *Everyone.* And here's my theory: non-addicts would have stories just as interesting, weird, varied, and crazy as addicts. We are all subjects of the human condition.

The Key to Step 5:

We have been alone for so long, cut off from our selves, others, and any sense of a Higher Power. We have lived with fear that if others knew what we were capable of, we would be alone forever. So we kept our secrets and kept ourselves alone for fear of being alone. The insanity of that ends now. Here is our opportunity to tell the Truth and be free. Humble yourself before another human being (usually your sponsor) and your Higher Power by recounting to them the story of your life. Be done with isolation. You are laying the foundation for the rest of your life. Leave nothing out. Have no more secrets. Realize you are a work in progress like everyone else. This is a massive detoxification of the mind-body. This is the pathway to purity. This work will bring great progress for all who approach it with heart. There is no failing. Only do your best.

Step 6: Were entirely ready to have God remove all these defects of character.

Having done our personal inventory and shared it with our Higher Power and another person, we now work on becoming ready to take out the garbage. This step is done quite quickly after the completion of a 5th Step as there is no need to pull back on the reins. Step 6 is about being in a state of readiness to let go of the parts of ourselves that no longer serve us. This is exciting! We are in the process of dumping a lot of dead weight. It is a shorter step than the previous ones. We sit and pray and simply become ready to be emptied out.

We have learned much about ourselves. We have seen where we have been selfish and dishonest. We have a good idea about our defects of character. Are we ready to let go of these things? You might think to yourself, "Of course I'm ready. Why would I want to hold on to defects of character?" You may fear letting go of some character trait because it still serves you in some way. Perhaps you do not know what life will be without it, and fear of the unknown influences you. What if you let go of selfishness? What if you let go of egotism? What would life be if you did not act out sexually? How would you feel if you did not try to be perfect all the time or if you set better boundaries in your relationships? We are talking about a big shift in perspective. It may feel like a sort of death to let go of these things but in actuality it will be a rebirth of your spirit. You will be creating a lot of space by letting go of these destructive energies. If there are things that you just do not want to let go of, turn to your practices of prayer, meditation, and yoga, and ask your Higher Power to help you become ready. Consciously work at this. And trust me; if there is something you need to let go of that you simply will not release, it is likely that the Universe will concoct an experience for you that will help you to become ready to release it.

The Key to Step 6:

This Step corresponds to the moment between your inhale and exhale. Here you are preparing to exhale, to let go of the un-necessary. Become ready to release what no longer serves you! This requires willingness. Some people hold their breath because they do not trust that the next inhale will be coming or because they fear exhaling, which is the last thing we do before we die. Face the death of your defects of character while you are still alive, and have faith that there is freedom on the other side of this process. There is a great story about a person who is in the pitch black hanging on to a rope suspended over a ravine he imagines to be hundreds of feet deep. If he lets go, death is certain. He is terrified. A voice calls out, "Just let go," but he can't do it. The fear has him gripped to the marrow of his bones. Finally, he can no longer hold on, and in releasing the rope, he falls . . . the two feet to solid ground that has always been awaiting him. Heed the message of this story. You will not be dropped. Let go. Let go. Let go.

Step 7: Humbly asked God to remove our shortcomings.

In Step 7 we make a direct request of our Higher Power to take away the things that have been holding us back. We have gotten ourselves ready in Step 6, and here we make the direct request with humility. Humility is a great virtue. To be humble is to see oneself as "right sized." We understand our place in the world. We neither amplify nor diminish ourselves.

Part of the humility required here is to understand that we are not the ones doing the "removal of our shortcomings." We are not the doer. Remember that everything is a co-creation with the Divine or our Higher Power. We are saying to our closest and most powerful ally, "Here is my garbage. Would you be willing to take it away for me so I can live more freely?"

If you still hold on to some of your defects of character, do not worry. You will surely get another chance to experience them again in your life. This is the nature of personal growth. We are continually given new opportunities to practice the things we need to work on. Even when we are ready to let go of our shortcomings, they don't necessarily vanish. I remember praying to have my impatience taken away. I was not struck patient all of a sudden. Instead, I was given several opportunities to practice patience the following week. The first one came when I had to go to the DMV to renew my vehicle registration, which I had previously always done by mail. I went down there armed and ready with my newfound patience, and within about 15 minutes I had lost all sense of calm from my life. Fortunately, I had to go back to the DMV two more times before the matter was settled. Each time I did a little better than before. The Universe is funny like this. You will always be given an opportunity to learn.

The Key to Step 7:

Humility means to be approachable. When you humble yourself, you become "open for business." There is now enough space for you to become an exalted being. It's just like going through your closet and getting rid of old clothing that you don't like. You are making space for something new to arrive. You can now have more energy to put toward your heart's desires.

Part of the key to Step 7 is to make yourself into a person who is approachable by your fellows and also by your Higher Power. Bowing is an exceptional habit to develop. We do not like to do it too much in our society. I think it is because we are not comfortable being in devotion to anything, much less a power greater than ourselves. Yet in our addictions, what have we been if not devoted? We have given everything we could to substances and addictive behaviors. Now we embrace a different kind of devotion, one that leads to contentment and bliss rather than pain and suffering. This kind of devotion leads to great places. At the beginning and end of every day, bend your knees and place your forehead gently on the ground. Ask that your shortcomings be taken away. Even if you do not believe in a Divine force underlying all things, still ask. Make the request like a mantra or affirmation to express your intention to your highest Self that you are now moving beyond the things that have held you back.

A very simple way to look at Step 7 is see it as the relaxation step. Relaxation is simply letting go of the unnecessary. Once you have released all the unnecessary things from your life, you find yourself in a state of relaxation. Step 7 does that.

Flexibility is an invitation-only event. We must try not to attach to this outcome of our yoga practice. The purpose of practice is to practice and explore the now. Explore what is. Our flexibility is not in our hands. Yes, we show up to work on it but in doing so we humbly ask our Higher Power for greater flexibility in body, mind, and life. At some point, through humble devotion to our practice, we will be invited into greater flexibility. This is precisely our approach to Step 7. Show up for the practice of life. Ask for help to improve. Release attachment to outcomes.

Step 8: Made a list of all persons we had harmed and became willing to make amends to them all.

In Step 4 we made our personal inventory, explored our resentments, and saw the places where we had harmed others. Now we make a list of those people whom we have harmed. We may be concerned about people's reactions when we come to actually make our amends to them, but that is a 9th Step concern. In the spirit of remaining present and doing what is in front of us, we remind ourselves that we are on the 8th Step. We must remain focused on simply listing names and becoming willing. We must not allow fear of facing the amends process to derail our progress.

Finding willingness to go through Step 8 is made easier by the promise of extraordinary rewards. Given what we release—dis-ease and psychic pain—and what we gain in its place—relief and freedom—we are encouraged, even excited to get on with this challenge. Yet our ego flares up. It is difficult to imagine looking someone in the eyes to let them know that we have done them harm, in some cases very big harm. This is not normal behavior. This is exceptional behavior, but it comes at a cost: the leveling of our pride and the facing of fear. Just make the list. The strength to act on it will be there when you need it. Continue to have faith.

The Key to Step 8:

As we have discussed, all dis-ease originates in constipation of one form or another. It could be in the bowels, in the arteries, in the energy body, or in the mind. There is a blockage somewhere. Prepare now to clear away the obstructions caused by past mistakes that resulted in harm to you or to another. Return to the yogic principle of *ahimsa* or non-harming. Step 8 is where we become fully present to our impact upon others. This is a transformative process. True harmony comes when our perception of ourselves matches our actions and other people's perceptions of us. When these three things are in alignment, we find harmony in the three primary relationships—self, other, Higher Power.

Observe what is without passing judgment on self or other. The energy of the past must be released. Whom have we harmed? Become willing to claim responsibility. Own your part in it all. Soon there will be freedom.

Step 9: Made direct amends to such people wherever possible, except when to do so would injure them or others.

An amends is not an apology. An apology lets someone know that you feel bad for doing something. An amends is significantly more. The word "amends" means to make better by changing. In making amends we are presenting ourselves as a changed person. Yes, we are sorry for what we have done. We also want to make reparations to set the matter straight, *and* we will not behave this way again. We have changed. We are taking life on life's terms. And this is the next thing that life has presented.

All the first eight steps—the work, searching, writing, praying, and action we've done to this point—have readied us to go out into the world to repair heartache, broken connections, and misunderstandings between us and our fellows. When I started to make amends to people I had harmed, that's when I started to see some pretty profound changes in my life.

It is very powerful to look someone in the eye and say, "I've stolen from you. I've cheated on you. I've lied to you. I'm telling you this because I want to make it right. What can I do to make this up to you?" The most exceptional healing took place through this process. I got to let go of a big fear that I had been holding on to for practically a lifetime: that if people knew what I was capable of, I'd be alone for the rest of my life. I had gotten through part of that fear when I read my 5th Step to my sponsor. Yet in approaching different people out in the world to make amends, I found even greater relief. The phrase my sponsor used was "You will be able to look anyone in the eye."

I approached my family members and friends. I visited store managers at stores I had stolen from. I approached old girlfriends I had cheated on or been dishonest with in some way. I approached it the way my sponsor told me to and did my best to clear things up. In a few cases, people were still angry and unforgiving, but generally speaking, they were more than ready to hear from me. I definitely blew a few people's minds and left them speechless. It is a rare thing for someone to admit wrongs to you and then go the extra step of making an offer to do whatever it takes to set the record straight. A couple of people I made amends to did not remember the incidence of harm. Here is one such example. I had stolen a small amount of money from a guy I knew as a teenager. He was going out with a girl from my school, and I was at his house buying some pot from him. He went to the bathroom and I lifted $20 off his desk. I knew he would miss it when he got back, so I went to the trouble of taking off my shoes and putting the bill in my sock under my foot. When he got back, he did notice it was gone. In his frustration, he even asked if I would empty my pockets, which I happily did. It had been eight years since that incident when I called him. He remembered me and asked what it was about. I told him I needed to speak face-to-face and asked if he could take 15 minutes out of his day to meet with me. There in his office, I recounted the tale of my cheating and fraud. He sat there with his jaw agape, utterly amazed that I was taking the time to see him and also that I felt the need to see him. He had no recollection of the event. I placed a $20 bill on his desk. He didn't want it. I explained that it was important to me as a symbol that I leave it. What he did with the small sum was up to him. Shaking his head in disbelief, he accepted it and insisted that I not think any further about it again. I shook his hand, wished him well, and was off.

The point here is not that he didn't remember the incident. The point is that *I* had remembered it. I felt shitty that day. For the eight years since, on some level, I carried the energy of being a cheat, liar, and fraud. I am not those things but I have behaved in those ways. Something had to be done to release the energy of that. I had to own up to it face-to-face and let it go.

It is no accident that the famous "AA Promises" show up in the Big Book in the 9th Step. I will list them here so you know what the suggested rewards of doing this work are. The 12 promises could be summed up in one sentence: "If you do this well, you will be free."

The Promises of Alcoholics Anonymous[4]

1. If we are painstaking about this phase of our development, we will be amazed before we are halfway through.

2. We are going to know a new freedom and a new happiness.

3. We will not regret the past nor wish to shut the door on it.

4. We will comprehend the word serenity and we will know peace.

5. No matter how far down the scale we have gone, we will see how our experience can benefit others.

6. That feeling of uselessness and self-pity will disappear.

7. We will lose interest in selfish things and gain interest in our fellows.

8. Self-seeking will slip away.

9. Our whole attitude and outlook upon life will change.

10. Fear of people and of economic insecurity will leave us.

11. We will intuitively know how to handle situations which used to baffle us.

12. We will suddenly realize that God is doing for us what we could not do for ourselves.

Are these extravagant promises? We think not. They are being fulfilled among us—sometimes quickly, sometimes slowly. They will always materialize if we work for them.

The 9th Step was a turning point for me. By cleaning up the wreckage of my past, I started to align my outer actions with my inner values. It is one of the most important things I've done in my life. I wish everyone would take the time to do it. The goodwill that could be created from these actions alone could be enough to tilt our world in a lasting, significant way toward peace.

The Key to Step 9:

This Step is the step of the guru. "Gu" means darkness. "Ru" means light. "Guru" means a teacher or teaching that moves you from dark to light. The time for hiding in the darkness is gone. Now you will look in the eyes of the people you have harmed and completely own your past behavior. By claiming it, you will be freed from it. Through this important work, you will release yourself and others from the energy of the past. You will also be able to release your shame and guilt and develop forgiveness. When you get on your yoga mat, you practice what you are going to do when you get off your yoga mat. We are all a work in progress.

Yogi Bhajan used to teach that one of the keys to being a successful person in this age was to "recognize that the other person is you." This is a deep teaching that reminds us that we are inseparable from each other. And it goes quite a bit further than that. We are instructed to actually realize that the other person is us and we are them. Adopting this attitude brings a whole new level of understanding to the 9th Step. We are putting ourselves in their shoes and "being" them. This is the root of understanding. Compassion is not far behind.

Step 10: Continued to take personal inventory and when we were wrong promptly admitted it.

The 10th Step is a mini 4th Step that we do each day. When resentment arises, we take notice and focus in on our side of the street. If we have been dishonest and noticed it, we fix it as soon as is possible. Perhaps we were hurtful, impatient, or cross with someone. We apologize and own it completely.

Usually, I am unable to move forward when I make such mistakes. I feel it right away and get stuck in it. Recently, I went to a car wash to have my car detailed inside and out. I cannot stand the ArmorAll product they use on the inside of the car, so I asked the guy who was about to clean the car not to use any. He got the communiqué but ended up working on another car and forgot to pass the message along to the guy who replaced him on mine. When I got back to find the interior of my car covered in ArmorAll, I just lost it. I called the guy over. As it turns out, he was the shift manager. "How could this happen?" I asked angrily. He looked in the car and realized he had forgotten to tell the other guy not to use the product. He was profusely apologetic and offered to get me another detailing for free. I had to leave on a trip and knew there was no quick fix. I got so angry with this guy that I became *that* customer. It was imperative that I let this guy know just how big a fuckup this was. He saw that I wasn't going to let it go and just sat back and let me rant. I finally drove away, my veins filled with the chemistry of self-righteous anger. I slid my fingers along the now-slick interior of the car and continued to yell at this guy even though he was no longer there.

When I calmed down about ten minutes later, the most incredible anger hangover descended. I was filled with remorse for the way I had behaved. In my mind's eye, I saw the guy standing there with me yelling at him and it sucked for me. What was the fix here? I had to go back and make it right. Turning the car around, I returned to the car wash and explained in plain language that my behavior had been unacceptable—he didn't deserve that from anyone. His mistake was an honest one. It was my job to accept it and move on with grace, something I had been unable to do.

"Is there any way I can make it up to you?" I asked.

"Yes," he said. "Let us clean your car again when you get back from your trip. We'll fix the situation, and there will be no charge."

I shook his hand, met his eyes with mine, and the incident was over. When I make mistakes and notice them, I have to fix them. I have not been perfect with this. In some instances, I have carried things much longer than desired. However, a well-done 10th Step is an amazing gift to ourselves that allows us to stay on the path to becoming the version of ourselves we would hope to be.

The Key to Step 10:

Each day we have the opportunity to practice being born upon awakening. We also practice dying as we lie down to sleep at night. It is important to consciously develop the quality of awareness in your approach to being born and dying each day.

Sadhana means daily spiritual practice. It is the central practice of our life. It brings us into alignment with our Higher Power and sets us up for the best day possible. Each morning, we practice yoga and meditate, thereby linking our finite self with the Infinite Self. At the end of each day, part of our *sadhana* is to review what has transpired.

Stay current and examine your own life. Observe the way you end each day and prepare for bed. Go to bed clean—energetically clean. Step 10 allows you to achieve this.

Step 11: Sought through prayer and meditation to improve our conscious contact with God as we understood God, praying only for knowledge of God's will for us and the power to carry that out.

Through the practice of all the Steps to this point, we have hopefully begun to develop a more profound awareness of our connection to ourselves, to others, and to our Higher Power. Of course, this is something we will always be working on from day to day. I am thinking about my Higher Power almost all the time and working on being more conscious of its will. Sometimes I feel in the flow. Sometimes I miss it completely. I know that prayer and meditation work in my life. They have become a regular part of it, and that is saying something. I never used to pray or meditate but, ironically, I desperately needed to do both these things. Sometimes I feel like the whole purpose of me becoming a drug addict and then having to get sober was simply to make me humble enough to put aside my own ego and pray.

I sometimes have daydreams in which I am standing in God's office. The angel overseeing my case comes in to speak with God about me. "Excuse me, sir. Do you have any thoughts about how we can get Tommy humble enough to pray and tap into . . . well, you know . . . everything?" I never get to actually see God in these daydreams, but there "he" is behind a really messy desk. God replies to my angel, "Make him an addict. Then put him through the 12 Steps."

From a macro perspective, the whole 12-Step program is a call to prayer, but here the 11th Step suggests a specific form of prayer: "praying only for knowledge of God's will and the power to carry that out." The 11th Step urges us to align with and improve upon our connection with our Higher Power. The main idea here is to ready ourselves for the work that follows. Essentially, we are moving beyond selfishness into readiness. We will need more power. We will need to be clear in our intentions and in our prayers. We are going to be shown one of the biggest secrets to living a great life: to live in service to others. For those of us who have been quite selfish, and I count myself at the head of the pack, we need a system for getting beyond our own selfishness so we can experience the great joy of service. The system we will use to move beyond selfishness consists of all the Step work to this point and now prayer and meditation.

Does this then mean that to pray for one's own health or abundance is of no use? No. When praying for abundance, for example, one might express that prayer as follows: "God (insert your word for that here), please make me successful in business so that my success can inspire others and so that I can be more helpful to those around me." The idea of praying to be wealthy for the sake of being wealthy might actually work in some cases, but you might find yourself lonely once your ship came in. The idea is to express through prayer your understanding that you are connected to others and that if your prayers are granted, they will serve a greater purpose than just your own. The Big Book puts it like this: "We ask especially for freedom from self-will, and are careful to make no request for ourselves only. We may ask for ourselves, however, if others will be helped."[5] Therefore, the intention behind your prayers counts for a lot.

The Big Book does not speak extensively about meditation. Its several uses of the word seem to liken it to a form of relaxed contemplation in which we ask our Higher Power for guidance and then listen to the thoughts that follow our request. The more we perform this quiet act of listening, the more intuitive we will become. "What used to be the hunch or the occasional inspiration gradually becomes a working part of the mind. . . . Our thinking will, as time passes, be more and more on the plane of inspiration."[6]

So the 11th Step is the launching pad. Prayer and meditation are two of the methods we will employ to expand our spiritual life . . . for the rest of our lives. Through these practices we will continue to move beyond "fear, anger, worry, self-pity, or foolish decisions."[7] We are moving into the land of Divine will and intuition. Thus we are going to want to know everything we can about these practices. To a large degree, the inspiration for Recovery 2.0 was born out of my personal need to branch out and learn more about prayer and meditation.

The Key to Step 11:

Success in prayer is called prosperity. We can actually become great at it, but it takes practice, vigilance, and heart. Prayers are energy. Directing energy is the key. You can train your mind through meditation to increase your capacity to do exactly that. If you knew that prayer was actually the vehicle for change in your life, you would probably work very hard on becoming a prayer expert. Well, guess what: prayers *are* the vehicle for change in your life. Expressing your most deeply held beliefs and desires in the form of a prayer is extremely powerful.

Through meditation you build intuition, move beyond self-will into Infinite will, and access even more power to walk your destiny path. Do you have enough energy to live the life you are being called to live? In Part IV of this book I will discuss meditation in greater detail. For our purposes here, suffice it to say that meditation, in my opinion, is a requisite part of living a great life. In this day and age, with all the stimuli, pressures, and stresses of life, it is less and less possible to maintain your balance and find contentment without slowing down and taking the time each day to calm your mind and connect with your True Self. Great power, energy, and vitality are available in the practice of meditation. You do not need to wait until you reach the 11th Step. Start a practice as soon as you can. It will serve you in ways you cannot imagine.

Guru Nanak, the first of the Sikh gurus, said, *"Man jeetai jag jeet,"* which means "By conquering the mind, you conquer the world." Clear away the clutter and gain control over your mind so you can experience your own true nature. Come to know the Truth about yourself in this lifetime.

Step 12: Having had a spiritual awakening as the result of these Steps, we tried to carry this message to other addicts, and to practice these principles in all our affairs.

Imagine you are suspended in midair. One arm reaches up to the sky. A person above you has a hold of your hand and keeps you from falling. Above them is another person holding them up, and so on. Your other arm reaches down and is carrying another person and keeping them from falling. Beneath them is another person whom they are supporting, and so on. Such is the flow of energy from sponsor to sponsee from the beginning of the 12 Steps to this moment. The flow of energy, ideas, and teachings comes down through time in this way. We are here to learn and to share. We will need to do both to feel a sense of fulfillment. This is part of being human.

12-Step philosophy is built upon the principal that one alcoholic or addict can and must help others if they are to recover from this dis-ease. It is such a simple idea that it took millennia of suffering and pain before Bill Wilson (we) finally "received the download" in 1935. One person overcomes their suffering by helping another person overcome their suffering. What are the ingredients necessary to be of service to another in this way? Willingness. Compassion. Empathy. Love. All the other steps are there to make you more ready to be of maximum service to another person.

Some people read this step and become fearful that they are going to have to give up their life in service to others. They envision a life like Mother Teresa's and they think, *I'm not up for this task. I don't want to live that kind of life.* Take note of this: you will be of service to others when you are ready in the perfect way that suits you. We are not obsessive in our desire to help others. Opportunities present themselves. We see that we can help and we actually desire to. Having developed a sense of intuition, being tapped into the inspiration of our own heart, we simply go where we are told and do what is suggested, not because some outside entity forced us to, but because our own spirit wanted to go there. Remember: wherever you are on the path, more will be revealed. We stay open to what we are shown and demonstrate the willingness to help where we can. Sometimes this can be as simple as smiling at someone or putting a hand out to a newcomer in a meeting.

The Key to Step 12:

Seva means selfless service. This is the highest form of yoga—nothing cuts through the ego as efficiently and completely as this. As Yogi Bhajan instructed in his teaching Seven Steps to Happiness, the final step before achieving happiness is developing the strength to sacrifice. To sacrifice is to give up something of value in service to a person or ethical principle. Interestingly, when we make sacrifices, something of greater value is often realized, like, for example, when we sacrifice our time for another person and receive the joy that comes from giving.

Most people want to help others. It is in our nature to do so. However, when we live in the Frequency of Addiction, we have a sense of lack. Our needs are not being met and we focus more and more on that. We may find it hard to give of ourselves to another, especially without wanting something in return. Step 12 tells us: Forget your troubles and put your hand out to another. Do it without expecting anything in return. The most exceptional blessings will come your way. You may only be able to help a few, but you can still bless everyone. Perhaps the single greatest gift of recovery is that it prepares you to experience the joy of helping another person. You will become stronger, have more time, and be happier than you might believe possible.

These 12 Steps offer you a clear path to heal from addiction and transform. The only requirement is for you to be honest through the process and have the willingness to consider what life shows you. If you have that attitude, you will find what you are looking for and get to live the life you were destined to live.

CHAPTER 9

STAYING THE COURSE IN EARLY RECOVERY

I will never forget those first years in recovery in San Francisco in the '90s. I was attending five to seven 12-Step meetings a week, including going out to a café after each meeting with a whole crew of Deadhead friends who had gotten sober. The Grateful Dead were still playing and we were re-experiencing the magic drug free. There is something very special about being in recovery with people who were using with you before you got sober. We were aware then, and still are, that we have been fortunate in this respect. Many people get sober and have to make new friends because their old friends are incarcerated, dead, or still out there using. We had a posse everywhere we went. We were dedicated to our recoveries. Each of us had been very extreme in our drug use. We had felt a lot of pain and did not want to go back.

They say habits cannot be broken, only exchanged for other habits. I developed a new set of habits: the habit of attending

12-Step meetings, the habit of expressing honestly what was going on with me every day to a group of people who understood, and, of course, the habit of going through life without drugs or alcohol. With each passing day, I developed into a person who did not use drugs. As a point of fact, that is what I became. Along the way, I had therapists, healers, yoga, meditation, and a great community of friends to help me. On the days when I found myself wanting to use or having powerfully negative thoughts, I did mostly what I was told to do. I went to meetings, called my sponsor, connected with other friends in the program, worked out, read spiritual books, and wrote in my journal. Sometimes I did none of these things and still got through the day without picking up. It got easier for me over time.

The first thing I noticed was that I felt better. While my thinking was still erratic and at times overwhelming, it was much better than what I had experienced while using drugs. Using made it impossible to get a grip on much of anything. There was no foundation to stand upon. In recovery, I was able to establish a baseline: okay, here is how I am without drugs. Then from there I could say to myself, *Ah. This is how it feels when I go to the gym without using drugs. I like this feeling. I think I'll do this again.* I also started to develop some consistency and integrity in my life. When I said something, I actually meant it and mostly was telling the truth. If I committed to something, I was getting better at showing up and seeing it through. All of this transformation was gradual. *The most important reflection I can pass on about what helped me in my early years was my commitment to attending meetings nearly every day and working through the 12 Steps with a sponsor.*

THE KITCHEN-SINK METHOD OF RECOVERY

My sponsor, Mickey, was a godsend. I met him and asked him to sponsor me when I was two months sober. He was about four years sober, went to a lot of meetings, and had a strong commitment to recovery. For those first few years, he worked with me and took me through the steps. As most sponsors do, he had to field several thousand questions about everything that came up in my life that I found disturbing. My God, he was a saint to put up with me. The girl troubles! The money issues! Family! Resentments! Insecurities! Obsession! Change! He dealt with it all.

Mickey ran with a group of guys who were known to be "Big Book Thumpers"—very strict and rigid in their approach to getting sober. It was helpful to me in those days to have a clear-cut approach to things. You hit a lot of meetings. You helped newcomers whenever possible. You found a home group. You took on commitments. These were all positive aspects of being associated with this particular group of guys. There was an unwritten and generally held belief among this crew that the fellowship and the 12 Steps could take care of anything that life threw your way. No matter what you were facing, the 12 Steps would carry you through.

During those years, I was seeing a therapist I've previously mentioned named Joe Tolson. Joe was something like ten years sober and he understood addiction, the mind, and spirit about as well as anyone I've ever encountered. Joe's work with me would be categorized as spiritual psychology. I went once a week and reviewed my life with him. We talked about spirituality, religion, the 12 Steps, and every facet of life. Joe offered broad perspective and with a deep knowledge of personal development helped me along my path. He is one of the people I will always remember as an angel in my life.

Mickey and the guys in his 12-Step crew knew that I was seeing a therapist and on several occasions gave me a hard time about it. It wasn't traumatic or intense. They simply poked fun at me when they got the chance. The point is they truly believed that the 12 Steps would solve any problem. My seeing a therapist did not fit into their view on recovery and life. Personally, I needed something more and was fortunate to have Joe in my corner.

Mickey ended up relapsing when I was about three years sober. I don't know the particulars of his relapse. He had given so much to my life. He truly loved and cared about me. He was my rock, my strength for a long time. We all know relapse can happen anytime to any one of us, but you do not expect it from the person who has guided you. One wrongly assumes a sponsor's sobriety is unassailable. Of course, no one's is. It's definitely a weird thing to have your sponsor relapse.

It had been many months since Mickey had relapsed when he called me on the phone. He sounded fairly lucid.

"Tommy, it's Mickey."

"Oh my God, Mickey. How are you?" I said.

"You know I'm out, right?"

"Of course I know. Do you want to come back in?"

"No, I'm not ready."

"Oh . . . well . . . what's up?"

"I just really needed to tell you something."

"Tell me. What is it, Mickey? Are you okay?"

"I just needed to tell you that I am so sorry I gave you a hard time for seeing a therapist."

Then he hung up.

That call really blew me away. In the middle of Mickey's relapse, one of the things on his mind is the fact that he made fun of me for seeing a therapist. It bothered him so much that he had to call me and set it right. I imagine that he was carrying something painful, something he missed, and that seeing a therapist might not have been such a bad idea for him. Who knows? I lost touch with Mickey that day. My sense is he is still alive and hopefully sober and contented. I am sober, alive, and contented in great part due to his love, support, and guidance in my early years of recovery.

The great takeaway here for me is that we have to use everything in our arsenal, whatever is necessary to get sober, stay sober, and grow into the people we dream to be. 12 Steps? Absolutely! Therapy? Go out and get it! If you have a chemical imbalance and you need medication to help you along, then by all means—take it. If exercise makes a big difference in your life, do it. If hiring a trainer will help you, then do that. If yoga and meditation make you a saner, stronger person, go after it. Whatever help you need, ask for it. Whatever it takes. If you have the dis-ease of addiction, then the best way to treat it is holistically. Organize your life around your recovery. Certain doors that have been locked your whole life will begin to open.

My early recovery was truly a process of small steps. There is no way to express how tenuous it is to change and stay the course of transformation. Many of the lessons I learned and the experiences I had during this time have been essential to my recovery. I hope that the following ideas will help you find your way through some of the tougher days you will face.

ONE DAY AT A TIME

The popular 12-Step slogan "One day at a time" is more than a slogan. It is an important nugget of spiritual wisdom that is, in itself, a road back from hell. It can be the cornerstone of a life well lived.

At first glance one understands the necessity of living one day at a time and its particular relevance for people in recovery. In early recovery, we just need to get through each day sober without using our drug or addictive behavior of choice. Our main job is to go to bed at night without having used. Everything else that happens during the day just happens, but the main focus is to go to bed sober.

Because addiction creates a large amount of unmanageability, we have to train ourselves to take life in manageable chunks. The thinking that goes along with addiction is pretty twisted, as we have seen. Living one day at a time is how we begin to change our thinking for the better.

In my early recovery, I had the following thought in September: *In December, when the holidays arrive, I am going to want to use drugs. Since I know it will be very difficult not to use at that point, and I will likely cave in, why bother staying sober now?* That is a great example of "borrowing trouble from the future." I was a sitting duck for a relapse if I was left to my own devices with that thought. Luckily, I had been trained to speak with my sponsor about uncomfortable thoughts related to using, so I brought this up. Mickey quickly reminded me that today we were in the middle of September and that the holidays were a ways off. My job was to take life one day at a time and to do the next right thing today. "When we get to the holidays, we will deal with the holidays." All I had to do was to show up for life today and stay sober, come what may.

He asked me, "Can you manage that? Can you go to bed tonight without having used?"

The twisted addictive thinking was supplanted. "Yes, I can handle that."

When you pay attention to the present moment, time passes well. You are connected to it. Of course, we realize that everything happens in the present moment and that it is our minds that habitually pull us out of it. In an esoteric sense we have no choice but to live one day at a time. It's not as if we can get much done tomorrow because tomorrow never comes. Today, we can reference tomorrow as the day that will be here when more time passes. However, then we will be living in today, so you see that nothing will ever happen in the designation known as tomorrow. This key slogan and regular reminders from our support group help us to develop a reverence for each day, which is something we truly disrespect when we are caught up in our addictions.

There are some tough days when one day is too much. Even that increment is too grand. On these days, we get through difficulty one hour at a time or one minute at a time. Our sobriety and life in general can be that tenuous. Early on in my recovery, I would begin to practice yoga and meditation. And that was when I learned to really slow things down and pay attention to life one *breath* at a time.

MY INTRODUCTION TO YOGA

Yoga was one of the practices I found in my first several years of recovery. Not only did it help me through the ups and downs of the early stages, but it also became a nonnegotiable staple in my life. How I found yoga—and fell in love with it—is somewhat serendipitous. Basically, in 1991 I walked off the street into Janet Macleod's Iyengar class in San Francisco. I had never seen a person move with so much freedom. It was an outward representation of something I greatly desired. I wanted that right away. I had a bit of a problem at first: most yoga classes are 90 minutes, nearly the length of a movie, and I was stuck in a difficult relationship with time. I was terribly impatient. No matter where I was, I would try to bring the future here faster. How would I possibly get through such a long class? I'd be in those first yoga classes looking for the clock in the room. How much more time? The postures were very difficult for me. I had so much tension and tightness in my body. I'd be at my edge after only five minutes, trying to find my breath and listen to the teacher's instructions. I remember one teacher walking over to me with considerable empathy, assuring me that someday soon downward-facing dog would become a rest pose. All I could reply, as a waterfall of sweat poured off my head, was, "Well, not today."

Yoga was a thrilling challenge. I loved the athleticism and physicality of it. It made me feel something intense. Yes, there is intensity to yoga. You are burning through old habits, opening up channels that may never have been open before. You are stretching connective tissue and adding powerful breath and *Prana* (a yogic term meaning life force) into the mix. You have to focus, listen, and connect words with parts of your body. A teacher might say, "Press down into your feet in such a way that you feel the earth press back up." So I would bring my attention to my feet, press down, and begin to feel the rebound of energy up through my body. "Breathe more slowly and more deeply." And I would bring my attention there. Wherever the teacher directed my attention, I would learn to connect with that area of my body or mind. I would sweat out of every pore, and the detox of that felt amazing. I felt clean inside and out.

Ninety minutes later, having come through an intimate and powerful experience, I would be directed to lie down, relax completely, and let the full weight of my body rest upon the earth. This was *savasana* or corpse pose. The feeling was electric—energy humming through my body. I felt like blood was pouring into areas of my tissues that it had not been able to reach for some time. It was relieving and healing. It was subtler than the feeling from getting off on drugs, but it was detectable and lovely, and there would be no hangover, just a feeling of more ease than I could remember. I felt a warmth come over me similar to what I felt when I had done heroin, but far from the darkness of that insanity, this was pure light—a way through. When had I ever paid 90 minutes of attention to my breath and body? Well, in all honestly, there were plenty of times during a 90-minute yoga practice when I found myself distracted by someone else's practice or a sexy body. Nonetheless, over time I would learn to pay better and better attention to what happened on my own yoga mat. It was my universe for that time period.

One day many years later, classes started to go by without me noticing the clock. This was around the time when I no longer desired to use drugs and alcohol. A major shift had happened. My thinking had changed. My relationship to time had changed. I had changed.

LIFE ON LIFE'S TERMS AND THE RELAPSE NIGHTMARE

Another teaching that helped me in my early recovery was that everything that happens in your life has a lesson to offer you. Nothing is random or accidental. Things happen so you experience, learn, and grow. You are never a victim. You are a very creative individual, and you have created the circumstances of your life in collaboration with your Higher Power, which is within you and everywhere else. If you do not like the circumstances of your life, you can learn to create something else. In recovery we recover the ability to create something amazing for ourselves. Start to look at life in this way and things will change beautifully for you. This is what it means to take life on life's terms.

I have had some hard times in recovery. I've lost relationships, my parents both died, and friends have gotten sick and some have died as well. No one relishes having to experience these difficult things. Yet some of the greatest lessons of my life came from these losses. The pain we feel seems unavoidable. Our suffering comes from an insistence that things be other than what they are. This is avoidable. Taking life on life's terms, we feel our feelings as they come up for us. We share them; we get support around them; we process them out of the body with the help of yoga and other mind-body healing techniques; we move on.

Several years into my recovery I started to have a recurring nightmare. The dreamscape was amazingly realistic; it was my life, except in a dream. I'd smoke pot and feel all of the guilt, anxiety, and worry that came with losing my "clean time." Within the dream, I would go to bed and wake up the next morning. I was saddened and overwhelmed. I hid it from my friends in the dream and experienced another day of living with the confusion and guilt of relapse. I'd go to bed and wake up yet again, still within the dream, and so it went. By the time I actually woke up for real, I was absolutely convinced that I had relapsed. I could not tell the difference between the dream reality and my waking reality. Consequently, I was overcome with guilt and confusion as I tried to piece together where I had smoked pot and why it had happened. Each time I had this dream, it took several hours before I started to realize that it was in fact a dream and that I had not actually smoked pot. My sobriety and recovery were still intact.

Sometimes I'd say to a friend, "I have to ask you the damnedest thing. Did I relapse last night? Did I smoke pot?"

They'd think I was joking. "Tommy, we went to an AA meeting and then to the movies last night. Don't you remember that?" I would piece it all together in my mind and the most incredible relief would come over me. I was so grateful to have my recovery.

I believe I was detoxing on a deep psychological level. Marijuana had been embedded deep in my psyche; it makes sense that it would take a lot to get it out. These dreams went on for a while, though. With each successive one, I felt all the more confused and sometimes quite certain that I had used again. When I describe this phenomenon to people in recovery, I find that many of them have had these experiences.

My therapist, Joe, told me that these dreams were a gift, an opportunity to experience the feelings that went along with a relapse without having to relapse. *He was reminding me to take life on life's terms. Even these dreams were not random. They were a blessing. What could I learn?* First, it was clear that being sober actually meant a lot to me. Also, I realized just how mentally ill I had been.

Drug addiction had hit me hard and deep. I was fortunate to have escaped its jaws. Upon realizing this, tears came. I was overcome with a sense of gratitude for everything and everyone that had helped me get to this point.

Shortly after the period when I was having these dreams, I woke up one day to realize that I no longer thought about using drugs and alcohol. The charge around it was gone. I knew I wanted to be sober and that I was going to be sober. Each day, my confidence grew. I have never become cocky about my sobriety. I am simply reporting that my thinking had changed dramatically. From a person who could not have imagined a day without drugs, I now could not imagine a day that included them. I did not fear doing drugs, nor did I obsess about it. I was confident about being a person in recovery and could openly discuss it. I had a running dialog with the Universe around me. I call it a connection with my Higher Power. There was newfound possibility in my life. I had had a spiritual awakening. Everything the 12 Steps promised had been delivered to me.

PART III

THE BIRTH OF RECOVERY 2.0

CHAPTER 10

ADDICTION
BY ANY
OTHER NAME

A part of me wishes that I could have ended this book here and reported to you that the 12 Steps worked their magic and I lived happily ever after. But, you see, that is exactly the problem. The very idea of "happily ever after" is as much an illusion as the idea of "a cure" when it comes to addiction. We are all looking for a quick and complete fix, a cure. We want to be able to say, "I was this way before and now I am better. It's great and that's that." Yet we know enough to know that life doesn't work that way. I'm 23 years sober. Of course I'm confident in my recovery, but I still choose to take things as they come, one day at a time. For me, every day means observation, focus, and concentration on what is happening, inside and outside. This means that my process of evolution is ongoing. I once believed that the 12 Steps would take care of any challenge life presented. Somewhere along the way, I must have missed the memo: "Tommy, you will encounter things in life that the 12 Steps cannot address." Some of the challenges I was going to face had been ingrained in my psyche over the course of my life. The fact I was sober and followed the 12 Steps did not mean that I was "cured" of my particular approach to being human. The 12 Steps are really the first step. They are the work that readies you to do the rest of the work that you get to do, and must do, in your life.

You really need to understand this if you are to thrive in recovery. Critiques of 12-Step programs cite a very low success rate. First of all, we need to understand that we are dealing with human development. True success cannot be measured on the outside. If a drug addict manages through sheer force of will to abstain from drugs and alcohol for a full year, but is miserable, does that count as a success? It really depends how the person feels inside. The true measurement of success is whether a person is able to find peace, contentment, and fulfillment in their life or at least make strides toward this goal. To me, *that* is success. We must also realize that there are going to be good days and bad days, good periods and challenging periods. For me to have sustainable recovery has required the 12 Steps as a beginning foundation and then a continuing process of growth in which I address the most important areas of my life. To see the 12 Steps as the be-all and end-all is to misunderstand their place as a foundation in the lifelong process of recovery and personal growth. Just knowing this will make the 12 Steps more successful.

I learned the hard way that one can recover from severe drug addiction and alcoholism but still live life in the Frequency of Addiction. It was alive in me through at least the first 12 years of my recovery. Since becoming aware of this in my own life, I've begun to notice it in most recovering addicts. We seem to be great at remaining in the Frequency of Addiction. We continue to engage in activities—smoking, overconsumption of food, codependent relationships, sugar, coffee, gambling, and pornography—that demote us rather than promote us. Maybe some people can live this way and get away with it. For people in recovery, these behaviors keep us stuck in the Frequency of Addiction and perpetuate our vulnerability. Many people have relapsed because they did not have the full picture of recovery in mind. It was not the fault of the 12 Steps that they relapsed. They just had no further plan in place or understanding that they needed one when life showed up and kicked their ass.

I had many great times in early recovery and hard times as well, but looking back, the thing I remark upon most is that my thinking still really messed with me. I was stressed much of the time and rarely truly relaxed because I didn't know how. Through my crazy, sugar-addled childhood and drug-addled adolescence, I had never learned how to turn it off.

Once I found recovery, I certainly learned and changed a lot, but I was not struck "enlightened." I still had a thinking problem and now there were no drugs or alcohol to quell it. Things started to get difficult again. There are really only two ways to go when a person reaches this point: the path of devotion or the path of commotion. The path of devotion leads to contentment, peace, and bliss. The path of commotion leads to friction, hardship, and more lessons in the school of hard knocks. I would choose the path of commotion. The good news and bad news is that the Universe in all its wisdom is happy to provide us with plenty of opportunities to learn.

In the world of human experience, two of the main "theaters of war" where people struggle are sex and money. And, as it turns out, for people in recovery these are the two biggest triggers. I'm speaking from direct experience.

RELATIONSHIPS AND SEX

It is a longstanding suggestion in 12-Step society that people not begin new romantic relationships in their first year of recovery. Part of the reason for this is because relationships and sex can be amazingly distracting and may pull people's focus away from their program of recovery. Relationships also bring up powerful feelings that, under the best of circumstances, can be overwhelming and trigger emotional issues and unresolved trauma. And when things don't work out well, all manner of drama often ensues.

Another important point is that in early recovery, we are moving through a rather broad and often rapid process of transformation. The version of us that we present to someone when we are one month sober is bound to be quite different from the person we are at three months or six months or nine months sober. We have not yet settled, if you will, upon solid ground. Our identity is being built or rebuilt to a great extent. We are perhaps not yet clear about who we are and what we want, which leaves us vulnerable to poor decision making and pain. Nonetheless, despite strong suggestions from sponsors that their sponsees take a hiatus from romance for a little while, people will be people.

Through my early recovery, I never stopped pursuing girls, relationships, and sex. The power of it all was too great for me to resist, even for limited amounts of time. So I disregarded my sponsor's advice on this topic and got an opportunity to learn a lot about myself through the experience of great joy and great pain. As with all things, sex and relationships involve light and shadow. The bright side of this story is that I shared love, learned a lot, and was able to grow through it. The not-so-bright side is that through immaturity, selfishness, dishonesty, and fear I hurt some wonderful people whom I truly loved and almost lost my mind in the process.

I had an interesting pattern. When I was single and "free," I longed for a deeper relationship with one woman. Sex was fine and all, but empty in comparison to the feelings of being in a committed relationship. When I was in a committed relationship, on the other hand, I felt trapped and wanted to be free. The confines of a relationship would not allow me the freedom to pursue other women, which prevented me from gaining the feeling of excitement, distraction, and self-worth that doing that always gave me. Eventually, I would leave the relationship and return to the freedom I thought I was seeking—but it never seemed to be there. I know many men who struggle in this way.

I went back and forth in this pattern for years, rarely finding true peace within myself. The level of pain I was experiencing in my relationships seemed to increase over time. Right around three years sober, I fell in love with an amazing woman and spent four years with her. I could not have loved anyone more, yet I was stuck in my pattern of discontentedness. She couldn't fix it. I couldn't fix it. I was so unhappy and confused that finally we broke it off. It crushed me. My heart hurt, literally, for months.

After that relationship I concluded that I was broken. I looked out in the world and saw plenty of people who had "found each other" and seemed to be very happy together, but apparently this was not something I would ever experience.

HOW NOT TO APPROACH A RELATIONSHIP

A few months later, I started to date a girl, but I was determined not to let the same thing happen again. Thus I told her up front that I was not to be counted on for true love. I wanted to spend time with her and be intimate together, but I frankly explained that I was not going to fall in love. Thus I headed down the road toward what would end up being a death-defying relationship filled with all the trappings of codependency, sexual obsession, addiction, manipulation, and dishonesty.

We started to have a lot of fun together, but in the early months of our relationship I was not faithful to her even though I had said that I would be. About a year into our relationship, I was about to make my annual pilgrimage to New Orleans for the Jazz Fest and I plainly told her that I wanted to go without her. I was thinking about some of the flirtations that might happen and that having her with me was not what I wanted. This prompted her to ask me point-blank if I had been faithful since we started dating. I told her the truth. "At the beginning of our relationship, I was with someone else, but that was nearly a year ago." She was understandably hurt and angry. Strangely, in that instant my connection with her deepened. I could see that she really cared about me and I, too, cared about her. Nonetheless, I headed off to Jazz Fest by myself. Upon landing in New Orleans, though, the most powerful feeling came over me. I missed her and felt I had made a big mistake in not inviting her. I called her to apologize and ask if she would consider flying down. Her distant tone said it all. She would not be flying down to be with me just because I had suddenly seen the light. No. I had shaken her trust to the core, and I would spend the next 18 months in a psychotic tailspin trying to win it and her back. The whole drama was elevated to the next level when I learned that she had started dating another person. We were still seeing each other and the sexual energy remained strong between us, but from that moment forward sex took on a dark quality. It was no longer about love and connection. Now it was more about manipulation and control. I wanted it. She had it and controlled it. And that dynamic created a huge addiction in me. Consequently, I descended into a level of relationship psychosis and sexual obsession that deserves mention.

Each day, I woke up with her on my mind and would begin to scheme my way back into her good graces and into her bed. I'd live with this obsession most of the day and night. It owned me. My friends, meanwhile, started to become concerned. After months of this, many of them told me flat out, "Tommy, we can't hear any more of this. You simply have to stop talking about her. Whatever it is you need, we don't have the answer." Unfortunately, I couldn't let it go. I couldn't stay away from her in my mind. On a daily basis, I was consumed by jealousy, fear, and sexual thoughts of her. I could not be with any other woman, didn't think about any other woman. She was the only woman in the world as far as I was concerned.

I started to fear for my own sanity. My ego was taking a beating. I felt guilty and shameful. It was like any other addiction I had ever known, but even more intense. There was a substance, in this case a person to whom I had become addicted. I felt I could not live without her and refused to let go even though the consequences of hanging on were considerable. I had built up an addiction story around her. "She's the only one. This has to work. I've caused this whole mess. It's all my fault and I've got to fix it." Those were the hooks. I was swimming in the Frequency of Addiction and it was slowly draining me of life force.

All this time I was attending 12-Step meetings and working the steps to the best of my ability, but it was obvious to me and just about everyone else that something was wrong. Would I need medication? Was this a depression? I had never experienced anything quite like it before. The thoughts were upon me before I opened my eyes each morning. Drugs and alcohol had been removed from my life and my thinking had changed. Now I had no desire to use drugs and alcohol, but my thinking had descended back into a state of dis-ease, this time focused on a person. It was particularly alarming. Before, I had been able to blame drugs and alcohol for my insanity. Now what?

YOUR CASE IS BEING CONSIDERED

I woke up one morning after about a year of this insanity. The sexual obsession was at its peak. As I went through my day, there was the front that I presented to the world and then there was the horrific 70 mm pornographic film that was taking place in my head. Walking down the street in San Francisco, I ran into an acquaintance of mine. We exchanged pleasantries and then he asked if I wanted to join him for an art opening at a gallery nearby. I thought, *Yes. Art. Anything to get me out of my head.*

"What's the address?" I asked.

"69 Powell," he replied.

Involuntarily, my fingers tightened and rolled themselves into fists. "Powell" was *her* last name.

I stared into his eyes, trying to see if he was messing with me. "Are you telling me that 69 Powell is the address of the art gallery?" I asked.

"Yep," he said. "Meet me there if you like." And he was off.

I stood there on the sidewalk looking at the sky and suddenly burst into laughter, which led into tears. This was not exactly the hand of God reaching out of the sky, but it might as well have been. I had been cut off from my heart for a very long time, so alone. Here, in my lowest moment, was my Higher Power speaking in the language we communicate in—the language of synchronicity. It went beyond words. I felt immediate knowing and relief. I was not alone. My case was being considered.

I wrote a final note to this woman, which shifted the energy and ended my involvement in whatever our relationship had become by this point. Time passed, and I slowly climbed out of the dark place where I had been. Obviously, there was work to do. I could not find peace within the confines of a relationship, nor could I find peace as a single person. I felt close to my Higher Power, a real presence, but what had been the purpose of that whole episode? What did I need to learn? What had I missed along the way?

It is a common story that people who put down one addiction tend to pick up another. Over the past 25 years, I have observed in myself and countless others that just underneath drug addiction and alcoholism, codependency lurks. Remember, codependency is a form of addiction with regard to the way we relate to others. It is hard to pin down because people who struggle with it exhibit many different behaviors. Relationship issues of every kind seem to crop up for codependents. This is part of the reason so many people end up relapsing after years of recovery. They experience the unique and unbearable pain of codependent behavior, which includes terrible obsession like I experienced. I referred to it earlier as "the disease of the lost self," which makes a lot of sense in light of my story with it. I was fortunate to get out of that scrape with my recovery and sanity intact. It taught me that I had to address underlying relationship issues, which I had not addressed through my 12-Step work. I always felt that part of the reason I had to go through that relationship was to understand this important piece of the puzzle. For the time being, I didn't have a solution, but I was keen on finding one.

Addiction is not about a particular substance. If you stay on the path of recovery, you will come to the point where you see your vulnerabilities, the places where life challenges you. People who struggle with addiction in one area often struggle with addictive behavior in other areas. These are the places where you can work to grow into the person you hope and dream to be. *As people in recovery, our job is to look. At all costs, we must not look away.* That is where the trouble starts and addiction gets a foothold once again. As life makes us aware of the places where we are out of balance, we will need to address them or pay dear prices for looking away. Unfortunately, I was about to find out that there was another area of my life I had been looking away from for a long, long time.

(CHAPTER 11)

HITTING BOTTOM
IN RECOVERY

When I was 11, I went to the Bahamas with my mother and sisters. There was a casino downstairs and all I wanted to do was play the slot machines. It was a logical extension of my childhood addiction to pinball—bright flashing lights, music, and other loud, hypnotic noises—with the intrigue of winning money thrown into it. This really got my blood pumping, especially when three big red cherries showed up on the screen and quarters started falling out of the machine. I think I only won $10 that first time, but I might as well have won a million.

Later on, in my early 20s, I went to see the Grateful Dead in Las Vegas. What a combination of energies! All these drug-addled Deadheads in the madness of Sin City. I was already two years sober but very far from true recovery and dreadfully out of touch with myself. As I have previously mentioned, long after I had gotten sober and was on a path supported by the 12 Steps, I was still caught up in addictive thoughts and behaviors. I was setting the stage to bring a lot of pain into my life. Though I didn't know it at the time, I was about to get a real and true ass-whooping, and that weekend in Vegas I started down that path by winning $10,000 playing blackjack.

I floated through the casino like a god. Women loved me. Men loved me. I loved me. I treated Deadheads I didn't even know to massages at the casino spa. I bought dinner for 30 people. Whenever I laid money down, I won. It was uncanny. The climax of the mayhem came when I decided to wager $2,400 on one single hand, which for me was an unconscionable sum of money. I won the hand, my heart pounding out of my chest, and somehow managed to stop and leave Vegas with 100 hundred-dollar bills.

Back home in San Francisco, my cousin Roger Low and I got together and I told him about my incredible gambling skills. He smiled strangely and plainly said, "This was the worst thing that could ever have happened to you. Congratulations."

Roger had left Cornell engineering school after his first two semesters with a 0.0 GPA. Though he was a savant in many respects, attending college in a traditional setting was not to be Roger's calling. Instead he announced that he would be leaving to pursue a career as a professional backgammon player in the casinos of the world. The family was freaked out about Roger's decision but he had made up his mind.

Within a year or so, to everyone's amazement, Roger ascended to the top of the international backgammon rankings. He was world-ranked somewhere in the top three for most of his career. However, what makes Roger completely unique in the world of professional gambling is the fact that he was able to quit when he wanted to. After making a lot of money playing backgammon, Roger was approached by a money manager who took him on as a protégé. He figured that with Roger's understanding of mathematics, statistics, and probabilities, he would be a great asset. He was right!

Roger transitioned out of the world of casino gambling to another form of gambling with higher stakes and better odds. He applied himself to learn the business of trading options and had an outstanding run up until October 1987, when calamity fell. One

Friday morning Roger woke up with about $4 million in the bank. About a week later, when he lay down to "rest," he was $8 million in the hole. He had personally lost $12 million in a single week.

That was what gamblers might refer to as a "bad beat," a really tough loss that makes you want to throw up. A loss like that has post-traumatic stress disorder associated with it and it requires recovery to heal from it. Not kidding! It is traumatic. Well, Roger would have a chance to heal in every way. Over the next 23 years he would build a boutique options trading firm called Parallax Fund that would way outperform all indices. He would also have a hand in changing the course of my life.

WELCOME BACK, MR. ROSEN

Throughout my 20s, I continued a love-hate relationship with gambling. I never really obsessed about it unless I found myself in a place where gambling was legal—usually somewhere in the strange and twisted state of Nevada. I went there two or three times a year either for a Dead show, a business conference, or to ski at Lake Tahoe. Once I started gambling, as happened with cocaine, I could never stop until I was either too exhausted to continue or had lost all my money and couldn't get any more. It would end with me hitting my friends up for cash once I had exhausted all other possibilities.

And believe me, in the gambling world there are *plenty* of other possibilities. Once you run out of your own cash, you can hit up your ATM cards. Once you've maxed your daily limit on those, then it descends to credit cards. Here you can get into real trouble because when you use your credit card to get a cash advance in a casino, you pay large fees as well as finance charges. In addition, you often have to deal with a call to the credit-card company because despite the fact that you have only taken out $3,000 of your $10,000 credit line, your next request for a cash advance is declined. So you get on the phone with a representative from the bank that issued your Visa card and the conversation goes something like this:

"Yeah, hi. I tried to get a cash advance for three thousand dollars, and it was declined."

"Yes, sir. Well, it shows here that you took a cash advance from the Golden Nugget Casino for three thousand already this evening. Our system automatically freezes your account until we can verify large transactions such as these."

The whole conversation is embarrassing. You're losing money in a casino and taking out credit to gamble. You are totally aware of what you're doing (especially if you're sober), but all you can think of is getting more money so you can play games that you are likely going to lose while in an environment filled with the worst energy of all time. Worst of all, the person to whom you are speaking on the phone is checking to see if you are who you say you are and bringing to your attention your *total financial irresponsibility*. Finally the credit-card company grants you the right to pull out more cash and you decide immediately to risk it in the very same manner that you have done for the whole night.

Once the opportunities for credit-card advances have been exhausted, you get to take it to a whole new level: you get to borrow money directly from the casino. The communication between a gambler and a casino executive is one of the most twisted forms of human interaction. You walk into an office, which every casino has. It is the nicest room in the casino. It has a lot of dark wood and nice carpeting. It is somehow quiet and removed from the melee that is taking place just outside its door. The casino executive is friendly, understanding, professional, businesslike, and intimidating, like a rich, estranged family member you have to go to for money in a pinch. Face-to-face with a casino executive, a gambler does everything he can to appear as if he is fine. Secretly, he is glad to have the casino executive as a kind of friend/therapist at this moment, someone he can confide in. "It's been a hellish night so far," he might say to the casino executive.

"Let me take a look at your betting average for the night," says the executive. "You've been averaging bets of seventy-five dollars per hand. That is good! If you were averaging up more around a hundred dollars, we could comp you a better room and better food." You somehow hear the words *That is good.* Someone has just complimented you, made you feel better. You think, *He understands me. All this time I have been feeling desperate, alone, and terrible about myself, but sitting here in this office, I feel better. This guy deals with people like me all the time. This isn't such bad behavior after all. Everyone's doing it! I feel hopeful, lucky even. Okay, what next?*

"You've lost about twenty-five hundred tonight." That's precise, by the way, unless you have gambled at a table without volunteering to give them your ID. Why would you volunteer to give them your ID? Well, because they ask for it in a suave way, promising comps and other perks. That's the first hook they get into you. Meanwhile, in front of the casino executive, you think, *Jesus, what an amazing system they have! They know exactly what I've lost, and furthermore, they know the average money I'm spending on each bet. That's pretty fucking mind blowing!*

These folks know exactly what happens underneath their roof. They are great at their job of getting money from you—whether you are an addict or just someone looking to piss away some money. Once you have borrowed all you can from a casino, your bank account is virtually empty. Actually, no funds have yet been removed from your bank account, but they will be. The casino will put it to you like this: "Mr. Rosen, you owe the casino five thousand dollars. How would like to pay that?"

If you don't know to ask, you may not realize that you can have 30 days to pay this tab. Many people will therefore go to their banks, one of which is likely right there in Vegas, empty their accounts, and give the proceeds to the casino, satisfying their "marker" or debt. Others will take the 30-day option and then, once they return home, struggle mentally with the fact that they have lost all that money.

Right around 30 days later, when you have still not been able to bring yourself to give your money to the casino (if you still have it), the casino starts to generate and send reminder notices, which become increasingly harsh. You will end up having your credit ruined if you do not pay the casino back. Ironically, the casino does not want this option any more than you do, for if your credit is ruined, they will lose, at least temporarily, a good customer.

Finally, you pay the casino back. Then, at some point in the not-too-distant future, you return to the casino—a rejuvenated hero—to repeat the process. "Mr. Rosen, how great to have you back. Congratulations on being here again. Can we get you some free drinks? Food? We can't yet comp you a room, but we'll watch your average betting numbers over the next few hours, and why don't you come visit us this afternoon to see what we can do for you? In the meantime, good luck and let us know if you need anything at all."

"Well, there is one thing, actually! How about a marker up front so I can avoid credit-card fees?"

"Sure, Mr. Rosen. Come into the office and we'll get you squared away."

As you can see, I speak from experience. I weakened myself every time I set foot in Las Vegas. I weakened my body by consuming junk food, too much meat, sugar, caffeine, and little to no water while there. (And I wasn't even drinking alcohol or using drugs.) I would sit for long periods of time, eight to ten hours a pop through an entire sleepless night until I ran out of money or until I was too exhausted to see that happen. I would drink caffeine all night long, tea with huge amounts of sugar. Yes, I had some large wins, but they were never satisfying. It was a drug-like experience for me. I never wanted it to end. When I was up $1,000, I wanted to be up $2,000. When I was down $1,000, all I wanted to do was get back to even.

Regardless of how the financial end of things turned out, I knew deep down that I would return to this crazy, addictive place. *And* that I'd always be welcomed back. Despite having been sober for years, I was still drawn to addiction, making poor choices and operating in conflict with my own heart. It would be a while before I understood about the Frequency of Addiction and the need to attune myself beyond it. As was the case for me with drugs and alcohol, it was going to take something extreme to get me to see what was happening and to break the spell I was under.

NOT HITTING THE JACKPOT

I had married my incredible wife, Kia, in June 2003. In September of that year, my friend Gabe called me to make a proposal: "Let's go to Vegas to have a post-wedding bachelor party for you." Now, at that point in my life, I was gambling more regularly than ever before. For a couple of years, I had been taking my shot at Vegas. I armed myself with books on counting cards and decided, like so many other deluded folks since Vegas became Vegas, that I was going to win big. *There certainly are some people who have made a lot of money this way. Why not me?*

The problem, as I've already noted, was that I was a compulsive gambler. I was in it for the *high,* not the money. This translates into astonishing impatience, erratic betting, dreadful money management, and generally terrible choices at the tables. This also means I am unable to walk away when I need to. I do not have the temperament of someone who can win in Vegas even if the cards go my way. I am just a sitting duck, and over time *I will lose.* And, by the way, so will almost everyone else, even if they don't have my particular makeup.

When Gabe called me, he didn't realize that I was as deep into this sickness as I was. He, like most of my friends, was in recovery from addiction. We all knew at some level that going to Vegas was a way we could still indulge in a "high," something with some juice to it. So we made our plan to arrive in Vegas on Friday. Of course, I invited Roger, who planned to arrive on Saturday.

We got to Vegas as planned. I got my comped room, of course. Free food, of course. And a marker for $5,000 from the casino.

I began to gamble at the $300 minimum table. Anyone will tell you that unless you have about $30,000, it is foolish to gamble at a table with such high stakes. But I was in a rush to make as much money as possible as quickly as possible so that I could a) justify my gambling in the first place, b) buy my friends everything for the weekend and impress them, c) have some extra cash in my life (Yes, finances were not going well. What a shocker!), d) fulfill the fantasy I had that I could live outside the rules that everyone else was subject to, *and* e) have the illusion of control in my life.

I lost the first three hands in a row and was now down $900. On the very next hand, I decided to wager $900 by playing $300 on three different hands. The dealer got 21 and I didn't. I continued to mix and match like this for the next 20 to 30 hands, and within 15 minutes, I had lost all $5,000.

The three friends who were watching me were mortified. "Holy shit! You just lost five thousand dollars!" I neglected to tell them that I had borrowed it and now owed it to the casino.

I got up from the table to go have lunch with them. But throughout what should have been a relaxing and enjoyable meal, every ounce of my being wanted to return to the casino floor and win my money back. I didn't want to be with my friends. I didn't want anyone to celebrate me, and I certainly didn't want to eat. My stomach was in knots, adrenaline was flowing through my veins, and I knew I had a job to do. Only one thing was holding me back—my shame and embarrassment.

My friends, all addicts themselves, knew exactly what was going on with me. They were more than aware of the fact that this little trip to Vegas had been a mistake. But they had no idea just how big a mistake it was about to become.

To make a long, awful night short, when I finally headed up to my room at 3 A.M., I was $12,000 in debt to the casino. In addition to that, I had tapped my credit cards for another $3,000, and I was freaking the fuck out. Biochemically speaking, my body was in full-on fight-or-flight mode.

The next day proved to be an epic, drawn-out day of compulsive gambling. Rather than lose my money right away, I went up and down, up and down all day long. I was never able to get ahead much, nor did I lose all my money. I was playing with about $3,000, which was all I had left at this point. I couldn't get any more money from my bank, my credit cards, or the casino. This $3,000 was it, so I was terrified of losing it. As a result of this fear, my betting was even more erratic than usual.

I kept thinking of Roger, who was to arrive late that afternoon. I imagined that he of all people would understand and be able to comfort me. I imagined that with all of his wins and losses he would know what to do to help me get back out there and right this situation.

When Roger arrived, I asked to have a private meeting with him up in the room. We got into the elevator and I exchanged a few awkward words. "How was the flight? So glad you're here. Oh my God, this is so much fun!"

Once we were upstairs in the room, Roger sat down on the bed and from the armchair opposite him I told him straight up: "Roger, I owe the casino twelve grand. I got on a terrible run. I have three grand on me, and I am struggling to win the money back. I don't know what to do."

The shock in his face was immediately sobering. "I had no idea this had gotten so bad for you. I'm sorry." That was all he said. There was no tough love or consoling to be done. He looked right through me, knew that I had the sickness, and knew that I was in trouble. Now I knew I was in trouble, too. I saw my own dis-ease in his eyes mirrored back to me in a language that cannot be misunderstood. It was his soul communicating to mine. And the news was very painful. This party, and my life as I had known it, was going to have to end.

I was ashamed in front of him. I had figured he would let me off the hook emotionally: "Hey, it's okay. I've lost millions. You'll get it back." But he didn't let me off the hook. Instead he forced me to see what was happening. With one glance and a sentence or two, he made it loud and clear that it did not matter how much or little I had lost. What mattered was the addiction, the compulsion to gamble, and all the horrible feelings and consequences that went with them. I was sick.

But what Roger said next I never saw coming. "I will cover your debt of twelve thousand to the casino, and I will give you two full years to pay me back."

"Oh my God, Roger," I said.

"That's not all," he continued. "If you take me up on this offer, you commit to me that you will not gamble again in any form *from this moment forward* until you have paid me back in full. If you still want to gamble after you've paid me back, that is up to you. Until that time, however, and starting immediately, you will not gamble again."

I paused. The likelihood of me not gambling in Las Vegas while I was in debt $12,000 to the casino with $3,000 burning a hole in my pocket would be the same as me being able to beat Roger Federer, arguably the greatest tennis player ever, in a singles match on center court at Wimbledon. It was an amazing offer, but how could I take him up on it? His terms were implausible.

Furthermore, I just wanted to get downstairs and win back my money. It was exactly what any addict would be thinking. *It isn't over till it's over . . . and it's not over. I'm here in Vegas. I've got to see this thing through.*

On the other hand, the offer was compelling. Was I going to have enough energy and stamina to play long enough to win back all that money? How would I pay the casino if I didn't win? What would Kia say when I got back home and told her what had happened?

When Roger was done making his proposition, he told me that he was leaving. What would be the point of him hanging around? There was no celebration—there was only a decision to be made. I was going to think about his offer and would not gamble until I'd made a decision. And I would call him as soon as I did.

I went to dinner with eight of my friends that evening and laid out the whole story. I told them the truth, perhaps for the first time that weekend. I told them of Roger's proposition and that I did not know what to do. I asked each of them to give me their opinion. Of the eight people at the table, four of them felt I should take Roger up on the offer and the other four thought I should try to win my own money back. Some people I have spoken to about this since find it absolutely amazing that anyone in recovery would actually suggest that I continue down the path of gambling when I had a clean way out. I guess they might have realized that it was going to be impossible for me to stop. Perhaps they really wanted to see me get out of it on my own. From where I am sitting now, the sound advice would have been to accept Roger's offer. At the time this was anything but clear to me—and apparently it wasn't so clear to four of my pals either.

For an addict to stop using while in the middle of a run is amazingly difficult to do. All of your history with addiction, the habits you've created in reaction to your thoughts and emotions, are telling you to do more. Biochemically, you are living through an apocalyptic event. All that occurs to you is to prevent yourself from coming down at all costs. Coming down means facing significant physical and emotional discomfort. You feel terrible about yourself. You know you've covered no ground and lost much. The hopes and dreams you have for yourself sit inaccessible in trophy cases in your mind. Do not pass Go. Do not collect anything. You are a loser.

Roger's deal provided me with all the rope I needed to hang myself. The addict in me hated him for it. If I took him up on it, I was going to have one hell of a night, white-knuckling the rest of my time in Vegas. Then I'd head home, forced to take a good look at the dis-eased parts of myself with feelings of shame, remorse, and insecurity. If I gambled and lost, I'd just be another $3,000 in debt and would have chosen to remain in the energy of sickness a little longer. If I gambled and won all the money back, I could pay my debts, have one hell of a story to tell about the bachelor party that wasn't, and get to stay in the illusion of being okay a little longer. I might even be able to deny all of it to myself and write it off as a rough weekend: *Hey, look. Things got a little out of control, but thank God, I pulled myself out of it and next time, if there is one* (and there will be), *I'll be a little more prudent* (and, of course, I won't be).

BREAKING THE SPELL

There are pivotal moments in life, moments of leverage. This was one of them. The impossibility of the decision notwithstanding, I took the path of recovery and decided to call it a night. *The moment I accepted Roger's offer, I felt somehow empowered to carry it out.* There was no real struggle. I honestly can't explain this. I walked through the casino one last time on the way up to my room, and I saw it for what it was: a very dark energy that at best provided distraction and at worst ruined people's lives. I no longer wanted to be there at all. I was turned off. The spell was broken. I hated the place, the employees of the casino, the pit bosses, the executives, the dealers, all of them. I hated the whole reality of it and I hated the part of myself that was vulnerable to it. I had been pulled to places like this since I was 11 years old. I couldn't stand it anymore. I had given so much of myself to something that would never take me where my spirit wanted to go.

I gave my money to my friends to hold and went upstairs with a couple of them. I informed Roger that I would gratefully accept his offer, that I would not gamble again at least until I paid him back. I would be coming home on the first flight out in the morning. Roger sent a check for $12,000 to the casino. I spent the night in my hotel room with a few friends. We watched some movies, and eventually I fell asleep. It was over.

Roger never asked me if I had stayed true to my commitment. I guess he trusted me, which is amazing, because I did not trust myself. Or maybe he didn't want to police me, figuring that my penance was forthcoming regardless of what my choices were. I paid him back within the allotted two years and did not gamble in the interim.

I would later have one more gambling experience in New Orleans during the Jazz Fest. I was walking back to the French Quarter from a late-night show at the Howling Wolf on St. Peters and, what do you know . . . Harrah's casino was right there. I must have looked like the guiltiest man in history. I looked over my right shoulder and then over my left shoulder to make sure no one I knew saw me, and up the stairs I ran. Classic! I knew it was wrong but decided to do it anyway. I was nervous and uncomfortable the whole time. I should have listened to my body. I could not win anything, nor was I losing much. At some point, I noticed the surroundings, I mean *really* noticed and became aware. I was immediately put off. The charge was gone for me. I cashed in my chips, left the casino, and have not returned since. I finally understood that *when you gamble with money, you can literally never win.* I am now 11 years removed from it.

Your relationship with money is important. Money is energy, which can be put toward positive or negative things. If you overspend, are often in debt, or gamble, your relationship with money needs review. Money is one of the biggest triggers for unhappiness, stress, and relapse. It is, therefore, a relationship we must tend to in our recovery lives.

There was weirdness around money in my family growing up. As you may recall, there was plenty of money around, but it was associated with control and pain. For me, there was a real sense of powerlessness around it.

If there was ever a time I felt powerful, it was when I was winning in a casino. As I said, it wasn't about the money. I now realize it was to combat a dreadful feeling of insecurity and powerlessness. I didn't feel worthy of earning money, so I'd go after a big payout by gambling. With impatience, bad psychology, and a powerful addiction to distraction, I went after the long shot and it landed me flat on my ass.

Despite the fact that I was 12 years in recovery from drugs and alcohol, I'd earnestly followed the 12 Steps, and I'd had a powerful spiritual experience, I reached another bottom—this time in recovery. I had no understanding of what was happening to me, and you can imagine the quality of the inner chatter that began: *You're 12 years sober and miserable. Wow! That's fucking great! What's wrong with you?* My life of addiction had been a series of efforts to avoid coming down to face the present moment and myself. I was still making decisions based on avoiding some aspect of myself. I was now into another full-blown addiction that threatened my health, security, and sanity. The Universe had had about enough of my antics.

CHAPTER 12

LETTING GO
OF MY
DIS-EASE

Shortly after I returned home from Vegas, I was dancing at a concert when suddenly a very sharp, electric pain shot down into my hips, butt, and legs. The smile quickly left my face. Suddenly, I could no longer stand, much less dance, without pain. I focused my attention within to try to make sense of the feeling, but the explanation was elusive. Had I injured myself? What had I done? It was literally unnerving. I felt like I was losing control of my legs. I sat down. *What is happening to me?* I had absolutely no idea. Can you believe that it never dawned on me that what I had just experienced in Las Vegas might be connected with what was now happening in my body? It is humbling to write this now.

I'd had a tweaky back for years, but it never lasted for more than a few days. Typically, my back would spasm and then it would take three to five days for it to loosen up again. I would see massage therapists, acupuncturists, and chiropractors to help me with these episodes. The only chronic aspect of it was that I was pretty tight in my upper back, but this remained unknown or unnoticed to me for a while to come.

CHRONIC PAIN: PHYSICAL AND EMOTIONAL

My wake-up call to the need for an additional stage of recovery was my struggle with chronic pain. Each morning, my ritual was the same. Even before waking, I knew that the second I moved my legs underneath the light sheets, the pain would begin, and it would remain until I went to bed at night. I'd open my eyes and sit there at the mercy of the terrible tales my mind crafted about how I was never going to be able to move well again. The moment my feet hit the ground, the pain escalated, and for the rest of the day I was in purgatory, fighting against myself.

Unless you've been through debilitating, chronic pain, it might be hard to understand how depressing it is, especially for an athletic person who had managed to always find a way through challenge. My body had always bounced back. I had survived junk-food malnourishment, terrible migraine headaches, and acute drug addiction. Despite all the hard living I had put myself through, I had remained in pretty good shape. But that was gone now. I started to take three Advil tablets three to four times a day (not a good practice for the liver and kidneys). It took me about ten seconds to get up out of bed or a chair. There was extreme tightness around my hips and upper legs. And then there was that nervy, ringing sensation that made me feel like I had holes in my legs. If you had asked me to run across the street, I would not have been able to do it. With each passing day, I became increasingly fearful that I was going to be crippled for the rest of my life.

Waking up with chronic pain is a horror. At first, you think, *What can I do to make this better? There has to be something.* Maybe you take anti-inflammatory medications. You have probably been to a variety of doctors and healers. In my case, I only visited healers, but I went to any kind of healer I could find: massage therapists, acupuncturists, chiropractors, rolfers, neuromuscular therapists, bodyworkers, energy healers, Reiki practitioners, herb-alists, nutritionists, physical therapists, gym trainers, yoga teach-ers, and meditation teachers. Unfortunately, no one seemed to be able to "fix" me.

This was one of the lowest points of my life. Not making any progress by seeing healers, I looked into what Western medicine had to say about my condition. I went to a prominent hospital in Los Angeles to get an MRI. This was the court of last resort for me. There were two doctors—a radiologist and an orthopedic surgeon—present at the hospital when my wife, Kia, and I went to hear the results of my MRI. The doctors told me the follow-ing: "You have degenerative disk disease. It is progressive. We have never seen it get better, only worse over time. You also have se-verely herniated disks at L3–L4 and L4–L5. We are going to have to manage your pain with drugs for the rest of your life, and even-tually we will have to look to surgery."

Kia and I stood there dumbfounded. "What are you talking about?" I sputtered, frightened and angry. "There has to be a way to fix this without drugs and surgery. There has to be something." But the doctors shook their heads. They had nothing further to offer. From their perspective, there was nothing else to discuss. I felt like my life was over.

As the adage goes, if you go to the barber, you're probably going to end up with a haircut. Well, the adage applies to sur-geons as well: if you go to a surgeon, you're probably going to end up having surgery. This is not a slight against surgeons. Many of them are amazing people who save lives every day. If I were in a car accident or had any traumatic injury, I would be most grate-ful that surgeons and hospitals exist. But I knew using surgery to heal chronic pain in the lower spine was risky business indeed and only advisable in the worst possible situations. A close friend of mine who is a respected orthopedic surgeon in New York City told me, "Tommy, unless you are shitting yourself because of pain, do not ever, *ever* consider back surgery." Given that this was advice from someone who was in the business of surgery and saw every variation of this issue every day, I took his words to heart.

TENSION PATTERNS

My continued search for healing led me to the office of a network chiropractor named Lou Fabale.* I came into Dr. Lou's office with my MRI in hand and gave it over to him for his review. He told me that he wouldn't need to look at it. I pushed it across his desk again, explaining that I'd just paid a lot of money to see what was going on inside and surely he would want to look at it. He assured me once again that he would not need the MRI. I insisted that he look. He told me to sit down and delivered the following message. "You are holding on to your MRI just like you are holding on to your dis-ease."

I started to tear up because I knew he was right. I couldn't let go of what I was carrying. My approach to the world was off center, to say the least. There was something wrong with the way I processed the world around me. It caused me stress but I did not know what to do about it.

"What do I do?" I asked Lou. He told me to come in to his office three days a week and not to miss a session for three months. Consistency was not one of my strong points, but I committed to him that I would do that. Among the jewels of understanding that he gave me was this: "Think of your dis-ease as a neurological disorder rather than merely having to do with the structure of your spine." This was a huge key to my understanding and answered many of the questions I could not otherwise explain.

Dr. Lou told me that many, many people had the same MRI as I did but many of them never felt pain. That made no sense to me. If you had the same spine, why would some people feel pain and others walk around pain-free? That's a powerful question. It turns out our nervous system has the answer.

Think about what it takes to make a fist. Your brain sends an electrical impulse through the nerves in the spine and then out into the nerves in your arm, hand, and fingers and then communicates with your muscles, getting them to contract so you can

---

* Network Chiropractic is a more gentle and holistic form of chiropractic work developed by Dr. Donald Epstein in the mid-1980s.

make a fist. Make a fist now and hold it for about five seconds. Now release it. Next, imagine that stress of any kind will cause you to make a fist. It makes no difference whether you feel physical stress because you are running from danger or emotional stress because you have too many e-mails to get through at the end of a long workweek. Every time the stress response happens in the body, you make a fist involuntarily.

Once again, make a fist now. This time, hold it and imagine that no matter what you do, you can't release it. The thousands, perhaps millions, of moments when you felt stress have culminated in a continuous gripping. Somehow, your nerves are damaged and are not communicating well. Even though you want to release your fist, you cannot—no amount of exerted will can get the job done. *A tension pattern has formed.* You have a neurological or nervous-system disorder. Finally, imagine that instead of keeping an eternal fist, your body's tension pattern is focused in your lower back. You have constant tension there. You may not even be aware of it for a while. You do notice a bit of tightness or soreness now and then, but it's nothing severe. Over time, if you do not change, it gets worse and worse. For some, there may be extraordinarily stressful events that aggravate the tension pattern and elevate it to the next level.

Now let's revisit my 72 hours at the casino during my wonderful bachelor party. I sat on my ass for long periods of time, gambling with money I had borrowed from the casino, desperately trying to fix my broken financial life. It felt as if my life was on the line. The chemistry of shame, along with caffeine and sugar, was coursing through my veins the entire time. I was dehydrated, malnourished, and completely disconnected from my breath and heart.

This is an extreme example of the way I had been in life in general. My interaction with the world was filled with stress. Not to that degree, obviously, but it was there. Of course, I was having lots of fun along the way as well, which is why I was able to blow off the stressful moments as being normal. *But* stress is an intoxicant. It is poison to the body. It breaks down the nervous system. It will catch up with you eventually if you decide to ignore the early warning signs. *Stress is one of the factors that lead to addiction and, of course, to relapse.*

Once upon a time, we only experienced stress through perceived or real physical threats. In our modern age, we still encounter physical stressors, but our emotional stressors are more frequent, almost constant for some people, and our bodies cannot tell the difference between the two. When I made the decision to go to Las Vegas and engage in "acceptable" addiction, I was putting myself in a world where emotional stress was nearly constant for me.

With these new understandings, I began to see that through my own actions, I had put myself in this position. The pain in my body was the direct result of my addictive behavior. I was not a victim of some invisible thing. I had been living in the Frequency of Addiction. I had put away drugs and alcohol, but I did not know how to heal beyond that. My life got better for a while through the work of the 12 Steps, but somewhere along the way, my core issues caught up with me, and to avoid them I chose other addictions. I was still in the habit of looking away from the present moment, and the direct result of that was more dis-ease.

I see people in recovery making this same mistake every day. Some of them get away with it for a while and then are forced by circumstances to change. Others end up relapsing and some of them will die from addiction.

Dr. Lou helped me understand the nature of my dis-ease. I had a diagnosis that worked for me. I had a neurological disorder that was brought on by the stress that comes from living in the Frequency of Addiction. Most important, Dr. Lou told me that I could heal myself. I needed to hear that. There was a way to heal from this, but it was going to take some time.

There is a way to heal almost anything in the body, but in order to get on the path to that healing, you are going to have to change the way you approach the world. Why? Because the way you approach the world is why you are in chronic pain. It has to be in your hands! You have to take responsibility for what is going on; otherwise you will remain a victim of the thing that has no name and that no doctor can accurately diagnose or fix.

A LIFE OF SECOND CHANCES: MEETING GURUPREM

One morning not long after I'd met Dr. Lou, a friend approached me and said, "Tommy, if you really want to fix your back, you should go see this man named Guruprem." I cynically thought, *Oh, that's just what I need . . . a guru!* I envisioned the turban and the beard, the glasses and the robes. I politely thanked my friend but was clear that "Guruprem" was not going to be my next move. Later that evening, I went to dinner with Kia. At the table next to ours was a woman named Holly. We struck up a conversation with her and out of the blue she said, "So, I just came to LA to see this man named Guruprem."

The next day I called Guruprem and said, "Apparently, I'm supposed to come see you." He said, "Well, we'd better get you in here, then."

I arrived at his office in Beverly Hills the next day. When he opened the door, indeed it was exactly what I had imagined— there stood a seemingly pleasant man dressed in all white, including the turban, with a salt-and-pepper beard and glasses. I thought, *My God, it's him. It's actually him.* When he closed the door and I sat down opposite him, I immediately started to feel better. I was not cured—it was nothing so quick or miraculous. I just suddenly felt like everything was going to be okay. And maybe that is all I needed to realize I had found my teacher. The rest, as they say, is history.

The first question Guruprem asked me was, "Tommy, what is your favorite toy?" Guruprem has a great sense of humor, but with this question he was quite serious. I threw out a few guesses.

"Uhh . . . my mountain bike? How about my tennis racket?"

Guruprem just smiled and said, "How about something you spend all your time with?"

"My computer?"

Guruprem chuckled. "Tommy," he said, "when you are in a state of alignment and health, *your body* becomes your favorite toy. You get to be in it all the time. And when you learn the key aspects of navel intelligence and how to lead with the heart rather than with the head, being in your body will be a truly joyous experience."

Navel intelligence? Leading with the heart? Even though I could not fully grasp what he was talking about, his words and manner were compelling.

My back was killing me that day. I certainly did not feel like my body was my favorite toy, but I wanted to find out what that felt like. I remembered my first yoga class in San Francisco so many years before and how moved I felt upon seeing the elegant postures the teacher demonstrated. I had always been looking for freedom in my body, mind, and spirit. I had glimpsed it when I had first used drugs and then again in the earlier years of my 12-Step work, but my addictions had only been partially dealt with. And now I was paying a price for all that. I feared that I had blown it, that because of something I had missed in my development I would never get to experience the freedom I had been seeking my whole life.

From that day forward, every Wednesday at noon for five years, I arrived at his office and we sat opposite each other talking about life while I practiced breathing, Kundalini Yoga, and some meditation. Often at the beginning, I was in too much pain to move much, so he set up his massage table and spent the time talking with me as he massaged my aching back.

If it were not for the Universe giving me a second chance to meet Guruprem, I would have missed out on one of the most precious relationships I've known in this life. I also might not have been taught how to fully heal from the Frequency of Addiction and my chronic back pain. I see this as yet another example of the presence of a loving Higher Power in my life. Despite my own arrogance and closed-mindedness, I was still given this opportunity, and I am grateful. Though I did not yet realize it, Recovery 2.0 was being born during my work with Guruprem. Many of the things he taught me—and many of the subjects we discussed in our work together—have helped frame my understanding of what it takes for a person to move beyond addiction and become wholehearted.

SITTING, STANDING, AND WALKING IN "PREHAB"

Guruprem used to joke that if I had learned the lessons of Prehab, I might have avoided rehab. I don't think he meant this literally (in case you are now thinking, *Hey, all I have to do is learn the following lessons and I'll be cured of addiction*), but these are wonderful lessons to apply to your recovery. In my case, I learned the lessons of Prehab 14 years after rehab. Well, better late than never. In Prehab, we learn how to sit, how to stand, and how to walk.

Can you sit cross-legged on the floor or the ground with comfort and ease? For most people, the answer is no. In Prehab, we learn how to sit consciously. Our seat bones press into the earth, our navel supports our heart, and our spine is upright. We breathe consciously, directing the flow of breath by using our diaphragm. We literally connect with the earth beneath us and develop patience and the capacity to pass time productively. The physical practice of yoga was designed to help a person do exactly this: sit in meditation for long periods of time in relative comfort and ease. People who struggle with addictions (well, most people, actually) do not have this critical, basic skill.

You can tell nearly everything about people by the way they "carry" themselves around. Are you able to stand with your pelvis and spine properly aligned, your feet and legs actively pressing down into the earth, your heart uplifted and your chest open so your breath can flow freely and fully? In yoga, this is called *tadasana* or mountain pose. In Prehab, we practice this in order to develop the right relationship to gravity and the earth, to be in divine alignment. Guruprem likes to say that he has never met a gravitational atheist: "Everyone believes in gravity but nobody knows what it actually is." It's an example of a power that we must learn to work with. We do this work here in Prehab.

The deeper intention of the lesson is to learn what we "stand for" in the world. What are the principles we stand upon? What is the code we stand for? These are the parts of ourselves that we must look into as we move along our path.

Once we know how to sit and stand, we can progress to the advanced practice of walking. How is your relationship with gravity as you move through time and space? Is there freedom in your body and breathing? Are you leaving a "pleasant fragrance" in your wake, meaning are you leaving a nice footprint behind you, or does your manner of moving through life leave discord? In Prehab, we learn to walk with grace and in conscious connection with the spiritual aspects of our lives. And what are we walking toward? What is our destiny path and where does it lead? Once you know this in the very cells of your body, you have realized who and what you are. Addiction will then have a challenge getting a foothold in you.

This is a lifelong process. These are advanced lessons, but you can begin practicing right away. "To learn how to sit, stand, and walk," Guruprem told me, "we will first have to learn how to breathe." Later on, in Part IV, you will learn more about the breath as it is used in yoga and meditation practices.

THE POWER OF WORDS

As I continued to heal each week, Guruprem laid out teaching after teaching that resonated deeply with me. Slowly, without my realizing it, we got down to the spiritual nitty-gritty. In the presence of Guruprem's love and contentment, I was inspired to consider for real the meaning of my life and its purpose. He taught me the mantra *Sat Nam,* which means "Truth is my identity." When we say Sat Nam, we are connecting with the Truth of who we are in the deepest sense. This is the part of us that is infinite and Divine. The idea that I had Divinity within me was one of the most powerful teachings Guruprem passed on to me. You have it, too. We just have to recognize it and we transform immediately in the light of that Truth.

He also taught me the mantra *Ek Ong Kar Sat Nam, Siri Wahe Guru,* which roughly translates as "There is only one Creator inseparable from all creation. Truth is its identity. This great knowledge brings indescribable bliss." I began to see everything as energy, a conscious presence through all time and space that was somehow aware of all of its parts—even me. My Higher Power was within me as much as outside of me. It was everywhere. This was a revelation for many reasons. I started to realize that I actually had the godlike power to create, just as all human beings do. My beliefs, thoughts, and actions would cause reality to unfold for me in a certain way. I was not cut off from my experience of life; I was influencing it and responsible for it. I saw myself as a participant in the outcome of all reality in a way I'd never realized before.

I began to pay close attention to my words, becoming more and more aware of their power to actually create. I could hurt someone with my words. I could help someone with my words. The intention behind my words, the tone that I used and timing, would be important considerations.

The simple act of chanting these mantras in my meditations or in sessions with Guruprem, along with my yoga practice, changed the way I saw myself in the world. As someone who had spent 12 years calling himself an addict, I could no longer identify in this way. I saw that stating "I'm an addict" regularly was like saying to the subconscious mind that I believed I would remain so. It was a declaration of identity that would obviously be incorrect from my new perspective. I now prefer to say, "I'm a person in long-term recovery" or "I experience addiction" or "I am in recovery from addiction."*

I had come to Guruprem because of back pain, but in actuality he would introduce me to my True Self and teach me how to become a wholehearted person. *The path from addiction to recovery, I would learn, is the path from being brokenhearted to being wholehearted.* Most importantly, my thinking started to change again. That feeling of being consumed by my thoughts and swimming upstream lifted. Though my back pain was still there, my relationship to it had shifted. I was tuning myself out of and beyond the Frequency of Addiction. I was now in the flow of something I had been seeking my entire life.

---

* Most people in 12-step programs (read: nearly everyone except me) refer to themselves as addicts or alcoholics. If this is comfortable or necessary for you, please continue. I'm simply offering another perspective about the power of words.

THE DIGESTIVE-TRACT CLEANSE

Another pivotal lesson Guruprem taught me had to do with the art of relaxation. "In order to relax, Tommy, you simply have to let go of the unnecessary," he would say. This is profound advice for people who struggle with addiction. When we are using, almost everything we do and pursue is unnecessary. No wonder it is practically impossible for us to ever fully relax. What could I let go of in order to move toward a state of relaxation, a state of greater ease? My diet history held part of the answer.

I had been seeing Dr. Lou and Guruprem for two months when my wife and I embarked on a 30-day digestive-tract cleanse. It was my first such experience. I was drawn to try it because of the testimony of several friends who had seen rather unusual, profound benefits through the process. This particular program, Ejuva, incorporated a lot of plant-based medicinal herbs from the ancient Ayurvedic tradition in India. Ayurveda simply means "the science of living" and its core philosophy is balance. Ayurveda addresses the question: how do we bring ourselves into harmony with our planet and ourselves?

The cleanse required commitment and discipline. For one thing, it asked that we adhere to a 100 percent raw food diet, 100 percent vegan, 100 percent organic, with a regular schedule of herbs and shakes that we had to drink each day. The first week we could have three meals a day with all the freshly squeezed, low-glycemic (low in sugar) juices we could muster along with our regimen of shakes and herbs. The second week we could eat two meals a day plus juices, herbs, and shakes. The third week we could eat one meal a day plus juices, herbs, and shakes, and the final week it was just juices, herbs, and shakes, no solid food. The experience was a game changer. My digestive tract cleared out from top to bottom.

As is described in the literature that came with the cleanse, mucoid plaque that had formed inside my intestines as a result of poor diet and toxic environmental conditions started to come out of me, particularly during the final week. Suffice it to say that I let go of a lot, physically and energetically. Sorry to get graphic here, but "things" were coming out of me in the toilet that were definitely not feces but must have been in me for a very long time. I thought back to my toxic diet as a child and all my drug abuse. I felt that much of that was still with me, caught in a layer of plaque my body had created to protect itself from the harm I was doing as well as from environmental inputs, which none of us can avoid. When that stuff came out of me, I felt an enormous weight lift. It was like clearing out a closet full of old stale clothes you'd kept for your entire lifetime. They just take up space and hold you in the energy of your past. And that absolutely falls under the heading of "the unnecessary."

When I finished that cleanse, my back pain left me. It was just gone. That weird nervy pain has never returned. In the wake of my healing, my diet remained very healthy. I continued to practice yoga (Vinyasa and especially Kundalini) and meditation with newfound enthusiasm and intention. I was seeing continued benefits to the practice. I let go of smoking. After I had struggled for so long to quit, it was suddenly the simplest thing to just let go. My thinking also changed drastically. I'd always been positive at the surface with stress just beneath. Now I was a much more positive person at the deeper levels. This will sound weird, but I felt as if the chemistry of my whole body had changed. And a general sense of relief had come along with the new me. I can explain it like this . . .

Have you ever been in a place where there was some kind of background "white noise," such as from an air conditioner or fan that was suddenly turned off? You might have spent days or months or years living in that noise, but you barely even noticed it. Now that it is gone, however, the relief you experience is just huge. It feels as if you have taken your first deep breath in a very long time. A terrible annoyance has been removed. You remark, "My God, I'm glad that stopped! How could I possibly have endured living with that horrible noise for all that time?"

EVOLVING IN RECOVERY

Evolution is a natural part of life. We are changing constantly. Our bodies change; our ideas and beliefs change. We learn and grow. That is why we have come here. The sacred and unique life path each of us chooses will have many differences, but all of us are built to evolve through the circumstances of our lives. If we do not evolve, it's painful. Energy is meant to flow, not stagnate. Stuck energy becomes dis-ease. This has been playing out for a long time. It's all around us.

Addiction is an example of abject stagnation. Caught in its grasp, we construct a false story and make it our world. We think for sure we are on the right track, but we hang on too tight and for too long. The promise of comfort turns into the certainty of pain. Some of us have lost our minds along the way. Many of us have died. We will never know why. It is a mystery.

In whatever way it happened for you, or perhaps it's happening now, to have your story smashed upon the rocks is a real and true death. Moving from active addiction into recovery, we have all been through this. We have held on to illusion. We have been insane. We have stood in front of the world and told one lie after another. Perhaps this is what bonds us to each other.

Evolution is the swapping of one story for another. Out of the ashes, humbled, and in early recovery, we sought to make sense of a new story that we were freely offered. It took me a while to adjust to the new story, which sounded like this: "You have a disease of the mind, body, and spirit. You are powerless over your addiction. There is a source of power known as the God of your understanding. Create a relationship with this power source and you will not only get better, but you will also be free. Stay open-minded, follow these steps, and just show up. You will get to live a life second to none."

In my case and for millions of others, it worked. We got better. Healed. Life turned around. Relationships were repaired. Impossible things seemed to manifest for us. We had a new story, which carried us forward out of our addiction and into recovery. We built a relationship with the Higher Power of our understanding and sourced the power we needed.

For years, I did the work and lived this life. After a while, though, I realized that I had once again stopped evolving. I had a new false story. *It no longer made sense for me to proclaim, "My name is Tommy and I'm an addict." I was not sick any longer. I had lots of inner work to do, but that was more a part of being human than because I had struggled so badly with addiction. Much of what I had come to believe in my first decade of recovery no longer held true for me. At the beginning, the crystal clarity of my identification as an addict served me well. I needed to say that for many years, but there came a time where it stopped working. It had become a transgression to my heart to say those words. I had no idea what to do. There was no second-tier plan for evolution that I knew of in 12-Step society. The 12 Steps are the 12 Steps. There was no advanced manual.*

It took me 12 years and a lot of suffering to realize that recovery happens in stages and that I had become stagnant after stage one. Recovery 2.0 is a program of recovery that honors and includes the 12 Steps while also building upon their foundation. Here's the message: You do not have to stay mired in the Frequency of Addiction for 12 years like I did. You can find lasting recovery and thrive by working the 12 Steps and adopting the elements of Recovery 2.0 into your life now.

PART IV

RECOVERY 2.0: THE PATH TO WHOLENESS

CHAPTER 13

THE INCREDIBLE UPGRADE

If you ask most people in recovery why they stay sober, they will tell you they do so because they have to. Others will say they stay sober because they will die if they don't. Still others will tell you they aren't scared of dying as much as living through the pain of addiction. In almost every case, recovering addicts will cite the terrible things that will happen if they "use" again—if they go back. It is very rare to find a person in recovery who can look into their heart and tell you, "I stay sober because I want to. I have found true recovery, and I love my life as a sober person. I prefer this state of being to using drugs, alcohol, and acting out in other addictive ways." That person is rare indeed. So many of us have been clear about what we stand against but less clear about what we stand for.

If you are in recovery, you are certainly right to have concerns about what will happen if you return to a life of addiction. You have lived through an absolute horror show and know that within you lurks a kind of demon that has had the better of you, perhaps for as long as you remember. In my opinion, though, if recovery works, you will get an opportunity to build a life so rich that you wouldn't choose to go back even if you could somehow get away with it. You may still be caught up in the idea that you need something outside yourself to feel better: drugs, alcohol, a person, and so on. To imagine a fulfilling life without some kind of substance or behavior may be frightening to you. Perhaps you cannot imagine what would happen without your distractions and addictions. How would you pass the time?

What would you do if you could do what you truly desired? You'd do precisely that: You would have a mission, a sense of purpose. You'd show up as an activated, fully present person. You'd engage in the world in the way only you were meant to do. You would live, as you ought to live, according to your heart and soul. Ask yourself this question: Are you making choices out of fear or out of love? There may in fact be a period when you stay sober out of fear, but eventually, hopefully you will stay sober out of love for the life that you get to live.

Some people have asked me over the years, "Aren't you recovered now? Can't you drink or smoke a joint without getting into trouble with it?" My answer to them is simple: I have no desire to. I love my life as a sober person. I walk this drugless path, and I get to feel everything that happens in life. I get to truly experience what it is to be human—to fail, to be sad, to feel jealousy or envy, to have joy and connection, to love and be loved, to succeed, and to be useful to others. Whether I could manage it if I used again is beside the point. To me, the idea of using drugs or alcohol simply makes no sense. Why would I want to intoxicate myself with something that I consider bad for my body, confusing to my mind, and dimming to my spirit? *Why would I want to get high in a way that weakens my system, when I have, at my disposal, ways to get truly high that strengthen me at every level? I certainly have not given up getting high. I've had a massive overhaul in my methods of doing so.* I've experienced an incredible *upgrade* from the terribly destructive, inefficient, and wasteful methods I previously employed to get high. I have redefined, for myself, what it is to get "high" and have set my sights on doing so often. In getting sober, you think, *I am giving up my chosen method of navigating life. My medicine! They're taking away my medicine!* Yet the reality is that you're being given the greatest gift ever. Your medicine and your life are both being upgraded.

Part of the joy of being alive includes our ability to change our consciousness, to explore new ways of seeing things and rise above what can sometimes feel like a mundane day-to-day struggle. When we talk about "getting high," we're usually referring to using some substance to achieve a shift in consciousness. We want to "clean out the pipes," connect more deeply with our friends, partake in rituals, and gain new perspectives. Many of us have lost a sense of ease—or perhaps we never had one. Getting high relaxes us. It helps us let go of tension, inhibition, and worry. It can help us forget the burden of shame and guilt we may carry. If we get right down to it, we get high because we like the feeling. If we didn't like it, we wouldn't do it. Unfortunately, most of the methods we choose are destructive.

I am a big proponent of getting high in recovery, but not in destructive ways. If I were unable to change my consciousness, shift my emotional state, and achieve a sense of elation on a regular basis, I'm not certain my recovery would be as strong or my life as joyful as it is. It should come as very good news to people who are new to recovery that in getting sober, you are not going to give up the joy that comes from changing your consciousness. It is very important for you to realize that you can "get high" in recovery using much better methods than you employed while you were stuck in addictive patterns. It may take a while for your body and brain to heal and be ready for what I'm talking about, but you can get there, and once you do, things will get really, really good. Let's take a second here to lay down a definition and some suggested guidelines about getting high in recovery.

From the Recovery 2.0 perspective, to "get high" means *to engage in an activity that brings about a shift in consciousness that benefits a person in both the short term **and** the long term.*

The short-term gain, long-term loss approach to life is the hallmark of people who struggle with addiction. In fact, most people live life in this way, which is why there is so much dis-ease among us. If your form of getting high brings you short-term gain and long-term loss, it does not fit the Recovery 2.0 definition of getting high.

Let's start with alcohol as an example. Many people enjoy the feeling of ease that it brings. It makes them feel more relaxed and less insecure. It takes the edge off. However, there is no denying that alcohol is toxic to the human body in many ways and has negative effects that weaken your system. Alcohol drastically affects blood sugar levels and dehydrates you. It is a depressant, so contrary to what most people think, it is the worst thing to do if you are feeling depressed in your life. Usually, you feel the negative effects of alcohol in the form of a hangover the next day. There are other, more severe effects to drinking alcohol in excess, such as being violent, blacking out, driving while drunk, and generally behaving like an asshole. As I previously noted, alcohol has a lot to do with criminal behavior, car accidents, and premature death due to liver dis-eases such as cirrhosis. Surely, drinking alcohol cannot bring about a true "high," at least not according to my definition.

How about marijuana, that beloved and terribly misunderstood plant that has been a crowd pleaser for quite some time? I smoked pot for ten years. As you've heard, I was a marijuana scholar for a while. I grew it, sold it, bought it, smoked it, and lived a lifestyle that revolved around it. Marijuana can bring about some positive short-term effects, such as temporarily shifting challenging emotions like anger, creating levity, changing one's perspective, and calming the hyperactive mind. The negative effects of smoking pot include dehydration, dry mouth, demineralization of the body, weakening of the immune system, clogging of the lungs, blockage of emotional growth, short- and long-term memory loss, sluggishness, and demotivation. Over time, marijuana weakens the human body and dims the human spirit. The negative effects greatly outweigh the positive ones. Therefore, marijuana also cannot fit my definition of getting high.*

---

* Despite its negative effects, I believe there are medicinal purposes for marijuana use. I have no personal experience with treating a

My point is that no matter what your "drug" of choice, If you get something in the short term but give up more in the long term, eventually you will have to stop or you will continually weaken yourself, paying bigger and bigger prices. It is an unsustainable approach to life. This is true for any addictive behavior.

THE INFINITE PHARMACY WITHIN

So how do we get high, according to my definition? What is this upgrade that brings elation, euphoria, comfort, and ease in the short term while also strengthening our system in the long term? What substance do we use? Where can we find it? How much does it cost?

Once you understand this and experience what I am talking about, you will truly have the keys to the kingdom. For you will realize that you have the power to change your own consciousness. You do not need a drug or a person or sex or shopping or drama or anything. It is so simple that we have overlooked it. The secret is to use our own body as a vehicle for the experience and transformation we are looking for. Jesus said, "Behold, the kingdom of Heaven is within you." And so is the Infinite Pharmacy.

Inside your body is a pharmacy that is open 24 hours a day. The drugs you are *really* looking for are all right there within you. They are distributed throughout your body in the way nature intended, via the endocrine, or glandular, system. The head pharmacist is represented by the pituitary gland, the master of the endocrine system, which sorts out messages between the brain and body. Your endocrine and nervous systems work closely together to regulate and harmonize your experience. When all is flowing according to plan, your nervous system provides all its inputs to the endocrine system, which releases the right drugs in the

---

physical ailment with marijuana so cannot speak directly to it. But for those people who feel it helps them cope with cancer, chemotherapy, or other serious health issues, I hope they always have access to it. In their case, we are not so much talking about getting high as getting through.

193

right amounts to the right places at the right time. This is called feeling good. It is a natural process that I wish for you, the person in recovery, to experience once again. In your addictions you have tinkered with your nervous and endocrine systems to such an extent that it may take a while for you to experience what it's like to have a natural high and a smoothly running inner world once again.

There are so many activities that encourage the Infinite Pharmacy to do its thing well that have both short- and long-term benefit. This is what we are working toward in Recovery 2.0. Here are but a few suggestions:

- Take a walk in nature.
- Play sports.
- Go to the gym.
- Eat healthy food.
- Drink an organic green juice.
- Hug a friend or lover for a minute or more.
- Listen to and play music.
- Write in your journal.
- Hit a 12-Step meeting.
- Volunteer your time to feed the homeless.
- Read or watch spiritual, uplifting media.
- See a teacher, mentor, or therapist.
- Help someone who needs it.
- Dance, sing, chant, and pray.

Remember Guruprem's teaching that my body should be my favorite toy? Now I understand what he meant. Everything is experienced through the body—that is the nature of being in one. We need to clear out the blockages and become an open channel for the free flow of energy. *Part of the reason people relapse is that they do not go into the body through mind-body practices to clear out what is stuck there.* When it comes to detoxing and rejuvenating the nervous and endocrine systems, yoga and meditation are indispensable. They are the upgraded methods of changing my consciousness that I had always been looking for. Ultimately, connection, stillness, and contentment are waiting for you, too, through the practice of yoga. Through steady practice and letting go of what no longer serves, you will find a throne for yourself known as the "comfortable seat." From that throne you can actually realize your Self and be free of unnecessary pain and suffering. You'll still be human, but you will be awake enough to realize your own divinity and experience everyone else's.

In the chapters that follow, we will explore the elements of Recovery 2.0, which together form the basis of a holistic and powerful approach to recovery from addiction. These are the things that have elevated my recovery and life to the next level. These are the things that set me up for greater freedom than I had known before. These are the things that helped me attune myself out of the Frequency of Addiction and into the Frequency of Recovery. I wish that for you, too, now and always.

CHAPTER 14

RECOVERING YOUR IDENTITY AND LIVING YOUR TRUTH

Earlier in this book I presented the concept of the Addiction Story, that illusory narrative that convinces you of the need for an addictive substance or behavior in order to navigate life successfully. You must release your Addiction Story if you are to recover, because it is not based in Truth. In active addiction, you have lost your true identity. Without this, you cannot move forward, because it is impossible to continue to evolve if you are living in a lie. The Universe is not so much interested in your personal comfort, but it is very interested in your personal growth. Thus, if you veer from the path, the Universe has its ways of nudging you, gently or otherwise, back toward it.

That is what happened for me when my back went out and I was led to the next level of teachings. I recall my experiences chanting "Sat Nam" with Guruprem. As crazy as it may seem, that mantra, which means "Truth is my identity," helped me recover my true identity. I sat in practice after practice, meditation after meditation, workshop after workshop, and tuned in to my Self. If any of you are skeptical, I certainly understand. I did not ever intend to chant anything in my life. And yet, there I was, eyes closed and rolled up to my brow point, chanting words from an ancient language I did not understand, but it was working. I began to develop the capacity to sense *me*. Underneath my incessant thoughts there was space and silence. I felt great bliss in the quiet and stillness of those Kundalini meditations as I penetrated the deeper layers of my being. To feel such depth and meaning increased my awareness in general. I knew my identity was not that of a drug addict, but my newfound understanding went way beyond that. The plain fact was that this work was showing me what I was to become on this earth and where I would go when I was finished.

In order to allow for your own evolution, you are going to have to let go of drugs, alcohol, and other addictive behaviors. Furthermore, you are going to have to recover your unique and true identity. That's what the process of Recovery 2.0 is all about. You get to remember and recover your True Self. Without this, you will always be vulnerable to relapse. Please take this at face value: *You absolutely must do the work to live authentically and truthfully. In recovery from addiction you are recovering your identity so you can live according to your own unique Truth. This is called living your destiny path.*

Here are some beginning suggestions and realizations that have helped me reach this amazing place.

See the 12 Steps as the First Stage of Recovery.

Be aware that the 12 Steps are just the beginning of a multi-tiered, multi-stage approach to recovering your identity. They are the foundation, and while they may always be a part of your program of recovery, you will likely come up against situations that the 12 Steps alone cannot address. This is a blessing! Life and all its challenges are coming to heal you. They will deal up exactly what you need. You may uncover past traumas, come up against codependency, face mental and/or physical health issues, and need outside help. As long as you are willing to look at what comes up and ask for help when you need support, you will be able to find the next teacher or teaching to guide you along the next part of your path. Recovery happens in stages.

Don't Let the 12 Steps Become Your Life. Get a Life Because of the 12 Steps.

Along the same lines, you must be careful not to let your program define you as an individual. You are more than a person in recovery. You are more than just an addict or alcoholic. These things inform who you are, but they do not define who you are. As you go through various stages of recovery, what you need in order to thrive will naturally change. Remember: your relationships with mind, body, family, friends, the food you eat, your work, money, and the pursuit of your mission in the world make life worth living. These are the aspects of life you get to develop because of your recovery work. Use the 12 Steps as a launching pad toward the life of your dreams and realize that though the steps may always be a part of your life, they cannot be your identity.

Start to Practice Yoga and Meditation.

From the Recovery 2.0 perspective, yoga and meditation are required elements of recovery. You will simply be more comfortable in your mind and body if you practice. Addiction is dis-ease. Yoga brings ease. Addiction is disconnection. Yoga is union. Addiction is a thinking problem. Yoga calms the mind. There is no downside to it. This is purely a short- and long-term gain proposition. In particular, I have found a combination of Vinyasa and Kundalini Yoga to be very effective. I have found no greater one-two punch than the 12 Steps and yoga. Use them together. See them as complements to each other and practice them every day. The most amazing blessings will come your way.

Quit Smoking Cigarettes, and Mind the Caffeine.

Smoking cigarettes and consuming caffeine are historically prominent behaviors for people in recovery. Recovery 2.0 takes a strong stance against smoking because it is self-harming and keeps you in the Frequency of Addiction. As for caffeine, since it is addictive, you have to be careful not to get into overconsumption of it. It will mess with your sleep patterns and your ability to relax deeply. Having a cup of tea or a latte is a great pleasure in this life for many people. There's no hard line here. You will have to decide what works for you. That said, I definitely recommend having stretches in your life when you are living caffeine free so your nervous system can fully reset.

Understand That Food Is Not an Outside Issue.

I once spoke at a prominent and quite large 12-Step meeting. As usual, I spoke candidly about the importance of diet in my recovery. After the meeting several people expressed some anger that I had overstepped boundaries by speaking about outside issues. "Hey, man, we don't talk about those kinds of things here." Other people came up to me and said, "I have to thank you for addressing issues that really need to be discussed here."

If you think food is an outside issue in any recovery forum, I urge you to reconsider your position. Addicts of every kind will find greater happiness and therefore increase their chances of sustainable recovery by looking closely at their relationship to food. Make the connection between the food you eat and your recovery. Educate yourself about food and water. Learn how to prepare your food and properly nourish yourself. With your food choices, you can move toward vitality or dis-ease. You really are what you eat. This is not an outside issue.

Bring the Ethical Principles of Yoga into Your Recovery.

The main ethical principles of yoga, which we'll cover in depth in the next chapter, are known as the *yamas* and *niyamas*. These highly inspirational ideals guide us in our relationship with our outer and inner world. They are motivating in and of themselves and highly complementary and resonant to any path of recovery.

Be Devoted to a Daily Spiritual Practice.

Everyone is devoted to something. What do you spend the most time thinking about? What do you love and cherish? Drug addicts love and cherish their drugs. They are capable of intense devotion. Drug addicts will go to any length to get their drugs. *Any length!* And there is no such thing as inconvenience when it comes to getting more drugs. You'll never hear a drug addict say, "I could not go across town to get my fix. It was simply too inconvenient."

It's funny, though, that in working with many people in early recovery, if I suggest that we are going to practice 30 minutes of meditation in the early morning for a while, a riot ensues. In recovery, the idea is to show that same level of devotion to something that is uplifting and nourishing to the spirit as you used to show in going after your drugs of choice. By developing a spiritual practice that you do every day, something absolutely magical happens in a short amount of time. You fall in love with it, life gets easier, and you no longer want to miss this great experience. I'll talk more about this later in the book.

Remember That Consciousness Is Contagious.

Consciousness is not something you just get. It has to be caught. To varying degrees, we are all susceptible to the positive and negative influence of others. It is easy to catch a higher or lower frequency in our world. We go to 12-Step meetings looking for a higher frequency. We can also catch it from individuals who carry it. I call these people teachers. *One of the truest facts of my life is that I would be nowhere without my teachers.* If you want to develop as a person, it is helpful to be around other people who carry the consciousness you want to move toward. When you identify these people, hang around them and catch the goodness they put out so you can be uplifted and, in turn, pass it on.

Remember, too, that we can just as easily be dragged down to lower frequencies by hanging around people who carry those. The old adage stands true: you can tell a lot about people by the company they keep.

Participate Regularly in Immersive Experiences.

My recovery has been marked by periods of rapid growth because of my regular attendance at intensive workshops, retreats, trainings, conferences, and festivals related to recovery, spirituality, and personal growth.

Workshops can last a few hours or a weekend or a whole week. You will get to go deeply into a topic and have the support of a community along the way. Retreats often take place in a beautiful setting that permits you to step out of your normal lifestyle and rhythm. I used to refer to smoking pot as taking time out of time. Now, I refer to these immersions as the upgraded version of taking *time out of time*. It's important to break out of your routines on a regular basis to assess how you have been doing and make adjustments accordingly.

Continuing studies are precisely that—continuing. I will be studying yoga, meditation, and my life for the rest of my life. Every year, I carve out time for more study. I am a teacher, yes, but I am a student first and that never ends. I love to go as deep as possible. Thankfully, yoga is a very deep well.

Every year, make a point of participating in these immersive experiences. Especially if you are feeling stuck, consider taking some time to learn, relax, and rejuvenate. From yoga festivals to teacher trainings to recovery workshops, these experiences have strengthened my recovery and brought so much joy to my life. I have included suggestions for workshops and retreats in the appendices at the back of this book.

Follow Your Bliss.

Joseph Campbell gave us the now famous teaching "Follow your bliss." He derived this often-misunderstood concept from the ancient yogic texts The Upanishads, which spoke of the journey toward ultimate freedom and connection with God. The idea is that by pursuing what most inspires us, we will end up basically where we are supposed to and experience a sense of bliss. It is about coming to your "Sat Nam," to your true identity. The happiest people I know have a sense of how to use their gifts in the world. The least happy people are those who do not know why they are here and who feel a sense of purposelessness. In recovery, seek out your own unique place in this world. How do you begin? It will always have to do with what inspires you, what you are good at, and what brings you true happiness and fulfillment.

Leave Some Space for the Possibility of a Full Recovery from Addiction.

I believe it is possible to heal fully from addiction in the same way I feel it is possible to reach enlightenment. Not likely, but why not shoot for it? This is a controversial idea because most people do not believe it is possible. Furthermore, many people believe that this very idea is threatening to their recovery. Some people imagine that a full recovery from addiction would mean being able to drink and use drugs "responsibly" again. That's not my idea of a full recovery.

Full recovery means moving out of the Frequency of Addiction, recovering your True identity, and living in service to ideas and beliefs that are greater than you. This does not mean you are beyond the possibility of relapse. You are still subject to the human condition.

Adopting the belief that it is possible to transcend addiction has changed a lot for me. I've already gotten further than I ever imagined I would. Besides, who knows what's possible? Why not open ourselves up to the possibility of transcending addiction altogether? That's the journey I'm taking, and I'd like to encourage you to join me.

CHAPTER 15

THE YAMAS
AND THE
NIYAMAS

When you think about yoga, you probably envision the physical practice of various postures. We will certainly get there in this book, but first I am excited to share the ethical and philosophical underpinnings of yoga so you can develop a broader view of this amazing path.

The parallels between yoga philosophy and 12-Step philosophy are innumerable. Energetically, the two paths carry great resonance and complete each other. The 12 Steps offer people in recovery a foundation that yoga cannot offer. Yoga offers people in recovery critical elements that the 12 Steps cannot offer. Taken together, the two approaches form what I consider the most powerful and joyful approach to overcoming addiction.

I want to offer a brief analysis of yoga's ethical guidelines, which are known as the *yamas* and *niyamas*. These add dimension and depth to the ethical viewpoints contained within the

12 Steps. In active addiction, our ethics are locked away in rooms with neither doors nor keys to open them. In recovery, we gradually gain access to these rooms.

THE FIVE RESTRAINTS OR *YAMAS*

The *yamas* are the five restraints that guide us in our relationship with the external world. They generally provide us with guidelines for what *not* to do.

The Five Yamas

Ahimsa—Nonviolence
Satya—Truthfulness
Asteya—Nonstealing
Brahmacharya—Energy Moderation
Aparigraha—Nonpossessiveness

AHIMSA

Ahimsa means nonviolence or nonharming: inflict no harm upon others or yourself. When they hear this, the first thing most people think of is physical violence. But ahimsa also includes nonviolence in thoughts and words. It is impossible to carry resentment, for example, and live the essence of ahimsa. You have to face your resentments, as you do in the 4th Step, in order to live up to this ideal. This includes any self-directed speech or thought you may carry. Do not complete a negative sentence in your head about yourself. It is not always easy to refrain from doing this, given where some of your notions about yourself come from.

In stressful moments, my father used to say to me, "When you're forty, you won't have a pot to piss in." That was my dad's way of communicating his fear that I wouldn't find financial stability in my life and that I would suffer the way he had under the weight of economic insecurity. The truth was that he cared deeply about me and only wanted me "to figure it all out." Unfortunately, the words he chose and the underlying fear brought about a different kind of effect from the one my dad or I had hoped for. His words ended up being a curse, with energy and a life all their own, which rented space in my mind both subconsciously and consciously until much later in my life. As I approached my 40th birthday, those words became very present for me. I did not end up as my father had feared "without a pot to piss in." Yet I was not free either. I would have to admit that I had made these words true in my mind to some extent and they had to be reworked into something more positive. I came up with this: "You are surrounded by abundance and opportunity, Tommy, and I trust you to find your way, and that your way is your path and it is the right path for you. I love you." I like to believe that this is what my father actually meant.

On a subtler level, violence and harm originate with a disconnection from your heart. This creates a friction within you that is harmful in and of itself. So another aspect of the practice of ahimsa is to establish and maintain a connection with your heart.

Addiction is inherently harmful; we are taking a substance or choosing a behavior that is harmful to us. By extension, our addiction can harm those around us. My 12-Step path helps me to see where I harm others. My adherence to the path of yoga reinforces my commitment to grow along spiritual lines. Clearly, we all have work to do, but I feel it is our willingness to self-reflect and self-correct that keeps us headed in the right direction. Both paths help with this.

SATYA

Satya means truthfulness in words and thought. Everyone has told a lie at some point. As it turns out, addicts tell a whole lot of lies. They are attached to their Addiction Story, which is, in itself, untrue. Addicts need to be dishonest, so they develop the habit of being untruthful. One of the first lessons I learned at Hazelden was the importance of telling the truth, especially to myself. The ideal of rigorous honesty is one of the major tenets of 12-Step programs. Again, while we may not have always been truthful in our lives, we can aspire to the ideal of satya.

Satya also extends to the idea of being free of illusion. However, to be in active addiction is to live in a great state of illusion. Let me provide one such example: One Monday morning in Boulder, Colorado, in 1987, I headed to my bank to withdraw $200, my weekly allowance, which my mom sent to me like clockwork each Friday. I went to the ATM to find that the balance in my account was $0.00. I went into the bank, approached a teller, and with great self-righteousness exclaimed, "Someone has taken my money, and I need you to figure it out." The teller asked for my ID and asked, "What exactly seems to be the problem?"

I explained that there should be $200 in the account and it wasn't there. The teller looked at the account and said the wrong thing to me at that moment: "The money isn't there because you took it out around two o'clock yesterday morning."

"I took it out? What are you talking about?" My voice rose, attracting the attention of the manager of the bank. "Are you not listening to me? I've just told you that someone else has accessed my account and taken this money."

The manager came over and I went through it with him. He asked, "Sir, are you saying that someone else stole money out of your account in the middle of the night over the weekend?"

"I guess this would be the first time in history that someone has taken someone else's money?"

"Are you absolutely certain that you cannot account for this withdrawal?"

"Do you think I'm sitting here lying?" I was now yelling. "Do you think I'm insane? Would I not remember taking my own money out of the bank? Yes, I'm certain someone has stolen this money."

"Okay," the bank manager said, "we're going to have to search through the ATM security camera tapes. Whoever took your money out will show up on the camera. Please take a seat, and we will be back in about fifteen minutes."

Bank business, which I had awkwardly interrupted, returned to normal, and I had a quiet moment to myself sitting on an ugly, uncomfortable bank couch. The chemistry of self-righteous anger coursed through my veins. The injustice of it all!

After a moment, I began to calm down. Suddenly, in a flash, the weekend's activities came back into my memory. With some clarity I recalled a 24-hour session of partying that included a lot of marijuana, cocaine, and alcohol. I couldn't remember going to sleep, only that I had recently woken up and it was Monday morning. I had blacked out at some point but couldn't tell you much more than that. What I can tell you now, however, was that in fact I had paid a visit to this bank at around 2 A.M. on Sunday to take out my $200 allowance, which I spent on a bunch of cocaine.

I had been living in a paranoid, self-righteous, annoyed state caused by my constant pursuit of insatiable desires and fantasy. I was obnoxious, rude, and quite insane. Without hesitation, I calmly skulked my way toward the bank door, exited, and never went back.

The episode in the bank says a lot about living in "thought-illusion." In active addiction we have this little problem of not seeing things clearly.

ASTEYA

Asteya means nonstealing. Let's look at it in energetic terms. We do not want to take (read: suck) energy from our fellows. People's possessions or energies can include property but also their reputation and accomplishments. To inappropriately take energy from another person can never bring happiness. Reaching for the ideal of asteya, we want to stop comparing ourselves to others and stop seeking what they have. We want to avoid gossip, which affects a person's reputation. Where business is concerned, we make a conscious effort not to take advantage of people. In the spiritual sense, we do not own anything. So we adopt a different view of money. We see it as energy to be responsibly circulated rather than to be controlled or hoarded.

I stole money and shoplifted many times in my addiction. After I got caught once, I can remember my mother saying something to the effect of "We just don't steal. Someone else's property is someone else's property. Don't you realize that?" These were sage words, which I could not hear at the time. Recovery is a return to the principle of asteya. The 9th Step amends process opens the door and permits us to grow into people who can live by this wonderful principle.

BRAHMACHARYA

Historically, *brahmacharya* has been interpreted as abstinence from or control of sexual activity. A more modern interpretation would be "energy moderation." The big question brahmacharya asks us is this: how do you choose to use your energy?

Being wise about how and where one uses one's energy, particularly one's sexual energy, is an art form in this life. Observance of brahmacharya means we use our sexual power responsibly. We try to keep it sacred. We are encouraged not to separate the sexual part of our life from the spiritual part of our life. To do so seems to ask for trouble.

You must realize that everybody has difficulty with regard to sex. Appetites and opinions are extremely varied on the topic. We get an opportunity in our 4th Step to do a sexual inventory and create a sexual ideal for ourselves. "In this way we tried to shape a sane and sound ideal for our future sex life. We remembered always that our sex powers were God-given and therefore good, neither to be used lightly or selfishly nor to be despised and loathed." I've always appreciated how balanced the Big Book is on this issue and how aligned it is with the principle of brahmacharya.

Most people grow up with strong ideas about right and wrong, particularly regarding ways to approach and treat the opposite sex.* Yet it is rare indeed to encounter someone who actually has developed a framework and a working strategy to navigate these

---

* To any readers who are part of the LGBTQ community, please forgive the heterosexual orientation of this teaching. I am coming from my own perspective. No offense is intended.

relationships. If we are in a monogamous relationship, how should we behave toward a member of the opposite sex whom we find attractive? What is a responsible way to manage that energy and the powerful feelings that go along with it? What if we're single? Then what do we do? Is it okay to pursue or allow ourselves to be pursued by everyone we come across whom we find attractive?

Here is a teaching that provides a framework for looking at your alignment to the opposite sex. It will not be right for everyone, but if it resonates with you, bring it into your consciousness as you walk through the world. It has helped me create clearer boundaries and has taken my relationships to the next level. Plus it has shown me parts of myself that I didn't realize I possessed.

Whenever you meet anyone, they will always fall into one of four categories: Men will only ever meet mothers, daughters, sisters, and a wife/lover. Women will only ever meet fathers, sons, brothers, and a husband/lover.

This means that, as a man, my job is to know which person I am dealing with and then to treat her with the appropriate energy. If I encounter a "mother," I become "the son" and must treat her with love, care, and respect. If I encounter a "daughter," I tap into my paternal instincts and treat her with love, kindness, and protection. When I encounter a "sister," I treat her with brotherly love—platonic, protective, helpful. And last but not least, when I meet that special someone with whom I want to develop a deeper connection, I can choose to call upon that sacred part of myself that has been honed just for her. She gets to know me in a way that no one in the other three groups has access to. For women, this all holds true as well.

The concept of "brothers" and "sisters" can get a little blurry because sometimes these people come in rather alluring packages. So it takes clarity of purpose, discipline, and awareness to check yourself, stay on track, and call up the proper energy in that moment. Remember: no one is perfect.

For many addicts, and I count myself among this group, regulation of this energy toward members of the opposite sex has, at times, been very problematic. And this often leads to problems with sex itself. If you have ever experienced sexual compulsion or addiction, you know it is no laughing matter. The act of sex becomes like a drug, creating mental and physical imbalance. Much shame goes along with this form of the dis-ease. All of this is made worse by the new addiction epidemic, Internet pornography.

Consuming sexual imagery regularly places you in a fantasy world that bleeds into your mind and your life. You become "imprinted" with these images and carry their energy with you into your interactions with people. These behaviors influence your communication and can create mental obsession. Guruprem said it best: "We put our prosperity toward something which ends up weakening us."

Most of the guys I know in early recovery are watching pornography often and doing so without a thought that this could be weakening them and leading to future pain. The land of fantasy may be okay to visit once in a while, but when it becomes a regular destination, you are likely living in the Frequency of Addiction and on the way to some pain. The healing from this is to come into connection with your heart. You learn practices that help transmute sexual energy into creative energy and gain perspective from masterful teachings on the topic.

APARIGRAHA

Aparigraha means noncoveting or nonpossessiveness. This principle instructs us to acquire only what is necessary and nothing more. Rather than constantly striving to have and do, we cultivate and appreciate simplicity. Simplicity is one of the greatest gifts we can give to ourselves. Revered yoga teacher B. K. S. Iyengar said, *"By the observance of Aparigraha, the yogi makes his life as simple as possible and trains his mind not to feel the loss or the lack of anything. Then everything he really needs will come to him by itself at the proper time."*[1] In active addiction, we do the opposite of this. We have a sense of lack. We do not trust that our core needs are being met. We want more. We grasp after it. No amount can ever be enough to fill the hole we seek to fill through our addictions. We create complexity and commotion.

Aparigraha brings our attention to the energy of grasping. We feel we need something. Perhaps we see someone else who has this something and we become envious or jealous. Aparigraha is connected to the development of trust that we will get our needs met. If we can accept this, we gain freedom. We can let anything go and trust that whatever is needed will come through next.

Working with our exhale helps in practicing aparigraha. We hold the breath out for a moment before taking in the next inhale. This willingness to be empty comes from the trust that we will receive the next inhale. Letting something go always makes room for something else to come through. Aparigraha creates spaciousness in our lives. In releasing old patterns new ones can form. By releasing our Addiction Story, for example, we can re-create ourselves.

THE FIVE OBSERVANCES OR *NIYAMAS*

The *niyamas* are the five observances that guide us in our relationship with our internal world. They are internal attitudes and/or practices that set us up for personal growth.

The Five *Niyamas*

Shaucha—Purity
Santosha—Contentment
Tapas— Inner Heat
Svadyaya—Self-Study
Ishvarapranidhana—Surrender to the Supreme Being

SHAUCHA

Shaucha means purity or cleanliness of body and mind. It also has to do with keeping a sacred quality to the environment around you, such as your home, bedroom, office, and so on. It is essential for health, happiness, and thriving. Obviously this is a big idea when it comes to recovering addicts, for we have intoxicated ourselves to a great degree. Detoxification is central to the Recovery 2.0 perspective. The adage "Cleanliness is next to godliness" has relevance. We have been so disconnected in our addictions; now we want to connect. Our quest is to connect with our heart, which is connected to our Highest Self, which is connected to our Higher Power. We bathe every day. We brush our teeth and floss. Many of us have forsaken these practices through our addictions. Now we bring them back into our daily lives. We work to release our resentments in our 4th and 5th Steps. We get clean through our 9th Step amends, and we stay clean each day through the practice of our 10th Step. In Recovery 2.0, we add yoga, meditation, and breathwork to our regimen so we can detoxify at even deeper levels.

We also improve our relationship with food, eating healthier, nutrient-dense, alkalizing foods and letting go of junk food and overconsumption. We clean up our language, becoming wordsmiths and masters of tone. We are careful not to consume media that stresses us out or creates imbalances.

Think of it from the perspective of "attunement." If we are unclean in body or mind, we are "intoxicated" at some level, lowering our frequency. Some form of blockage is going on. What we are after is the free flow of energy, in which nothing gets stuck. Keeping a clean body and mind, therefore, helps us have greater consciousness and attunes us beyond the Frequency of Addiction. There is a direct correlation between being "clean" and being connected. In 12-Step language people who have put down drugs and alcohol might refer to themselves as "clean and sober." The principle of shaucha asks that we review our own concept of what that means and then take it to the next level.

Remember: we improve over time. These are not all overnight shifts we can hope to make. In our early recovery, we remember that our program, meetings, and Step work come first. Later on in our recovery, we will likely realize that there are things we need to change to continue down the path to contentment and fulfillment. Striving to live by the principle of shaucha has been a wonderful mission for me. Obviously, I am a work in progress, but just to have a high bar to shoot for and work on has been most helpful.

Bringing this principle to mind in small ways in your life each day makes a big difference.

SANTOSHA

Santosha means contentment, but not just regular old contentment. It means having the ability to look at your life in its entirety and be in such a state of acceptance of what you find that you wouldn't change any of it. You realize that all your challenges are there so you can learn and grow. Everything in life is happening for you and not to you. So it would make no sense from the perspective of santosha to want any of it to go away. Now, that's a high bar. Again, you work toward the ideals of the yamas and niyamas. They are guides that help you know what to shoot for.

Here, we realize that by this definition we may never have been truly content before. Contentment is something we have to work on. Like building muscles at the gym, we work the muscles of contentment by consciously bringing acceptance and gratitude into our mind as often as we can. When we are stressed, dissatisfied, angry, and resentful, we are lacking in acceptance of what is. We may not be able to accept a situation in our life, but we work at it.

This past January I went on a hike and got a dreadful case of poison oak. It was so severe that I had no choice but to take steroids to help my body fight it off. Returning home from the doctor's office, I showered and then stood naked in front of the mirror to assess. I saw epic patches of irritation all over. They were terribly itchy and painful. Even with steroids, there would be no quick fix. I was going to have to put up with it for many days.

I had a moment of panic when I realized the gravity of the situation. I was amazingly uncomfortable (and stuck) in my own skin. I couldn't get away. How long would I be here? How would I sleep? How would I get through it? This was dreadful. I brought my mind back to the present moment and, despite all the pain and discomfort, accepted my lot. Yes, this would suck. No, there was nothing to be done about it, but I would heal. My attitude changed. My story of suffering turned into a story of acceptance. The dread was gone. Of course, I would still suffer for a few more days. I still wished things were different, but I had made great strides toward santosha.

Now, this is an extreme example. In our everyday lives, we have the opportunity to practice santosha in each moment. Our bank account may not be what we want it to be. Our relationships might be challenging. We can work the muscles of santosha and eliminate the need to have something more or something different in order to find contentment. We can still work toward our dreams, but santosha suggests we do so while finding contentment at each step of the journey.

TAPAS

Tapas means heat and refers to the inner fire that results from spiritual practices such as physical yoga, meditation, and other disciplines, which are necessary to burn away the things that block us. My friend Nikki Myers, who founded the Yoga of 12-Step Recovery (Y12SR) program, says, "Tapas helps to get the issues out of your tissues." I love that. We have spoken a lot about stuck emotional energy in the body and how critical it is to process it through. With 12-Step recovery and verbal forms of therapy, much is achieved. With the addition of tapas that results from yoga, you have a powerful combination on your hands that can help you "burn through" the past and have greater success on this path of recovery. It is said that tapas cultivates the capacity for discipline in the mind and body. Tapas even includes the mental discipline to return to presence when you notice you have lost it.

Remember that discipline simply means to follow or be a student of something. We surely need this quality as we go through our lives and walk a spiritual path. Tapas puts our desires in check and *helps us move beyond craving.*

Through practices that generate tapas, we also cultivate tranquility and balance, two qualities that are lacking from the character of most active addicts. I remember going to my friend Bryan

Kest's class after a long hiatus from practicing yoga. Bryan is a strong teacher with a great sense of humor who delivers an uplifting and challenging power yoga class. I was sweating before the class began, but Bryan's masterful teaching style kept my mind on the practice, my body, and my breath. I worked in that class—gave it my all. After the 90 minutes were over, I had left an ocean of sweat not just on my mat but two feet out from it in every direction. The people next to me, also soaking wet, looked at me as if I had defiled their space . . . and I kind of had. Bryan came over, pointed down at the mess, and at the top of his lungs exclaimed, "Holy shit!" All I could do was laugh. I felt new after that class. Rejuvenated. In just 90 minutes, I was able to get my mind and body back into balance. I'd carried a lot of stress that previous month or two and I had left it all on the floor in Bryan's studio.

The inner heat I've had to generate to burn away the insanity of addiction has been considerable. I like to think I've sweated out the karmas of many lifetimes. It certainly has felt that way through my practice these past 20 years.

SVADYAYA

Svadyaya means self-study and also refers to the study of spiritual texts.

All spiritual paths require self-reflection and the study of what is actually taking place within. How will you manage your mind, thoughts, and emotions? How shall you conduct yourself to reach a deeper, clearer understanding of your purpose in this world? What are your beliefs? Why do you have them? What is your relationship with the seen and unseen parts of life?

Svadyaya is a central component of the 12-Step Path. At every step of the way we are asked to self-reflect and to contemplate our connection with a Higher Power. We are looking for a spiritual experience because we have been told that this is required to recover from alcoholism and addiction. I believe this is true. Without a connection to your spiritual side, I think true recovery from addiction is implausible, never mind recovery from the human condition. We only need to be open to looking at or studying what life throws our way and be in the questioning of it all. This is enough to move forward. Svadyaya encourages us to find the divine within. That might be an offensive idea to some religious people who think it blasphemous to consider themselves divine. Perhaps a better way to put it would be that svadyaya suggests that we have a piece of divinity within us, which is connected to the Infinite Divinity in all.

This concept of having the divine within is central to yoga philosophy but is not meant in the egotistical sense of "I am God"; there we get into a bit of trouble. Rather, the realization of having God within us can help us move beyond shame by understanding there is something inherently amazing in us. We are not inherently bad. We also have "God-like" capabilities to create our own reality. By this I mean that we are living in a participatory universe. Our beliefs, thoughts, words, and actions affect the way reality unfolds before us. We have that kind of power. It is best that we learn to use it to create rather than destroy.

ISHVARAPRANIDHANA

Ishvarapranidhana means surrender to the Supreme Being or God. I have said several times in this book that one does not have to believe in God to have a spiritual experience and that a spiritual experience is required to recover from addiction. By this point, I am hoping you are open to the idea of such a thing.

Today, I am open-minded about spirit and God. I subscribe to Yogi Bhajan's statement that "if you can't see God in all, then you can't see God at all." I have beliefs about God, but I do not know. I see the signs of God everywhere, but I cannot explain it. I didn't always believe in God. Part of that is because I didn't know a way of relating to it that worked for me. Once I found that way, my heart and mind opened to a greater "perception" of things.

There is a wonderful, beloved Kundalini Yoga teacher named Guru Singh. He has this to say: "How much more evidence must you accumulate before you surrender?" For me the evidence has been overwhelming. There is wisdom and strength in surrendering to a power greater than myself, even if that simply means living in awe of my own heartbeat and in reverence to the unseen power that gives me breath.

Guruprem talks about "the thrill of the subtle." He describes it as a sense of excitement for subtler experiences that we often gain as we mature along the path of yoga. *As I have developed sensitivity to the spiritual side of myself, I have felt what he is talking about. The practice of Ishvarapranidhana and the entire 12-Step process are there to facilitate a spiritual experience through which we become more aware of and thrilled by the subtle.*

Here is what makes sense to me: God is formless, beyond description. We can relate to It through a form that makes sense to us. God, in my book, is an aware and conscious force field threaded through all reality. It cannot be seen as you might see with the eyes. It cannot be touched as you might touch with your hands. It can take any form and, in fact, it takes every form. God reveals Itself to each person in Its own way. You have heard several examples in this book of times I have felt the undeniable presence of my Higher Power. It was undeniable to me and me alone. This simply means I can't make you feel or know what has been made known to me, but hopefully, I can encourage you to take on the practice of yoga, which will help you to observe your life with greater sensitivity and awareness.

And do not worry if you don't believe in a Higher Power or God or anything. Remember: I was the one who refused to say the Lord's Prayer at Hazelden because it triggered my religious prejudices. I'm the one who balked at seeing a guru when it was suggested I go see Guruprem. I'm the one who questioned everything about the 12-Step path. If there were ever a person who was not cut out to get this thing and move beyond addiction, it would be me.

Go from where you are today and take one step forward and another and so on. The most important thing is to consider and ponder what life shows you rather than shutting out ideas without looking at them. With this approach you will find your way through any block.

PRACTICING YOGA

The path of yoga takes a person from darkness into light, from dis-ease toward ease, and ultimately to liberation from all suffering. Yoga does not discriminate. It is accessible to anyone who wants to grow along spiritual lines and, as I have stated, it is particularly relevant for those in recovery from addiction.

The purpose of yoga is described in classical texts as "the calming of the fluctuations of the mind," which sums up the entire path of yoga. Since addiction is seated in the mind, this goal is precisely what we are after. We have to settle the disturbances of the mind so we can move beyond the suffering of addiction. We can achieve this through the physical, mental, and spiritual practice of yoga. Thus, yoga is an asset to anyone on a path of recovery.

Provided you have the right attitude and the right teachers, the comfort and ease you have been waiting for are available to you every single day through this practice. You will breathe better. You will move better. The systems of your body will heal, making it easier for you to be comfortable in your own skin. You will get physically stronger and mentally clearer. You will be challenged in the ways you want and need to be. Yoga is a lifelong process. No matter how much you practice, there will always be more to experience one day at a time. Strangely, you will find that through the physical practice of yoga, other areas of life such as your relationships with people, food, and money will improve. *And* you will get to experience the bliss of being free from your mind and getting to know yourself much better.

There are many different forms of yoga. These include Ashtanga, Iyengar, Kundalini, Tantra, Bhakti, Sivananda, Viniyoga, and Power Yoga, to name but a few. These are all wonderful styles that complement one another and benefit all. The important thing is for you to find a practice that resonates with you. Kundalini and Vinyasa are the two main styles of yoga I have practiced these past 23 years, and I will focus on these in the pages that follow. But no matter what form of yoga attracts you, they all have one thing in common: all yoga begins with a connection to the breath.

THE IMPORTANCE OF THE BREATH

One day early on in our teachings together, Guruprem told me that he knew how I was going to die. Somewhat cynically, I said, "Okay, Guruprem, tell me. How am I going to die?"

"On an exhale," he plainly stated. My mind quickly ran through a number of death scenarios, and I found the statement to be true. There is only one way to go; we all will go that way and that is . . . on an exhale. He then followed this up with "And of course, you were born on an inhale like everyone else."

This was Guruprem's introduction for me to the importance of breath in our life. Our whole life sits between that first inhale and that final exhale. In the hierarchy of needs in the body, breath is number one. We can go without food for several months and water for several days, but to be without breath for even a few minutes is cause for dismissal. *As it turns out, breath is one of the keys to healing from addiction. In fact, addiction cannot take root where there is conscious awareness of breath. The more we are aware of our breath and its importance, the closer we will be to ease and the further we will be from the dis-ease of addiction. Once you know how to manipulate your breath, you will even be able to change your emotional state at will.*

Most people do not breathe very well. Their breaths are quite shallow and what little breathing they do causes their shoulders, spine, and heart to lift up on an inhale and drop down on an exhale. They look like they're inflating and deflating with each breath. Of course, our lungs inflate and deflate, but our heart should remain lifted and supported by the navel, our diaphragm should drive our exhale, and our spine should remain in integrity throughout. The fact is that most people live in thoracic incarceration. They have not learned how to breathe, how to use their diaphragm, how to free up their rib cage, how to maintain a healthy spine, and how to strengthen their core muscles to support their heart. All of this can be fixed with practice and leads to much greater ease.

Our breath has five main purposes:

1. Brings in the goods—oxygen and *Prana* (life force)

2. Discards the waste—carbon dioxide and *apana* (eliminating force)

3. Carries our words (on our exhales)

4. Alters our mood and consciousness and helps us enter meditative states

5. Attunes the body-mind system to the Frequency of Recovery

Taking a look at this list, let's pause for a moment to appreciate all the breath does for us. Our inhale draws in oxygen and Prana. It is our primary form of nourishment. People who become disconnected from their breath (almost everyone) lack something pretty significant from their lives, namely ease and comfort. I am suggesting here that most people in the world are disconnected from their breathing and that if they focused more on their breath, they would have more energy, be more contented, and have less reason to look outside of themselves to try to feel better.

With our exhale, we get to release what no longer serves us: carbon dioxide and other waste products. Of course, most people are not aware that our exhale is capable of carrying a lot more than just waste. It carries our words. There are few things we possess that are as powerful as our words, whether we think them, write them, or speak them. They are one of the main ways we relate to each other. They can destroy or heal, denounce or uplift. In yoga we pay a lot of attention to this particular use of the exhale as we try to develop greater awareness and compassion around our speech. I saw a great T-shirt recently that read, "Exhale only Love." I thought, *What a difficult practice that is. All your words would have to come from a place of love.*

The ancient tradition of yoga emphasizes the connection between our breath and our thinking. If we can control our breath, we can control our mind. The better we get at doing this, the better our life will be. After all, we are slaves to our mind. We get identified with our thoughts and, as we have seen, this is where addiction really takes off. If learning some breathing techniques can calm my mind's chatter, sign me up. Learning how to use the breath to focus and control my mind has been a huge part of my recovery, and I have included a number of breath exercises and meditations in the Appendices at the back of this book.

The breath is also one of the keys to changing your emotional state. When you are anxious, angry, or depressed, your breath becomes shallow. This sends a signal to your body that your primary needs are not being met. This, in turn, creates a chain reaction in the body, resulting in lower energy and higher stress. By deepening your breath and applying certain techniques, you can reverse this and create relaxation and calmness. You can have control over your reactions to various emotions, and in wielding the breath, you can even shift them.

I have spoken a lot about the Frequency of Addiction. The breath, as it turns out, is a major catalyst when it comes to changing our attunement. This is important to understand. If we use certain breath techniques regularly and become better at breathing in general, we will benefit from our primary source of nourishment. We will become stronger and clearer in thought, and we will break free of the Frequency of Addiction by re-attuning ourselves to the Frequency of Recovery. This is why I call the breath a game changer: it literally changes everything in your experience once you start to practice.

VINYASA YOGA

The physical practice of yoga is one of the great blessings in my life. In most yoga classes across the United States, you will find a teacher leading students through a series of physical movements with an emphasis on connecting the breath with each movement. This is the practice of Vinyasa Yoga, which simply means movement coordinated with breath. If you are looking to experience freedom, bliss, strength, peace, self-love, and progress, start to practice Vinyasa Yoga.

In our addictions, we have undergone great stress and trauma. We have weakened ourselves. Vinyasa is particularly important for people in recovery because of its strengthening and detoxifying capabilities. Vinyasa will make you very strong from the inside out. If you are of the opinion that yoga is a mellow workout and could not possibly get you into "real shape," you only need to step into a moderate-level Vinyasa class and your opinion will change in fewer than ten minutes. Through the physical challenge, you will sweat and detox. By focusing on the breath you will develop presence and mental acuity.

Remember, too, that addiction is rooted in trauma and that unprocessed emotions get stuck in the tissues of the body. Well, Vinyasa Yoga is one way to get deep enough into the tissues to release and process those stuck energies out. Sometimes people will burst out laughing or crying in their practice. When questioned about what happened to create that response, very often they will tell you that they have no idea. It didn't seem to be connected to any particular thought at all—it just came out of them. This is the release of stuck energy. I hope you have an opportunity to experience it for yourself.

KUNDALINI YOGA

In addition to Vinyasa Yoga, I practice and teach Kundalini Yoga, which was brought to the West by Yogi Bhajan in the late 1960s. Yogi Bhajan was a master of Kundalini Yoga, deemed so by his teacher when he was just 16 years old. As the story goes, he had become a customs officer at the New Delhi Airport and was watching thousands of Westerners come to his country searching for wholeness in their lives and looking in all the wrong places: drugs, alcohol, and sex. He would see these young people arrive in India and then see them leave some time later with less vitality and less connection than they'd had when they arrived. He decided to come to the West to teach Kundalini Yoga. This form of yoga had never been taught publicly in groups before. Upon hearing that Yogi Bhajan was teaching Westerners Kundalini, his peers cursed him and said, "If you keep teaching this yoga, you'll be dead within one year." Guru Singh was one of Yogi Bhajan's first students and was there when Yogi Bhajan reached his one-year anniversary of teaching in the United States. He reports that in reference to the curse that had been placed upon him, Yogi Bhajan said, "Guru Singh, I knew it was bullshit."

In the early years, Yogi Bhajan taught many people who struggled with drugs and alcohol. It was the early 1970s, and there was a lot of that going on. He formed a rehabilitation center in Tucson that was one part ashram and one part primary-care facility for recovering addicts. It was a powerful combination. People got sober in an atmosphere where everyone was meditating, chanting, practicing yoga, and eating a vegetarian diet. It helped many people over the years, but as the insurance landscape shifted, it ultimately ended up closing for financial reasons.

Yogi Bhajan would build an entire society around his yogic teachings over the next 35 years until his death in 2004. From day one, he continually told his followers, "I am not here to gather students. I am here to create teachers." The 12 Steps are built upon a similar idea. Really, we get sober to help others get sober. This is a bit of a simplification, but it expresses that same idea of passing on the teachings so that the maximum number of people can benefit from them.

So what's the big deal here? Why the need to create teachers? Why the pointed effort to spread the teachings of Kundalini Yoga or the 12 Steps? The reason is simple: we are in trouble.

Yogi Bhajan correctly prophesied that in the 21st century, life on earth was going to become overwhelming and unmanageable for most of its inhabitants. There would be great suffering and higher and higher levels of stress, addiction, and dis-ease. His intention was to raise the consciousness of his students as quickly as possible so they would be able to show people how to manage the coming challenges. He referred to Kundalini Yoga as a technology. It would be powerful enough to heal a person from their addictions, their neuroses, and their pain. It would take a person fated to hardship and elevate them onto their "destiny path" so they could live out their life's mission guided closely by intuition and in service to others. This is the effect these teachings have had upon me.

I never met Yogi Bhajan. He died just as I was getting turned on to Kundalini Yoga by one of his students . . . Guruprem.

You've heard a bit about my awakening over the five-year period visiting with Guruprem. We practiced Kundalini Yoga and talked about life. I cherish the memory of that time as my body and mind released the patterns that no longer served me. I practiced challenging postures, and when we were done I felt a sense of total release. It was as if the tension in my body had dissolved straight out the bottoms of my feet. Over time, I started to move more freely. I was actually changing the way my body moved in physical space. The joy of this is indescribable. While the practice of yoga was integral, our discussions were no less important. I had some terribly misguided ways of looking at the world. The perspectives Guruprem shared with me make up much of the philosophical foundation of the Recovery 2.0 approach to life.

Kundalini Yoga offers a time-tested, advanced user's manual for the human body-mind system. Its primary purpose is to help you reach your potential as a human being. From the Kundalini Yoga perspective we all have potential energy stored at the base of our spine. As we awaken that energy and distribute it through the main energy centers of the body, we awaken to a more whole-hearted existence.

Through addictive behavior we weaken our nervous system and endocrine system. We turn off our intuition. Our physical body becomes weak and we are susceptible to dis-ease. Addiction robs us of our health, vitality, and power. It also disconnects us from our heart and spirit. It is no wonder that we come to be "powerless." As we've discussed throughout this book, we are looking for more power. Kundalini Yoga strengthens us physically and mentally. It repairs and builds upon the capacities of all the systems of the body. It increases intuitive capabilities and ultimately connects us with our own divinity, giving us access to more power than we might have realized was possible.

Kundalini Yoga practice includes such elements as physical postures, *pranayama* (breath exercises), meditation, chanting, and deep relaxation. Like Vinyasa, it is taught in classes all over the world. I have found it to be a powerful complement to 12-Step work and helpful for anyone on a path of awakening. On the 12-Step path we practice certain rituals such as prayer and going to meetings in order to have "a daily reprieve" from our dis-ease. On the path of Kundalini Yoga, we build a daily spiritual practice known as our *sadhana*.

SADHANA—ATTUNE YOURSELF TO THE RIGHT FREQUENCY EVERY DAY

Sadhana (pronounced saad-nah) means daily spiritual practice. Its purpose is to "attune" you in such a way that you connect with your Highest Self, the part of you that is Divine in nature. You can then live your day from this place of reconnection. Once your thoughts descend, it becomes increasingly difficult to "meet yourself," which is why people often practice their sadhana first thing in the morning.

Your sadhana will consist of elements that help you to maintain balance in your life, strengthen and detoxify your body, and calm your mind. Ultimately, when you do your sadhana you will feel great, have less or no pain in your body, increase mental clarity and intuition, and feel aligned with your highest purpose. Sadhana is an addiction buster! It will help you to attune yourself to the Frequency of Recovery.

Yogi Bhajan said, "The greatest reward of doing sadhana is that the person becomes incapable of being defeated. Sadhana is a self-victory." He also expressed the power of doing sadhana in a group setting. "First, the isolation which can hit anybody and make them go totally crazy is defeated. Secondly, when all of you meditate on God, the total effect of your sadhana becomes multiplied by the number of people participating . . . If you have to do sadhana alone, imagine yourself surrounded by millions of people."

Yogi Bhajan constantly stressed the importance of sadhana as a daily practice, particularly before the sun comes up, between the hours of 3:30 and 6:00 A.M. This time of day is referred to as the *amrit vela,* or ambrosial hours—the sweet hours of the day when fewer people in your area are awake. There is less psychic energy, more calmness. It is thought to be the most powerful time to meditate. *Do not worry!* I am not suggesting that you regularly wake up at 3:30 A.M. to meditate, nor do I feel it is a prerequisite for having a great life. That said, saints and sages have used these hours throughout history to get an edge in the effort to gain mastery over their minds. The times I have done yoga and meditation in community during the ambrosial hours have been powerful, transformational, and filled with joy. I suggest you try it sometime.

My sadhana consists of physical yoga practice to activate my body by bringing Prana, or life force, into my spine, organs, and tissues; meditation and chanting to help me gain mastery over my mind before it has a shot at mastering me; and prayer to help me connect with and express myself to my Higher Power.

So, any given morning you have a choice: get up and float through life, roll with its ups and downs, and try to manage your mind—or attune to the Frequency of your Highest Self, activate your creativity, and go through the day on purpose, guided by intuition. Having a steady morning sadhana is a recommended part of Recovery 2.0 life.

DESIGNING YOUR OWN SADHANA

Sadhana elements can include yoga, meditation, pranayama (breathwork), chanting, singing, dancing, journaling, reading spiritual literature, and anything else that connects you with your Highest Self. The elements of a great sadhana will vary from person to person depending upon spiritual beliefs, schedule, lifestyle, and needs. Sadhana can be short—even three minutes can make a huge difference. The main thing is to adopt a practice every day that you can manage. As with all new endeavors, a little bit of discipline goes a long way. You will come to love this practice so much that you will choose not to live life without it. All of this can be a little overwhelming at first, so in the Appendices of this book you will find a few suggestions to help you choose a sadhana that works for you.

HOW AND WHERE TO PRACTICE YOGA

All forms of yoga have something to offer. As with diets, lifestyles, and approaches to recovery, there is no one right yoga practice for everyone. Google yoga in your town. Connect with the owners of a yoga studio and ask them for some guidance. Go out and try a class. See how it feels. Do you feel safe, excited? Is it fun? Do you want to go back? That's usually a good sign. If you hit a class that's too easy (boring for you) or too hard (couldn't catch your breath, thought you were going to die), try another one at a different level, perhaps with a different teacher. The teacher is key. You will surely find teachers with whom you resonate and others with whom you do not. You may also opt to have a few private lessons. These can be expensive, but you can learn a lot very quickly, and it's a great way to jump-start a practice if you are nervous about going into a class environment. It's also rewarding to tap into a yoga community, so make sure to get out to a class when you can. If you feel that yoga classes are too expensive, visit a donation-based yoga class in your town and drop what you can in the box on the way out.

Of course, these days there is also a ton of yoga available online. We are fortunate to have this kind of access to so many teachers and styles of yoga. Nothing is holding you back.

CHAPTER 17

MEDITATION

The classical path of yoga leads to meditation, which is the means by which we achieve true freedom. From the perspective of the ancients, yoga and meditation are not separate from each other. In fact, the physical practice of yoga was traditionally used to ready the body to sit comfortably in meditation for long periods of time.

I cannot overstate the extent to which I have needed meditation in my life. The signs have been everywhere. One day I was in a New Age bookshop and came upon a book called *The Secret Language of Birthdays*. It breaks down your life horoscope not just by your astrological sign, but, more precisely, by the actual day of your birthday. I was born on May 31, which is referred to as "The Day of the Cutting Edge" in this thick tome. There on the page in plain black print it states, "All forms of escape pose grave dangers to the health of May 31 people. . . . Those born on this day have a marked tendency to seek solace in alcohol and drugs . . ." This hit a little too close to home to just blow off as astrological nonsense. The rest of the page was filled with other interesting tidbits, which I also found bizarrely relevant to my life, and then there at the bottom of the page it offered the following: "The most successful May 31 people learn to bring the extremes of their personality into harmony with each other. . . If not successful at this, they appear as souls in torment, constantly struggling against frustration and unhappiness. Neither the oblivion of ceaseless activity, nor temporary escape from problems gives them rest in the long run." This rang completely true for me, and the words that came into my mind were *Tommy, you have to meditate.*

Meditation is a universe unto itself with countless forms, practices, and goals. For our purposes here, I define meditation as a practice of focused concentration or of mindfulness that leads to a clear, calm state of mind, the development of contentment and compassion, and ultimately liberation. As we have discussed, the 12 Steps do not offer much in the way of meditation instruction, but they do encourage us to seek outside help where necessary.

EVERYTHING IS CREATED IN THE MIND FIRST

Everything in the world is created twice. First it is "seen" in the mind, and then it is made manifest on the physical plane here on earth. Think about an architect's process when she is hired to build a concert hall. She first has to envision the space and the materials. What will it look like inside and outside? How will people access it? How can the right acoustics be achieved? She directs her mind to imagine possibilities. Her power of imagination is of course a central component of her ability to create.

All human beings have the ability to create, whether they have developed that ability or not. When we get inspiration or vision, it comes from our "creative ability" or, put another way, our ability to tap into the "great mainframe." My writing this book right now is happening like that. I'm sitting and writing what comes into my head. I'm focusing on the topic at hand and words are showing up, but it does not originate with me.

People struggling in addiction are like our architect, only in their case, their imagination leads to the creation of dis-ease. Addicts have incredible minds, amazingly powerful imaginations.

They are very creative people. Their creativity is skewed in ways that lead them toward pain and suffering rather than toward harmony and bliss. They are disconnected from the great mainframe. They are not creating concert halls in their mind. They are creating their next shot of alcohol, hit of crack, or codependent relationship.

It is encouraging that the classical path of yoga recognizes and addresses the issue, which all addicts know to be *the* issue: the mind. We know that a conscious approach to the 12 Steps treats the condition of addiction and reconnects us with the great mainframe. Then, through meditation, we can forever build upon our connection, develop focus and compassion, transform our thinking, and teach others to do the same. When our thinking transforms, we transform and our world transforms.

MEDITATION, ADDICTION, AND TIME

We live in a world that is constantly gearing up and going faster, and for most people this leads to stressful relationships with time. We may be caught in resentments, which draw us back into the past, or we may be anxious or worried about the future. All people who struggle with addiction seem to have a strange relationship with time. Recently, a sponsee told me, "I cannot wait for the future to get here. Time is not passing quick enough, but I also feel like I'm behind. I'm thirty-eight years old and I feel like I'm running out of time." My sponsee is not alone in this feeling. I believe most people can relate to it. And what do we do about it? Well, we do everything we can to get time to pass. The problem is that if we always press for another experience that gives us the illusion of time passing more quickly or more pleasurably, our life depends upon constant action, constant movement. Something will always have to be there to help us pass the time. So addicts, who rely upon addictive behaviors to move things along, have truly lost the ability to pass time well (if they ever had it at all).

Guruprem is constantly reminding me that we are searching for the comfortable seat and that the real action is found in the "subtle." Well, there is not too much that is comfortable or subtle about the way addicts think and behave. One of our main characteristics is to be extreme in almost everything we do. Yet this is not necessary. We can develop into human beings from our current state as "human doings." We can find the present moment and the bliss that comes along with living in it. The more present we become, the more we will be able to find true compassion and contentment.

In recovery, we must reclaim and cultivate the ability to be still and live in the present moment. Meditation holds the key to overcoming the beliefs, thought patterns, and behaviors that undermine this process.

THE FALLACY OF IF-THEN THINKING

One of the thought patterns that many of us have to break out of is "if-then thinking." This causes us to postpone our happiness, contentment, and joy until life arranges itself in a way that meets our demands. "If I get the right job and make the right money, then I'll be happy. If I get the right girl or the right guy, then I can start living. Once I reach this goal or that goal, then I'll relax." The problem with if-then thinking is that we set ourselves up to miss the whole trip. The end seems to be the only place where we stand a chance at happiness. Of course, once we are "there," we find that we have blocked our happiness with something else. The journey is the point. That is where our healing is. That is where our joy is. That is where our love is. Meditation has been the practice that has shown me how to break out of this destructive pattern. Meditation will help you to enjoy the journey as you live it.

THE SHITTY COMMITTEE

Another thought pattern that exerts control in our lives is what people in recovery often refer to as the "shitty committee," that cacophony of heinous internal voices that makes life unpleasant.

The first thing to understand about the shitty committee is that *all* people have a problem with it. We all have a thinking problem in that we are identified with and dominated by our thoughts, quite often negative and painful ones. To identify with a thought gives it weight and meaning. We follow the thought and perpetuate it, thus giving it power over us. Imagine you are thinking about eating an entire chocolate cake. The thought unto itself is not a problem. It has no basis in reality. It is just a thought. It has no power except the power you ascribe to it. If you start to think about the icing on the cake, for example, or the feeling you had when you first tried chocolate cake, the thought sticks around a bit and starts to gain weight (no pun intended). The more thought energy you throw at it, the more you become stuck to it. Now you enter the realm of temptation. Remember: you have the ability to take a thought and make it manifest here in reality. Suddenly, you are very tempted to demonstrate this ability. This is what plays out in the mind of the addict from nanosecond to nanosecond until he or she becomes overwhelmed by it.

For most of us, the shitty committee gets its start bright and early in the morning, and unless we take action (read: do our sadhana), we may be at its mercy for the rest of the day.

CHANGING YOUR MIND

Yoga and meditation teacher Anand Mehrotra tells us, "Sincere meditation practice is a responsibility for our planet. All we know of ourselves is as the mind. To be identified as mind we have no choices. Once we develop the capacity to tell the difference between our thoughts and our Selves then we begin to have choice."[1] This is a beautiful way of looking at it. In addiction we have no choice. We are compelled to do something, which feels out of our control. Anand suggests that with a strong meditation practice, we can restore our power of choice. So we see how the addictive mind is the opposite of the meditative mind.

Meditation builds our capacity to reflect and focus. It trains us to witness rather than react, and it builds our nervous system by teaching us to resist impulse and temptation. Through meditation we learn to delay the gratification of doing something about this thought or that.

Imagine you are sitting in meditation when a terribly uncomfortable thought comes into your head. Maybe you feel ashamed for having done something you know is against your principles. The thought comes to you and it's difficult to bear. And it isn't just one thought, is it? The first thought comes and you run with it. You envision the thing you've done over and over again until you are all but crawling out of your skin. You think, *I've got to do something. This is awful. I can't bear the thought of it. Meditation sucks!* Yet if you sit there long enough, you will usually find that the thought passes. It will have shifted to something else and you will be stronger for having watched your mind and resisted the temptation to do anything about it.

The same is true of physical sensations in the body. Have you ever had a terrible itch during meditation that you tried not to scratch? What about when pain or tiredness comes into the picture? Do you observe the sensation or do you scratch, fidget, and move to try to get rid of it? If you can hold on, you may note that the pain or other sensation has moved, shifted, or gone away completely.

The main point here is that addiction is seated in the mind. Since we know that the mind is where the problem lies, adding a meditation practice to your daily recovery regimen is an excellent idea and a part of Recovery 2.0.

In my seeking, I have practiced various forms of Buddhist meditation as well as Kundalini meditation. These practices have brought about the most profound changes in me. The biggest difference I've noticed has been the development of my capacity to simply sit still, especially in the face of discomfort—whether mental or physical. Meditative stillness has further allowed me to cultivate intuition. Meditation has led me to a greater understanding of the addictive aspect of my mind. I can isolate it now and when it rears its head, I tell it, "I see you." This has led to self-forgiveness and compassion.

KUNDALINI YOGA–BASED MEDITATION

Of all practices I've known, Kundalini meditation has been the most transformative for me. As I've said, being in the Frequency of Addiction causes you to attract certain thoughts into your mind. I envision a massive thought cloud in the sky and each of us draws down thoughts from it. Imagine that as you enter recovery, you begin the process of dealing with a lot of difficult thinking. As you move down your recovery path, the hard thoughts still come, but you deal with them better and better. Eventually, your thinking changes altogether. Not only are you an expert at dealing with the hard thoughts, but now fewer of them show up. What is coming down the "thought pipe" is more intuitive and aligned with your newly attuned self. Without knowing how to explain it any other way, I believe these Kundalini meditations break the Frequency of Addiction and give you access to ideas and intuition you might not have had otherwise.

There are thousands of meditations offered within the Kundalini Yoga tradition that focus on breath, mantras, mudras (hand positions), chanting, and visualization. The particular focus of these meditations changes from one to the next. Sometimes they are intended to build intuition or aid in deep healing. Other meditations help you master certain parts of your mind or ego. Chant-based meditations might be used for protection or building your auric field or for blessing yourself. There are even meditations specifically for overcoming cravings and addictions. These are specific practical tools that help you reduce stress, increase vitality, and clear energy.

In the Appendices of this book you will find several accessible Kundalini Yoga meditations as well as information about where you can find my Yoga, Addiction, Recovery DVDs, which include my favorite meditations and instruction on the breath.

THE THREE MINDS

Within the powerful teachings of Kundalini Yoga there is the concept of the three minds—negative, positive, and neutral.

This teaching has been instrumental for me in my recovery. It has given me a framework to view and better understand the workings of my mind. This new perspective has helped me improve the quality of my thinking.

Let's say you have a decision to make, such as whether to cross the street or not. The negative mind shows up saying things like, *Are you sure you want to cross the street? There's a lot of traffic and you might get hurt. What's so special across that street anyway?* Despite its name, the negative mind is neither bad nor good. It is the part of your mind that tells you the reasons not to do something. The negative mind is the protective aspect of your mind.

The positive mind adds its two cents: *Wow, look over there. It's amazing across that street. You've never been hit by a car before. Why would you get hit now? Doesn't look dangerous at all. It's an adventure. Let's have at it.* The positive mind also is neither good nor bad. It simply tells you the reasons to do something. It is the creative, adventurous part of your mind.

Then there's the neutral mind, which you access through stillness and meditation. The neutral mind is like a judge who hears the testimony of *both* the negative and positive minds. It perceives the full picture and from an informed place makes a decision. Yogi Bhajan used to say that if people are tapped into the neutral mind, they should be able to make any decision in nine seconds or less. So when you are making decisions, you want to access the neutral mind. This is a way of connecting more deeply with Higher Power or with your Highest Self. You can develop this capacity through meditation and calmness. With practice, you will improve your decisions and the way you navigate through life.

People who lean too heavily toward their negative mind are overprotected. They are risk averse and will miss some opportunities that life presents, but they rarely get burned. These folks can be dominated by fear and stay in their comfort zone because they are mostly aware of what could go wrong.

People who lean too heavily on their positive mind rarely miss an opportunity life throws their way. These folks are adventurous and willing to take risks. They have a hard time seeing what might go wrong, so they do receive a solid whooping from time to time.

Ask yourself which mind is your dominant mind. Do you lean toward the negative mind—more easily seeing the reasons not to do something—or toward the positive mind, where you see all the reasons to do something? I lean toward the positive mind. My general approach to life has been to ask, "What could possibly go wrong?" And many times, I've had to find out the hard way. "Lots can go wrong!" This means I am working on developing my ability to hear the testimony of the negative mind and drop into the wisdom of the neutral mind in order to approach life in a more informed, balanced way. *When you hear the testimony of both the positive and the negative mind, you move toward greater awareness and intuition.*

And how about addicts who are in a state of craving? Are they leaning toward their negative or positive mind with regard to the substance or behavior they are craving? Of course, in that state, people predominantly hear the testimony of the positive mind— all the reasons they should go after it. For an active addict in the throes of addiction, it is as if there is no negative mind. That's the proverbial "mental fog" we spoke of earlier. You cannot summon a reason not to do this thing, so you return to the addictive behavior again and again.

The great teacher Swami Rama wrote, "Meditation is not what you think, for it is beyond thinking. You do not meditate on your problems in order to solve them, but through meditation you see through the problems you have set up for yourself."[2] The state one achieves in meditation is the opposite of the state of addiction. *In meditation there are presence and focus, witnessing. In addiction, there are identification with one's thoughts and reacting to everything.* If the thought arises that you should have that chocolate cake we talked about earlier, you'll just have it. There is little separation between thought and action, no discernment.

MINDFULNESS MEDITATION: INVITE THEM ALL IN

In addition to Kundalini meditation, I found that mindfulness meditation was particularly powerful in my recovery. In this practice, you open up your awareness to experience all that is going on within and around you. You allow all the voices to happen and even though you ignore them at first, you are aware of them. *I am thinking many thoughts,* you might notice. Maybe a particularly painful, funny, or strange thought arises. You might remark without judgment, *What an interesting thought to have had!* You feel sensations in the body and might label them as *pain in my left knee* or *tension and tingling in my lower back.* You are becoming aware of all that is occurring for you in real present-time awareness.

This is really the end of illusion. You enter the present moment, which is the only moment you can actually experience; ironically, it's the one most of us seek to avoid. You leave the fantasy of past and future altogether and have a method of discerning true from false. Without judgment, you develop more awareness of what is and who you are. Numerous studies over the years have shown how effective mindfulness meditation is in managing stress, depression, and a host of other medical and mental disorders, including smoking. These meditations are outstanding complements on the path of recovery. If you are drawn to them, please look up *vipassana* or mindfulness meditation and begin to work closely with a teacher. Noah Levine, the founder of Refuge Recovery and author of a book by the same title, is a wonderful meditation teacher with profound understanding of addiction and recovery. Many other outstanding teachers offer classes, workshops, and retreats all year long. As is the case with yoga, having an immersive meditation experience is central to my recovery. I would not like to know what my life would be like without a yoga and meditation practice.

CHAPTER 18

THE ROLE
OF FOOD IN
RECOVERY FROM
ADDICTION

Your relationship with food is directly connected to the way you experience life. It doesn't matter if you are a drug addict, alcoholic, sex addict, compulsive gambler, or emotional food binger; there is an intimate connection between what you eat and how you think, feel, and behave. *Your diet correlates directly with the way your life unfolds.* Food is not an outside issue when it comes to any form of addiction. It is one of the core issues. Therefore, any holistic approach to recovery must include a deep look at your relationship with food.

The connection goes much deeper than you may realize. Your energy levels, mood, thinking, actions, immunity against disease: all functions of the body and mind are affected by the food and water you consume. In a recent interview at the Recovery 2.0

Conference, world-renowned nutrition expert David Wolfe had this to say: "The quality and intent that's behind the food we eat, the way it was grown, the way it was produced, the way it was delivered to us, the way it was prepared, the way that we ate it—all that has a strong impact on the quality of our life and the quality of our behaviors and what we value. It affects the choices we make moment to moment and day to day. It even affects our character and integrity."[1] For people who struggle with addiction, diet carries that much more significance because our diet can attune us to the Frequency of Addiction or the Frequency of Recovery, depending on our choices.

I am a foodie. I love the ritual of eating, of gathering, of experiencing different cultures through their cuisine. One of my greatest joys in life is sharing a great meal with friends and family. I would not want to give it up, and thankfully I do not have to. When you start to address your relationship with food, you may fear that you are giving up the joyful part of eating. You may imagine some tasteless, joyless approach to eating and focus on all the things you have to give up. Nothing could be further from the truth. In fact, once you really start to build a healthy relationship with food, a whole universe of exciting possibilities opens up. Get psyched!

THE GREAT DISCLAIMER ABOUT DIETS

People can be opinionated in many ways, but you really open the floodgates by asking practically any person what they think you should eat. Ask 100 people and you will get 100 opinions. In Los Angeles, I can tell you a pinnacle has been reached when it comes to people telling other people what to eat. Without going into details, I can tell you that some of it gets really weird.

With a thousand diets floating around, how would it be possible to find the right diet for you? The answer is simple. The right diet for you is the one that gives you energy and keeps you healthy and vital. You don't get sick. You generally feel good. Your mind is sharp and working well. If you are lethargic, bloated, flatulent, low in energy, often sick, unfocused, or confused, or if you have mental disorders such as addiction, bipolar disorder, or the like, you need to take a close look at your diet. Remember: food will either play a part in your healing process or it will be a contributor to your dis-ease. The way to figure it out is to experiment, pay attention to how you feel over a period of time, and make tweaks along the way.

I strongly recommend that you work with a physician throughout this process. He or she can get your blood work done to assess your health more completely. Blood tests can help you and your doctor analyze the enzymatic and mineral composition of your blood, hormones, cortisol levels, adrenals, and thyroid, among other things. Your level of nutritional fitness will also be reflected in your blood, and you will learn much about what is out of balance. Then with the help of a few good books or a great nutritional coach, you can make the right decisions about your diet and begin to feel better at every level of your being.

Your own observations and life experience will be the teacher that shows you what works and what does not. Here are a few ideas to help get you started on your exploration.

THE PRINCIPLE OF GRATITUDE

My teacher Guruprem once said, "A child cannot be spoiled if he is grateful for the food he eats." This statement has stuck with me for a long time.

As a child, I was raised eating meat and junk food. Now I eat consciously. That is to say, I am aware of what I am eating and why I am eating it. I have huge gratitude and express it in words every time. The words I use, whether aloud or under my breath, are not important other than to express that I am thankful for the blessing of the food I get to eat.

My diet is mostly vegetarian, but I also occasionally eat eggs, chicken, and fish. Guruprem is a strict vegetarian: no meat, no eggs, no fish. I once asked him if he ever wondered why I some-times eat meat. He thought about that for a moment and then replied, "I suppose you eat it because you feel like you need to." It was a great answer, surprising in its lack of judgment. He followed this statement up with "Tommy, only fools argue about what to eat. You can't eat your way into heaven. What matters most is that you are grateful and that you say a prayer before eating." This has been one of my guiding principles in developing a new relation-ship with food.

WHAT *SHOULD* I EAT AND DRINK?

There is no one answer to this question. Just as there are many approaches to recovery, there are many approaches to diet, and the right approach for you today may change over time. However, you can observe a few guidelines and principles that will be help-ful to you on your path of recovery from addiction. The following ideas are meant to inspire you to relate more deeply to the food you eat.

My friend Kris Carr, the best-selling author who is thriving alongside cancer, has taught a lot about the importance of diet in the process of recovery from dis-eases that people aren't sup-posed to recover from. She speaks about inflammation being one of the biggest culprits. She teaches an anti-inflammatory way of living, and diet is central to her message. We want to eat a diet that is non-inflammatory to our body, she tells us. When we eat poorly, our body reacts as if it's facing an unwant-ed intruder. This means the immune system has to go to work. The body expends energy protecting itself from something that is supposed to be nourishing. You may not feel it right away as such. Maybe you feel bloated or just tired, like you want to crash. Many people have food allergies, so they feel symptoms that go along with that. Learning about the foods that make you feel bad is just as important as learning about the foods that make you feel good.

Go Green with Organic Salads, Veggies, Juices, and Smoothies

Greens are where you are going to get your minerals and counteract the acidic, inflammatory foods that most of us consume. The idea is to eat a wide variety of vegetables, put lots of different colors in your food, so you get lots of different minerals, vitamins, and life force. If you can't afford organic, consider letting go of some processed foods you may be eating and put your savings toward buying organic produce instead.

Eating raw vegetables is great for your health. Lightly cooked vegetables are as well. And you don't have to just *eat* your veggies. Having fresh organic juices and smoothies filled with the right ingredients is one of the most delicious, efficient, and powerful ways to increase alkalinity, re-mineralize, and create optimal health in your life. You can experiment with superfoods, fruits, vegetables, seeds, nuts, nut butters, and other healthful ingredients to create the most wonderful concoctions.

One rule here is to be mindful of the sugar content of the ingredients. Carrots, beets, pineapple, bananas, and oranges are high-glycemic, meaning high in sugar content. Even though they are natural sources of sugar, I like to use mostly mid- to low-glycemic options such as green apples, blueberries, grapefruit, all green leafy vegetables such as kale, chard, and lettuces, and herbs such as parsley, basil, and cilantro.

You will need two things in your kitchen for juices and smoothies—a juicer and a blender. These are not inexpensive items, but they are worth it for the endless enjoyment and health they'll bring you. There are many juicers on the market. Champion and Breville are two great ones. As for blenders, I'd suggest you look into getting a Vitamix or a NutriBullet.

Eat Organic, Free-Range, and Grass-Fed Meat (If You Must)

If you eat meat, eggs, and dairy, eat the healthiest and most humanely treated animal products you can find. Also, experiment with eating less of them. Most of what you eat at any meal should be green vegetables (80 percent at least). No person on the planet needs meat every day, much less at every meal. As you explore new types of foods, you will be able to create totally satisfying, healthful vegetarian meals as part of your regimen. You do not have to give up meat if you do not want to, but experiment. Try new things. Explore the wonderful world of healthy, whole-food, and vegetarian options.

Tune In to the Wisdom of Superfoods

Superfoods are nutrient-dense plants, herbs, and fungi. In a world where it is more and more difficult to get the full spectrum of minerals and vitamins we require, people are turning more and more to these amazing foods. Since part of the key to being healthy is the re-mineralization of the body, I turn to high-nutrient superfoods daily. Very often, I have these foods raw in smoothies or salads. Superfoods include spirulina and chlorella, wheatgrass, seaweed, goji berries, chia, bee pollen, maca, acai berries, coconuts, and herbs and fungi such as ginseng, nettle, aloe vera, and reishi mushrooms. You can find superfoods at health-food markets everywhere, and today many companies are putting this goodness out into the world. One of the best ones is called Essential Living Foods.

Buy from the Farmer's Market

Go to the farmer's market in your town as often as possible to buy your meats and produce directly from farmers. If there isn't one, consider starting one for your community. The benefits are numerous. Small farms are disappearing. We want to support them because we want to support organic food grown with more care and attention than larger farms can afford to do. And small farms treat their animals with much more care than large factory farms do.

Fresh produce is delicious. Any organic farmer will tell you that nothing can beat the taste and nutritional power of a freshly picked fruit or vegetable. Tasting freshly picked food from my garden, I am always reminded of just how blessed I am to have access to such a thing. You may be able to hook up with the farmers in and around the area and cut some deals with them or create a community-supported-agriculture program with your neighbors, arranging for regular pickup or delivery of seasonal fresh produce from local farmers.

The idea here is to eat food as close to its source as possible. Once food is processed, packaged, or shipped, it loses a lot of its nutritional value. So much processed food has additives that are at best unhelpful and at worst may cause health problems down the line. Many of us also deal with allergies to things that show up in processed foods. Even "organic" so-called healthy processed foods are to be eaten with awareness and moderation. I definitely still eat a few things that are processed, such as breads and pasta. I do my best to get the best whole-grain breads and organic pastas I can find. That works for me and I enjoy it. At the end of the day, you will have to decide if the food you eat is helping or hurting your cause and adjust accordingly.

Stay Properly Hydrated

I have never met an active addict who was well hydrated. It's hard enough for most of us to remain hydrated throughout a normal day, but addicts have other more pressing concerns. Even for those in recovery, hydration just isn't a priority, but it ought to be.

For all of us, staying hydrated is one of the hardest things to do because we've lost contact with what it feels like to be thirsty. Try to imagine the feeling of being just a little bit thirsty—you may not know what that feels like anymore. Sure, you know what "very thirsty" feels like, but most of us regularly miss the earlier signs that we need to stop for a moment and drink some water. If you miss the first signs, the body does exactly what it is supposed to do: it sends a stronger message. Maybe your mouth gets dry or you begin to feel a bit lethargic. As you continue to miss the body's messages, it will keep sending louder and louder signals until finally something happens that stops you in your tracks and forces you to hydrate. You might get a headache, or worse, a migraine. If you have ever had the misfortune of having a migraine headache, you know that this qualifies as something that stops you in your tracks. It's much better to hear the body's warning signals early rather than get into your version of a migraine.

The best drinking water comes from natural springs and artesian wells. If you cannot access it directly, have it delivered to your house, in glass bottles if possible. Plastic can leach into the water and has a bigger environmental footprint than glass. If you are living in a city and prefer to drink filtered water, definitely get a great filter to treat your tap water to remove chlorine and other harmful chemicals. At the end of the day, while we are very fortunate to have relatively clean drinking water at all, we might as well choose the best water we can and stay away from environmental toxins whenever possible, as they add to the burden our body must manage.

I also want to encourage you to begin to look at hydration in terms of water *and* salt. Many people think, *Whoa now! Salt? Don't we already get enough of it?* Well, what we usually consume as table salt has been mined, stripped of its natural chemicals, and reformed to make a tightly bound kind of salt that is much less healthful and bioavailable than salt in its natural form. The best salt to consume is pure rock salt mined from pristine environments. Examples are Himalayan pink salt or Celtic sea salt. So every day, I take just a pinch of salt and put it in the water I am drinking. This helps hydrate me properly. Please note: you should always check with your physician first before making any dietary changes, especially if you have weight- or salt-imbalance issues.

Another wonderful practice is to begin each day with a glass of water with some organic lemon juice squeezed in it. This is a great way to flush the digestive tract and reboot the digestive system for its day ahead.

CAFFEINE AND BEING TIRED

When you feel tired, it's the body's way of saying that it needs to rest and rejuvenate. If you listen to the request, you allow your body-mind system to rest and utilize the amazing talents of your parasympathetic nervous system, the part of your nervous system that repairs and rejuvenates your cells and all the systems of your body. Most of the time, you are in your sympathetic nervous system, which is your get-up-and-go, get-it-done, fight-or-flight response to the world. The body cannot fully repair itself in this mode, nor can it find true rest and relaxation. What do most people do when they get a signal from the body that they are tired? Do they rest? Nope. They drink some form of caffeine, often with some type of sugar included.

When you consume caffeine and sugar, your heart rate and respiration increase, your adrenal glands fire, and your nervous system stays locked in fight-or-flight. This is called burning the candle at both ends. You are literally exhausting yourself, further preventing your body from healing itself and relaxing. What happens next? All kinds of things, actually. You become irritable and uncomfortable. Your thinking becomes less clear and less effective. You become more susceptible to stress, and ever more tired. Your energy is off. Your energetic defenses are down. You become attuned to the Frequency of Addiction. Of course, you can still sleep, but since you've been drinking a lot of caffeine during the day, you won't sleep as well as you should. Your nervous system is unable to let go. And the terrible cycle goes on and on. This is important for people in recovery from addiction to understand.

All the people I work with and observe in early recovery have a problem with caffeine. They drink coffee, tea, sodas, and energy drinks such as Red Bull and Monster. I cringe when I see addicts downing these drinks. I know they're setting themselves up to remain in the Frequency of Addiction for yet another day. Usually they don't realize what they're doing. They want the rush and the energy, which aren't yet available to them naturally because they're healing from drug addiction of one kind or another. So they go after the energy drinks and they wonder why they aren't feeling much better after a while, even though they have put down their drugs of choice.

When I make the following suggestion in retreats and workshops, there is usually an outcry. Nonetheless, here it is: Take 30 days off from all caffeine. Keep a journal of your reflections during this time. If you do this, you may be surprised to find how well you have been sleeping and how much more relaxed you feel. You may not want to return to your caffeine-drinking days. If you do, though, most importantly, write down in your journal how you feel once you resume drinking caffeine. These reflections, based on your own personal experience, will help you figure out whether there's a place for caffeine in your life. I can tell you from years of personal experience that I am better and happier without it. Furthermore, when I do drink caffeine, I'm not great at controlling my intake of it. Hmmm. I wonder why that is . . .

SUGAR: THE REAL GATEWAY DRUG

Sugar is a highly addictive, mind-altering substance. One of the most widely used sugar substitutes, high-fructose corn syrup, is also addictive and comes largely from genetically modified corn, creating potentially more danger than we currently know of. Here's a disturbing fact: 50 years ago, the average American consumed about 20 pounds of sugar and corn sweetener in a year. That number has now risen to over 130 pounds per year.[2] Overconsumption of sugar leads to many health problems, including heart disease, type 2 diabetes, and obesity. How is it not clear that our consumption of sugar and corn sweetener is a part of that? You've heard the story of my childhood, which I've described as "bouncing off the walls from one sugar event to the next." Well, this followed me into my adulthood, and it wasn't really until my first major cleanse at 35 years old that I was able to break through it and begin to operate on a different level where sugar and food in general were concerned.

I also believe overconsumption of sugar leads to other diseases and addictions. For example, I've noticed a direct connection between strep throat and sugar intake. If I eat a bunch of crap with sugar in it, I have, at times, gotten that terrible feeling in the back of my throat. Can't swallow, very painful. In my childhood, I took antibiotics for this, weakening my system even further. I remember the first time I beat strep throat by treating the condition myself with plant-based medicines and healthy food: removing all sugar from my diet, taking herbs, drinking medicinal teas, and using pure oregano oil. It was a revelation. It showed me something about the detrimental effects of sugar and my body's ability to heal if given the chance.

Over the past few years, I have done well by avoiding refined sugar and processed food. I eat lots of vegetables and salads and drink lots of juices. When I want to, I use organic honey or maple syrup, which are certainly high on the glycemic index but much healthier alternatives to white cane sugar. Sometimes I have a dessert, but it is pretty rare. I just don't need these things to be happy, and I am past feeling like I'm depriving myself of something by not eating them. I am so excited by the idea of health, living as well as possible, and helping others to do the same that it is actually less and less enjoyable to eat something that isn't good for me.

Now and then I'll "go there," and my friends like to poke fun at me when I do. Recently, someone brought a box of Krispy Kreme donuts to a party at my home. I knew the minute that box came through my door that I was going to have one of those donuts. I said a prayer and went in! I took in the starch, fat, and sugar. I went through the initial joy, which gave way to a sugar crash and, ultimately, a slight headache and hangover. I felt like I had done something to my system that was low-grade "uncool." Not really a big deal—nothing to feel guilty or shameful over! *But* also not something I'd like to get in the habit of. *And it's the strangest thing: for a while after having that donut, my mind chatter around donuts, cookies, and pumpkin pie increased. I noticed I was thinking more about sugar, and my sugar consumption had gone up a bit. The way out of this for me is always to start drinking green juices and return my body to a more alkaline state so the cravings will go away.*

I can hear the voices of certain friends who really like their sweets saying, "What is wrong with having a donut? Tommy, you've taken this a bit too far." For people who feel that way, maybe there is nothing wrong with having a donut, or 20 of them. For me, the second my mind kicks in and starts to work on me, driving me toward addictive behaviors, I know I need to pay attention.

Your food decisions can open or close doors for you. Make the connection between the food you eat and the way you feel. One's mental and physical health are adversely affected by overconsumption of sugar. Eating addictive foods is related to the development of addictive thinking and the neurotic behaviors that result.

As I just mentioned, the way to beat these sugar-fueled cravings and addictive behaviors is to lead your body toward alkalinity.

THE ADDICT'S QUEST FOR ALKALINITY

Human beings in general reach for processed plants, such as coffee and sugar-filled foods, to feel better. Drug addicts and alcoholics, being more desperate than the rest of the population to feel better, really go after the processed plants. Sugar, beer, wine, gin, vodka, tequila, whisky, marijuana, LSD, cocaine, methamphetamine, and heroin all derive from plants. In each case the plant-based source of these drugs is modified, processed, or engineered in such a way as to deliver a very powerful form of what the plant would normally deliver if ingested under natural circumstances. To chew on coca leaves, for example, produces quite a different effect from snorting cocaine. Addicts can take this even further by processing cocaine into freebase or crack. Processing is necessary in some cases. When it comes to the opiate family, we are very grateful to have access to processed forms of opium such as morphine when it's needed for traumatic injuries and operative procedures, but when it comes to addiction, opiates have the power to kill.

The point is that, as addicts, we erroneously reach for processed plants to find the means by which we can attain balance.

When I was mired in drug addiction, the more desperate I got, the more I needed processed plants—in my case cocaine and heroin. I was frantically trying to create balance in my body-mind system. Ironically, in order to speed up detox, restore health to the systems of the body, and recover fully from addiction, plants in their natural states play a big role. Let's explore this.

There is a connection between acidity in the body and disease. Acidity is caused by a diet that is rich in sugar, processed foods, and overconsumption of grains and meats. The mineral content of these foods has high amounts of sulfur and phosphorous, which are very acidic. So we need to bring in vegetables and herbs, which are high in alkaline minerals such as calcium and magnesium, to swing things back from a more acidic state toward balance. If you eat alkalizing foods that make you feel good, energized, and vital, you will have less of a reason to reach out for something to make you feel better. If you eat food that makes you feel bloated, lethargic, sleepy, and sick, you will have even more reason to reach out for something to try to feel better. You should eat with the understanding that it is going to have a big effect on the rest of your life in very tangible ways, especially if you are in recovery from addiction.

GREEN JUICE AND RECOVERY

In the same Recovery 2.0 interview I previously referenced, I asked David Wolfe what he would suggest to help a person who had just detoxed from heroin. What David said confirmed my own personal experience and has now opened up a whole new area of focus for me in my work with people who are struggling with addiction. First, David stressed the importance of cleansing and detox, that the colon and liver need to be encouraged to drop their toxic load. He emphasized drinking fresh vegetable juices and blended soups. Then David said something that just blew my mind: "There are opiates present in the entire lettuce family. Poppies are part of that family. When someone is addicted to opiates such as heroin, they are actually craving the soporific compounds that are in the lettuce family. So what I would do with a heroin addict is I'd get them drinking lettuce juice. Because that has the natural soporific compounds in the right balance the way nature has intended it." My personal experience with juicing and cleansing validates this critical perspective that David has put forth. Drinking juice made from organic vegetables has a calming effect, lessens cravings, and can be a powerful ally on your recovery path.

For recovering addicts (and everyone) I advocate the commencement of a daily juicing regimen to get fresh, organic, mineral-dense, alkalizing vegetable juice into the cells of your body. I believe that if you do nothing else and make no other changes in your approach to food, adding 16 to 64 ounces of organic green juice to your daily diet will make a big difference to you. Plants have intelligence, which you are taking in. They are packed with nutrients and alkalizing minerals. A 16-ounce green juice contains the distilled nutrition from a huge quantity of vegetables and is highly bioavailable to your cells without your body having to work hard to break it down. Green juice is an ally on the path.

These ideas are relatively new. I am not suggesting that putting addicts on a juice cleanse will cure them of their addictions. I am saying that plant-based nutrition holds part of the answer. It is relatively easy to implement and inexpensive relative to medical costs, and it has as-yet-unrecognized potential to help with detoxification and the promise of long-term recovery.

"CLEANSING" AS PART OF RECOVERY

As you know, I went on a 30-day digestive tract cleanse that I credit as one of the main factors in the healing of chronic back pain. I believe that cleansing can be of profound benefit to people in recovery from addiction, and I advocate implementing an annual cleanse, with a few key understandings and exceptions. Cleanses are to be done with professional supervision, usually in groups. Doing them well takes knowledge and experience, especially coming off a cleanse and returning to a more normal regimen.

Cleansing is contraindicated for people who struggle with anorexia, bulimia, and other food-control issues. For these folks, "controlling" their intake of food in the manner that a cleanse requires can be triggering for their addiction and dangerous.

NUTRITION IN TODAY'S RECOVERY ENVIRONMENT

The role of plants in today's recovery environment is virtually ignored. Primary treatment for drug addiction and alcoholism focuses mostly on the cognitive behavioral aspects of addiction. Typical treatment protocols for recovering addicts include individual and group therapy sessions, 12-Step meetings, professionally guided self-reflection, and writing. We are beginning to see some yoga and other mind-body offerings in a few rehab facilities. All these things are important aspects of treating addiction. However, I am not yet aware of any addiction treatment facility that uses the healing power of food—plant-based nutrition in particular—in its programs.

Overall, the food served at treatment centers is off target, from the sodas and chips one can buy in vending machines to the lack of organic, nutrient-dense foods or juices that would help with detoxification and rejuvenation. When it comes to employing the healing power of food, there is a big missed opportunity in our current treatment of addiction.

Furthermore, diet in 12-Step culture is thought of as an "outside issue" and therefore is not discussed openly. We see that coffee and sweets are the things people have at meetings. It's a part of the culture that unfortunately contributes to addiction, though the behavior is obviously so much less destructive than what was going on before. My point here is that caffeine is an addictive substance that can keep an addict in the Frequency of Addiction and prolong suffering. People who struggle with addiction would be able to make a lot more progress if they were willing and able to put down the coffee and sugar. Of course, to suggest such a thing at a 12-Step meeting would set off a riot, similar to how smokers reacted to bans on smoking in public places a decade or so ago.

I find healing, joy, and love in most of the food I eat. Previously, I mostly found dis-ease. That's a big transformation, and it is available for you, too. You want to be taking things into your body that increase your vitality and health. You want to eat foods with the greatest amount of life force in them that take the least amount of energy to digest. Each person will have to make up his or her mind about what is and isn't healthful. Ask yourself before you eat: Is this food good for me? Is it going to give me energy and vitality? Is it going to promote or demote my health? Will it contribute to my addiction or to my recovery? As Guruprem has said to me many a time, "If your food does not speak to you, don't eat it."

CHAPTER 19

DISCOVERING YOUR MISSION AND LIVING IN SERVICE

You need three things to reach any goal—desire, direction, and discipline. You have to have them all. Two of them will not cut it.

Desire here is not a simple desire: "I think I'd like to do this." No. When I say *desire*, I mean a heartfelt desire. It comes from your heart and connects with your soul's purpose. "I *really* want this. I think about it often. I would be great at it if I were to get my chance, and it thrills me to imagine myself achieving this thing."

I mentioned that when I was younger, I wanted to be able to catch a fly ball in the outfield. For months I tried but couldn't get it. When a fly ball came my way, I positioned myself as I thought I should, got my mitt ready—and missed it. I lacked direction. Direction comes from teachers: people who have been where you are and have acquired a skill you'd like to acquire. Teachers have the desire to help you because it feeds their souls' longing to uplift and elevate the people they come across who need help. Everything I've gotten has come from a teacher of some kind. Finding a great teacher means you're ready to receive great direction. For me, it was a camp counselor who had played baseball. He took me under his wing. He showed me how to judge the flight of the ball, how to hold my glove, and how to use both of my hands. I listened intently and began to put into practice the things he taught me. I showed discipline.

The root of the word *discipline—disciple*—means "student of" or "follower of." I became a disciple of the good direction I received. The desired result came quickly. Within three days of learning what to do, a fly ball came my way. I put out my mitt and caught it using both hands. It was probably not the prettiest catch, but my spirit nearly leapt out of my body, I was so excited. I continued to practice and became an expert. I have played baseball and softball throughout my life and still find it thrilling to chase down a ball in left field.

This brings up an important point about discipline. The flip side of discipline is joy. At first, being a "student of" may be a tedious process. Guruprem tells the story of how he learned the piano. He had to face what every musician has had to: the tedium of scales and fundamentals. His teacher had him do scales for a long time. He also practiced pieces of music, but scales were the focus. One day the teacher simply said to him, "Now just play." He was able to play music and got to experience the joy that came from his many months of discipline. So many joyful experiences in life await us on the other side of discipline.

Many people have missed opportunities because they were unwilling or unable to show up as a "student of" long enough for joy to show itself on the other side. For some reason, this is a real plague for addicts. Many of us just cannot complete things that require discipline over time. Part of the reason is that we are stuck in the Four Aggravations, especially procrastination and self-doubt. Nonetheless, in our recovery we find the support and resources to do things that would have been impossible otherwise.

What happens when we have direction and discipline but lack heartfelt desire? When your heart is not in it, you cannot find true success in your pursuits. It will feel as if you are swimming upstream . . . like all the time. You will be stressed because you know at some level that what you are doing is not right for you. Human beings have been trying to learn this lesson for many millennia. It is a classic pitfall. Since at least the *Bhagavad Gita* and *Oedipus Rex*, the idea that we must live our own unique destiny and the message "know thyself" have been well expressed. When we go down the road of living for someone else or seeking the approval of others, we have to pay a price. Usually we struggle for a while and then fail to achieve our goal. Occasionally, though, someone will go after "it" with great zeal and through focus and willpower they will achieve "success" even though their heart is not in it. What happens then?

Have you ever known anyone (perhaps you) who has gone after something to seek the approval of parents, other family members, or peers even though it is out of alignment with their own calling? You may not realize you are out of alignment at first. You may design your entire life around the idea that if you get to achieve your goal, you will then be happy.

A dear friend of mine had come from a conservative, well-off family and set his sights on becoming a successful banker. He really went after it and, to his credit, he "succeeded." He made huge deals and had a lot of money, a wife, the house, the cars, all the trappings. There was one trapping missing, however: contentment. Inside, something was nagging him. He was out of alignment with his heart. Even though he had reached the goal he set out to reach, he realized that he would have to change the course of his life or give up the idea of ever finding fulfillment. My friend is an amazing man. He was able to learn the lessons he needed in order to proceed on his heart's path. Humbling himself, he talked to many people and asked for help. He changed his career and the focus of his life. He and his wife got divorced, and some years later he married a woman who was exceptionally right. They have three incredible children. Their lives are examples of the blessings that are bestowed upon us if only we learn and then choose to live from our heart.

YOUR PERSONAL MISSION

Writing a personal mission statement is a great idea to help get you onto your path of destiny and structure your life to be its most fulfilling. Please take the time to write one. Your personal mission has to do with your heart's desires as well as your talents. What do you love to do? What are you good at? If you do not know the answer to these two questions, do not despair. Your mission will then be to find your mission—and that in itself is a great mission. If you are in early recovery, it makes sense that you may not be clear on where you fit into the grand scheme of things. For right now, your personal mission might be to get to a meeting and stay sober today. That is an excellent mission. As you move forward in your recovery and life, you will need a job so you have a place to live, food to eat, and the ability to pay your bills, but also so you can engage with life. As you develop further from this point, a sense of longing sometimes shows up. You've always wanted to start a business or write a book or cut an album or become a licensed drug and alcohol counselor. You have no idea how such a thing could be possible but there it is in your heart (and now your mind), yearning to be born in the physical world. How will you go about it? Where will you seek direction? Will you demonstrate the discipline to apply the direction you find?

I believe most people have not found their mission and purpose. I believe this is a cause of great suffering. It certainly was in my life. Not knowing what to do leads to not feeling useful. Not feeling useful leads to feelings of worthlessness and frustration. Powerlessness rears its head. I have felt so depressed at times around this issue. It is very important that people in recovery work consciously on this piece of their lives as soon as they are able. This will come at different times for different folks. When you are solid in your recovery and you feel a longing for greater usefulness, it may be time to work on getting clear on your mission and to get busy aligning with your heart, which is linked to your Higher Power. Once you make a commitment to your path of destiny, you will note that the strangest and most supportive things start to take place. That powerless feeling will be replaced by flow and ease. At first, you get sober and that is enough. Later, as a result of your commitment to a path of recovery, with desire, direction, and discipline you will grow into a person who is satisfied because you are on purpose and on mission. At that point, you might remark, "I would not go back to my addictive way of life even if I could get away with it." Now, *that's* what I'm talking about!

RECOVERY 2.0: A CASE STUDY

The following case study of a person's path from addiction to recovery is the best example I can give of why I believe Recovery 2.0 is so important.

On a fortunate day in October 2012, I met Matt, who had been living as a heroin addict on and off for many years and had been on the street for several months. His body was filled with infections, some of which had erupted in the form of painful abscesses on his butt and legs. His life force was very low. I believe that he was close to an unnecessary and tragic death. He had a good heart, though, and a bright smile when it showed up. He stood out to me in bold print as a brother who had lost his way but could have an exceptional life if only he could get beyond addiction.

Over lunch and two subsequent meetings, I spoke with Matt as the 12 Steps, therapy, and life have taught me to do. By some stroke of grace, Matt was able to hear it. The door to hope and possibility opened just the tiniest amount, but it was enough for him to embrace the idea that it might be time to kick heroin again.

On the Internet, I found a sober-living home run by an exceptional person, himself an ex–heroin addict with several years of recovery under his belt. Matt and I went to meet him to see if he would accept Matt into his sober-living home. I sat back and observed as this guy, covered head to toe in tattoos and with long dark hair and rocker clothing, lovingly, calmly, eloquently described to Matt how it could work for him to live in this home as soon as he could present himself detoxed off heroin and pass a piss test. Matt's parents, who had suffered his antics for the past ten years, agreed—with some trepidation—to take yet another risk on their son and cover the rent. The enduring love of family is one part of the puzzle that helps a person get sober if the blessed moment arrives. *But* many families can attest to the sad, hard fact that not everyone gets to have the gift of recovery.

This meeting was on a Wednesday, and all Matt would have to do was show up on Monday detoxed and sober. It was a long shot! I took him to a motel near my home where I could easily check up on him through the weekend. He had a small room with a shower, TV, water—it was a good setup compared to how he had been living—but he would be without his precious dope. And so his ordeal of kicking heroin began.

Every day was a bit nerve-racking for me, as it always is. I care too much to not get a bit strung out emotionally myself. Each day is a constant prayer: "God, please help this guy to find peace and recovery. Please help him get through this weekend. Please do everything you can for him."

I brought him some food, though he didn't eat much. He mostly slept. Maybe we'd walk around the block. I'd go home and Kia would ask how he was doing and I'd tell her, "I have no idea if he is actually sober, but he seems to be okay." Later, Matt would tell me that he used crack cocaine and heroin that first night and then actually began his kick the next day. Of course, there is nothing surprising about that. What is very surprising is that when Matt presented himself at the sober-living home on Monday, or it might have been Tuesday, he was reasonably detoxed and legitimately passed the piss test.

I saw Matt every day for those first months. As we all do, he needed a near-constant reminder that everything was going to be all right, that there was hope, and that life was going to get not just better but really good. Each day was a victory. We worked through the first few steps together. Matt had a lot of willingness. He did what I suggested, but not without a regular questioning process.

I might say, "I suggest you start to hit an AA meeting every day."

Matt would reply, "Every day? Well, you mean for right now, right? I'm not always going to have to do that. You *get* that, right?"

Or I would suggest, "You know, Matt, sometime you may want to give up smoking and drinking coffee."

"I don't really see that happening. Tommy, I don't want to be some fucking pure, happy person. Okay?" he would respond.

In actuality, Matt hated coffee. He winced every time he choked back his quadruple espresso. He didn't love smoking either, but it was something to do in the absence of anything else. He hung out around other folks who were smoking to pass the time. Somehow, he had gotten it into his head that he needed to do these things. The truth is that, like all addicts, he wanted to be impacted, hit hard by something. Addicts are used to the impact chemicals deliver. This is why it is so important to deliver impact to people in early sobriety, just not the same impact they have been used to. Matt needed to be inspired along a path that would give him that hit of something weighty that also would deliver health, strength, vitality, and self-confidence. He needed to be turned on to yoga and learn to sweat it out in conscious awareness of body and breath. How would this happen?

There were a few hurdles to Matt changing his lifestyle. For one thing, he slept late. He would happily sleep till noon or later any day. The rules in the sober-living home were that you had to be up by 9 A.M. whether you had something to do or not. It is fair to say this rubbed Matt the wrong way. On any given day when he had no responsibilities, he could not understand why he had to get up. He could not yet grasp the idea that getting up in the morning, facing the day, and engaging with life was going to be helpful to him and, more to the point, joyous.

Despite his sometimes challenging attitude, his consumption of cigarettes and coffee, and his love affair with being asleep, Matt started to heal from acute drug addiction. The magic of the 12 Steps, one ex-addict helping another addict, delivered on its promise. Matt got a month sober, then two, and then three. He struggled in the Frequency of Addiction. Each day this manifested as he continued to smoke and drink excessive amounts of coffee and energy drinks. This, of course, affected his energy, mood, and general outlook on life.

When Matt was five months sober, I presented him with a proposition: "If you are willing, I will pay for you to participate in my wife's week-long Kundalini Yoga and juice cleanse program." This was just intense enough for Matt, and I could see him get excited.

"What would I have to do?" he asked.

"Well, you will have to give up caffeine, stop smoking, limit your food intake to the daily juices we provide you, and one more thing . . . you'll have to be at the yoga studio at seven sharp every morning."

Matt tilted his head back and blurted out, "Man, that would be incredible. Can I do that? Would I be able to do that? What would that be like?"

Matt committed to the plan and, sure enough, showed up on time every day for yoga and stuck to his juices, quit smoking, and quit all caffeine. As I write this a year has passed and I am pleased to report in with the following update: Matt is still continuously sober. He is still smoke free. He likes his caffeine in tea form now. He practices yoga three to four times a week and goes to meetings three to four times a week. He has adopted a mostly vegetarian diet. He has learned to play the guitar, has been writing music, and is about to cut his first album. He is not sure exactly what his mission is to be, so he is working on that each day. In the meantime, he has a job to support himself. In short, his life is pure gold. Is he still vulnerable to relapse? Of course! Like all of us, he must work his program one day at a time to live in the Frequency of Recovery. The point is that he has Recovery 2.0 at one year sober. I didn't find it for 12 years. In Matt's own words:

> Experiencing this healing has enabled me to have a totally different perspective on dealing with the outside world and all the stresses that go along with that. My coping skills have increased exponentially, and that is a big reason I am able to

stay sober. There also has been a snowball effect with these practices. The deeper I get into my healing, the deeper I want to go and help others do the same. I have truly been transformed in every sense of the word. Mind, body, spirit. I am so grateful to have come across these teachings and will be reaping the benefits of them for the rest of my life. All I had to do was be willing to find out what resonated with me and then be willing to practice discipline in exploring it further.

THE POWER OF PURPOSE

I have been happiest at those times in my life when I have felt a sense of devotion to a *purpose* greater than myself. The hardest times were those points when I had no clue why I was here and how I fit into the scheme of things. This is true of human beings in general; we thrive with a sense of purpose. It is therefore not a surprise that the happiest people I know in recovery are the people who are pursuing their mission and live in service to others—just as many of us found when we experienced the desire to help others in our own recovery.

Living in service is a state of mind. It happens everywhere you are. Doing specific service work for others is powerful and transformative, but service work also takes place in homes, with families and friends, and in the workplace. I believe that when you find your mission, opportunities to be of service to others will present themselves anywhere you are. Interestingly, as you move down the spiritual path toward greater awareness, you will become more available and open to being of service than before. You will begin to look at all of life and ask, "What can I add here? How can I contribute?"

I believe that the essence of recovery is service to others. That is key. The final step on the path, the bodhisattva's vow, is to return again and again to help others transcend suffering. We extend a hand to another person to help them get past their acute addiction. We offer our time and our heart and our love. We also must stand as an example of victory. Not arrogantly, but simply to let others know that there is somewhere to go that is much better than where they may be at that moment.

It is my mission to help as many people as possible with Recovery 2.0, which today consists of an expanding global community of about 60,000 people. The community comes together each year around two online conferences, a variety of retreats, workshops, classes, and festivals.

For the near future, I envision holistic treatment centers, online educational tools for people in recovery, 2.0 clubhouses, and a global network of people walking the holistic path of recovery from addiction.

Addicts are extraordinary people with great sensitivity, passion, and enthusiasm. We have all experienced the results of our efforts focused toward the dark side. If we were to embrace the light, imagine what we could do. There are tens of millions of us in the U.S. alone. If we continually move forward on our unique evolutionary paths, we will find our true identity and our purpose on the road to the light of our own hearts.

CONCLUSION

You will remember that at my workshops I ask people if they struggle with addiction in any form. After I explain the Big Six addictions and then the Four Aggravations, there is often someone who is still hanging tough. "I can see how those aggravations are harmful, but everyone has them. I don't think I'd run to the next 12-Step meeting because I sometimes procrastinate or I'm resentful toward my boss. I don't see myself struggling with addiction in any way."

My response is always this: "Well, you may not be struggling with the Big Six, and you may not be stuck in the Four Aggravations, but you certainly are caught up in the most prevalent addiction in the world—the addiction to the belief that we are separate from each other, from the entire universe, and that our individual actions do not affect the whole."

This belief of separateness underlies and fuels the Four Aggravations and all the addictions and problems of our world. Our misperception of the interconnected nature of reality is responsible for war, famine, poverty, and disease. It is the main addiction we must all face if we are going to bring about true recovery and peace for all. Dr. Martin Luther King, Jr., wrote, "It really boils down to this: that all life is interrelated. We are all caught in an inescapable network of mutuality, tied into a single garment of destiny. Whatever affects one directly, affects all indirectly."¹ It starts with the individual. It starts with you.

At your core, you are not a drug addict, nor are you an alcoholic. You are not a compulsive overeater or gambler. You are not a codependent. You are not a sex addict. These may be behaviors you have chosen to help you along through difficulty, but these are not the truth of who you are. You are not meant to remain an addict. That is not your destiny, but you could make choices to make it your fate.

I believe you are a divine being. It makes no difference where you have been or what you have done. There is *Spirit* inside you as there is in everything in the universe. You are connected to everything through the Spirit, which lives in you. It makes your heart beat. It gives you your breath. Some refer to it as God, the Supreme Being, Great Spirit, the Universe, the Divine, or Higher Power. Others do not know how to refer to it or prefer not to refer to it at all.

Whatever your beliefs, if you are stuck in addiction, you have been chosen for something. You may think, *This is horrible, I cannot seem to get out of this. When will the pain stop?* And yet, the pain is there to help you see something that, once seen, will end up being your currency for transformation. It will be the thing you look back upon and say, "That was a turning point for me. Something happened there. I was a certain way before that time and then after I came through it, I was different."

If you have ever had one single thought that you wanted something more for your life, please heed that thought. I believe it is the voice of your own heart asking you to become whole again. Yogi Bhajan said, "Creation is ready to serve you if you just be you. Please take away the ghost of your life and stop chasing around. Consolidate. Concentrate. Be you!"

Please understand that the powers of the Universe are constructing something beautiful. It takes time for these constructions to unfold. Hang in there, get support, move toward love, *always move toward love,* and you will soon enough find that you are in a new place. Though perhaps it's far different from where you thought you wanted to be, you will be able to see the elegance of the design that was created for you, even though before it had remained hidden and required your faith.

Thousands of years ago, through extensive meditations, the ancient yogis beheld the truth of our reality. This great truth has been passed down through scripture and from teacher to student ever since. It has been like a road map for me to understand my place in the world as a human being.

There is only One Source of all creation, from which all has manifested. Its identity is Truth. Your spiritual identity is also Truth. That part of you has never been born and it will never die. We are inseparable from the Creative Source and from each other. Knowing this brings indescribable bliss . . .

. . . And everything else is just your story.

May you stay on the path of recovery and experience a life beyond addiction. May you answer the call of your destiny and uplift others to do the same. May we share love with each other and may all beings be free.

Sending Love and Strength to you,

Tommy Rosen

APPENDIX A:
THREE GAME-CHANGING
BREATH EXERCISES

The more we are aware of our breath and its importance, the closer we will be to *ease* and the further we will be from the dis-ease of addiction. This is a simple lesson that is powerful enough to combat addiction and change the world. How is this possible?

All addiction comes from a sense of lack, a core feeling that something is missing. And when we feel this lack subconscious-ly or consciously, we tend to breathe poorly. Ironically, when we breathe poorly, we inadvertently send a signal to every cell in our body that, in fact, our most core need for Prana, or life force, is not being met. There is a lack. Every part of our being picks up this sig-nal, and it creates a pattern of tension. Since people who struggle with addictions usually breathe poorly, they tend to reinforce the underlying sense of lack with every shallow or rushed breath they take. In yoga practice, as we begin to pay closer attention to the breath and apply techniques that help us to deepen it, we send a new signal to the mind-body that communicates a sense of whole-ness. This begins the process of true recovery, and it is one of the most powerful ways we can stack the odds in our favor against relapsing into destructive patterns.

*The three breath exercises you find here are game changers.** Put aside any preconceived notions about what you think will heal you, and put your focus on learning to breathe like an expert. You can do these exercises as often as you like—they will never let you down! Ideally, they will become a regular part of your daily routine. If they do, in the not-too-distant future, you just might find yourself living the life you've always wanted. *Do not fall prey to the negative thought that this is too simple to be effective.*

PLEASE NOTE: In these exercises and unless otherwise specified in yoga practice, we will breathe in and out through the nose only.

BREATH EXERCISE #1: THREE-PART BREATH

Part 1: The High-Rent District of the Lungs

Sit up tall and cross-legged (Easy Pose), and place both your hands on your stomach. If Easy Pose does not feel so easy, please feel free to sit up in a chair with your feet flat on the floor. Here we have to get rid of the cultural impulse to pull our stomachs in. Why do we pull our stomachs in all the time and create tension there? It is because we believe on some level that to have a flat, toned belly will bring us the right guy or the right girl or the right something. Please take a break from that nonsensical fantasy.

Allow yourself to fully relax so that your belly spills into your hands. Really release your abdomen completely. Adopt a positive attitude right now. Regardless of how big or small your belly is, tell yourself how grateful you are to be on a path to greater health. Enjoy the feeling of relaxing.

Take a deep inhale through your nose, focusing it down to the bottom of your lungs, so that your belly naturally presses out into your hands. It will press out because your abdomen will expand as

---

* You can practice these exercises along with me on any of my DVDs, available on my website, tommyrosen.com.

air enters your lungs unless you breathe exclusively up into your chest, which we want to avoid here. Pause for 2 seconds at the top of your inhale. Experience the feeling of being filled with oxygen and Prana. Exhale slowly and completely, again through your nose, pulling your navel point in to squeeze all the air out of your lungs. Pause here with empty lungs for 2 seconds. Experience the feeling of being empty. Inhale again, focusing on the bottom of your lungs so that your abdomen once again expands, pressing out into your hands. Pause at the top of your inhale for 2 seconds and again exhale completely, pulling your navel point in to squeeze the last bit of air out of your lungs. Pause at the bottom of your exhale for 2 seconds.

Repeat this breath 10 times, and then sit quietly with your eyes closed.

PLEASE NOTE: You may feel a little light-headed as you breathe in this way because you are taking more oxygen into your lungs *and* to the lower lungs than you are used to. The lower lungs are great real estate—the high-rent district. There are more capillaries there, which translates into more oxygen entering your bloodstream. You are also regulating your breath and therefore changing your regular rhythm and sense of things.

Part 2: Getting Out of Jail Free—Breathing into the Mid-Lungs

Since most folks do not know how to breathe, they live in "thoracic incarceration," which simply means that the tightness of their rib cage literally prevents them from taking a deep breath. In order to get a full breath, we have to breathe into our mid-lungs and generate the force to expand our rib cage outward and upward.

Still sitting in Easy Pose, place your hands on your ribs at the side of your body. First, inhale through your nose downward into your lower lungs, as you just practiced. Continue your inhale so that your ribs expand outward, pressing into your hands. In the first exercise you focused only on your belly expanding; now we are focused on the expansion of both the belly (lower lungs) and the ribs (mid-lungs). Pause again at the top of your breath for 2 seconds, noticing how your ribs have expanded. Exhale all the air through your nose, and gently draw your ribs and navel point in. Pause for 2 seconds at the bottom of the exhale, and then begin another cycle of breath. (You might not immediately be able to control the flow of air into different parts of your lungs. With practice, you will quickly notice your progress.)

Repeat this breath 10 times, inhaling and exhaling completely. If you become slightly light-headed, take a few long and deep breaths until you feel grounded again.

Part 3: Filling Up the Cup—Adding the Upper Lungs

Sit up tall in Easy Pose with your hands on your knees, palms face up and your thumbs and forefingers touching. Through your nose, inhale ⅓ of your breath to your lower lungs, feeling your belly expand. Pause momentarily. Inhale the next ⅓ of your breath to your mid-lungs, feeling your ribs expand. Pause momentarily. Inhale the final ⅓ of your breath to your upper lungs, feeling the expansion all the way up under your collarbone. Pause momentarily. Notice how lifted you are. Your heart is lifted, your chest is open, and your shoulders are drawn back and relaxed. Keeping this sense of lift, exhale slowly so that all the air leaves your body. Remember to pull your navel point in to squeeze the last bit of air out before beginning your next inhale.

Repeat this wonderful breath 10 times. Again, you may feel light-headed here because you are breathing into the full capacity of your lungs for the first time in a long while, perhaps for the first time ever. These breaths are nourishing. They bring more oxygen into the body, and that is a very good thing. Where there is steady flow of oxygen in the body, there is health and comfort and *ease!*

Three-Part Breath has many applications in recovery from addiction. It expands lung capacity and exercises the diaphragm to keep it fit and functioning. It sets a calm and balanced tone for the day and can help us deal with anxiety and stress anytime we have to face them. It also strengthens the habit of using an internal control mechanism to manage our thoughts, feelings, and reactions to life.

This breath shows you where your power lies. Often in recovery we speak about our powerlessness. Once we learn to use our breath to change our mood and elevate ourselves, we will never have to reach outside ourselves for a pill, or a him or a her, or a this or a that. We have the power to change the way we feel.

BREATH EXERCISE #2: LONG DEEP BREATHING

Once you have become familiar with Three-Part Breath, you can remove the pauses between each section of breathing to experience what is referred to as Long Deep Breathing.

Sit up tall in Easy Pose with your palms face up on your knees and your thumb and forefinger touching. Close your eyes, and bring your focus to the third-eye point between your eyebrows. Releasing all tension from your abdomen, inhale through your nose so that the first part of your breath travels all the way to the bottom of your lungs, pressing your belly out. Continue this breath so that you feel your ribs expanding outward. With your shoulders drawn slightly back and your heart lifted, let the air fill your upper lungs so that the area under your collarbone expands. Pause for a split second at the top of the breath and, keeping the lift in your heart, begin to exhale gently and steadily. Toward the end of your exhale, draw your navel point in toward your spine to squeeze the last bit of air out so that your next inhale can be as full as possible. Pause for a split second at the bottom of your exhale. Continue this breath for 3 minutes. Open your eyes after 3 minutes and bask in the sense of calmness that comes with breathing well.

BREATH EXERCISE #3: BREATH OF FIRE

This is one of the most powerful breaths in all of yoga. It is used frequently in Kundalini Yoga and has played a prominent role in my own recovery. It is one of the main practices I used to heal my back and to excel physically and mentally. It strengthens your core, increases your lung capacity, detoxes the cells of your body, and gives you great energy.

Once you have some experience with Three-Part Breath and Long Deep Breathing, you are ready to try Breath of Fire, a breathing exercise that is powered by abdominal contractions, which provides a great workout for your diaphragm and lungs. Breath of Fire is often likened to pumping a bellows. It does not take much effort and should not be a strain. Your shoulders, neck, and chest should feel relaxed all the way through.

To do Breath of Fire, sit down cross-legged or in a chair, if you prefer. Inhale through your nose. When you come to the top of your inhale, exhale as you draw your navel point firmly toward your spine. Then release your abdominal muscles and allow your belly to expand as your next inhale comes in passively. Exhale powerfully again by drawing your navel point in. The inhales and exhales are relatively short, producing a fast breath. You are not inhaling all the way to the bottom of your lungs as in Three-Part Breath or Long Deep Breathing. Simply allow the air to flow in by releasing your belly after your powerful exhale. Start slowly at first until you get a rhythm, then you can gradually increase your pace until you feel like you have found the rhythm for you. You can build toward doing about 2 to 3 cycles of breath per second. You can start doing Breath of Fire for 1 minute and build up to 3, 7, 11, or even 31 minutes.

Congratulations, you have discovered one of the greatest tools to take control of your mind and your life: your breath. This is one of the most important lessons of Recovery 2.0.

APPENDIX B:
KUNDALINI YOGA SETS
AND MEDITATIONS

I have listed a few of my favorite Kundalini sets and meditations here. These yoga sets, known as *kriyas,* and the meditations were passed on to us by Yogi Bhajan, who masterfully presented them to address certain needs in the physical and/or energy bodies. Kriyas are generally designed to energize your body, center you, and balance and strengthen your nervous and endocrine systems.

I have written here why I chose these particular sets and describe some of the benefits they offer.

To practice these sets along with me, visit **tommyrosen.com** where you will find Kundalini Yoga and meditation videos in my video library.

TUNING IN . . .

Before practicing Kundalini kriyas or meditations, please take a moment to tune in by chanting the following mantra 3 times: *Ong Namo, Guru Dev Namo.* It means: I bow to the Divine spark

---

* To hear a recording of this mantra so that you know how to chant it correctly, please visit tommyrosen.com.

in all things. I bow to these Divine teachings, which take us from darkness into light.

This sacred mantra sets the space for what is to come. It puts us in the right energy to participate in these wonderful teachings. By chanting this, we honor all the yogis, saints, and sages who have come before us.

KUNDALINI YOGA KRIYAS

The Basic Spinal Energizer Series

As the yogis say, "You are only as old as your spine." No matter what your actual age, you will always be able to remain young if you keep a healthy spine. This kriya is accessible to almost anyone and profound in its effect. This was the most important kriya that Guruprem turned me on to in order to heal my back, but it will prove strengthening and invigorating to all who practice it, whether they struggle with back issues or not. I think of this set as a morning constitutional. It takes about 30 minutes to do, and it will turn on your central nervous system by getting energy to flow along the spinal energy channel. It will activate and balance your endocrine system, tone your lungs, and put you in position to have an outstanding day.

The Healthy Bowel System

This is a powerful series that will twist the issues out of your tissues and help you to maintain healthy digestion. It will detoxify and strengthen your organs through contraction and release and powerful breath work. People who practice this set develop the ability to let go of that which no longer serves them physically and emotionally. I've included this set to emphasize the importance of healthy digestion and the removal of waste. Try this every day for 40 days, and you will note some pretty significant changes.

The Nabhi Kriya for Prana-Apana

This is an excellent kriya that focuses on the navel point and the heart. It will strengthen you and is also great for digestion. The mixing of prana (nourishing energy) with apana (eliminating energy) at the navel point is a key practice in Kundalini Yoga whereby one's potential is unlocked. Hence, this kriya really gets right to the core of the practice. It has elevating properties, combats mild depression, and is deeply healing.

Surya Kriya

Surya is the Sanskrit word for sun. Here we will be invoking that expansive, action-oriented energy. This is one of my favorite kriyas, and it really never fails to deliver. It is also relatively short. You can do it in about 30 minutes. In the beginning, you will practice a brief pranayama (breath control) exercise, then you will use one of my favorite mantras: *Sat Nam*, Truth is my identity. It ends with a meditation that brings me into deep connection with my Higher Power. This is one of those kriyas that gives me a powerful sense of something beyond the physical. They all do this to some extent, but Surya Kriya is something special. You will not want to miss out on it.

KUNDALINI YOGA MEDITATIONS AND PRANAYAMA

The Basic Breath Series

This basic series of breath exercises will elevate you to the point where you can begin to direct your own mind. First, by controlling your breath you will come to experience the differences that are caused by breathing through one nostril versus another. This is where you begin to develop your capacity to go more deeply into meditation and to change your emotional state. As an aside, breathing in and out through the left nostril only is a calming breath and can be effective against cravings. This is a series you might try doing every day for a while. The changes that it brings in your overall consciousness and health are profound. Such is the power of conscious breathing.

The Meditation to Remove Stress and Clear Past Emotions

This is my go-to meditation when I need to calm and center myself. It establishes a steady 5-5-5 breath rhythm and sends a signal to your mind-body system that all core needs are being met. For this reason, I consider it to be one of the more important meditations for people in recovery from addiction. It is easy to do, and its effects cannot be denied. Start with 5 minutes. You won't need more to feel it, but build your way gradually up to 11 minutes to reap the full benefits this practice has to offer.

The Learning to Meditate Meditation

Excellent for beginners and accessible to all, this is an example of a meditation that uses an internal mantra, *Sat Nam* (Truth is my identity). Your eyes will be closed, and with your right hand you will be sensing the pulse on your left wrist. While this may seem rudimentary and simple, make no mistake, this is a profound meditation that can calm even the most scattered mind.

Please remember that you can find videos of all these practices at **tommyrosen.com.**

APPENDIX C: BUILDING YOUR OWN SPIRITUAL PRACTICE (SADHANA)

I want to make it super easy for you to build and start a spiritual practice that hopefully will become a part of your wake-up routine each day.

Step 1: Choose a length of time that works for your life.

Way too often I hear the story of the gung-ho seeker who takes up a 2-hour sadhana practice right off the bat only to back down three days later wondering where their resolve went. To begin to build a sadhana practice, choose a length of time that you know you can handle and create the conditions for success to take place. Some people start with a 5-minute meditation and build from there. Others choose a set of yoga they love that takes 15 to 30 minutes, and that becomes the central pillar of their practice. You have to start somewhere and take small steps for the rest of your life.

Step 2: Choose the elements that serve you the best.

You can choose from different forms of yoga, meditation, pranayama, and chanting. The main point is to choose a practice that centers you, strengthens you, and connects you to the Truth in you that becomes obscured as soon as your thoughts and the day get some momentum.

Step 3: Make a commitment to do this for 40 days and then review.

Try the same sadhana each day for 40 days, which is the length of time yogis believe it takes to establish a new habit. It is powerful to get into a routine and to see how you grow through the process over time. People who struggle with addiction often struggle with routine. Doing something (other than drugs) for 40 days can be unthinkable to a newly sober person. Yet, once you achieve this, the feeling is amazing.

After 40 days, decide whether you want to continue with this sadhana, add to it, or build a new one from scratch.

Here are five sadhana options for you. Try these or build your own.

SADHANA #1

Length of Time: approximately 12 minutes
Elements: Pranayama and Meditation

a) Tune in with *Ong Namo, Guru Dev Namo.* (2 minutes)
b) Three-Part Breath (pages 274–277) (3 minutes)
c) Long Deep Breathing (page 277) (3 minutes)
d) Ego Eradicator* with Breath of Fire (pages 277–278) (3 minutes)
e) End by chanting one long *Sat* followed by a short *Nam* on one breath.

---

*   Visit tommyrosen.com to learn Ego Eradicator.

SADHANA #2

Length of Time: approximately 15 minutes
Elements: Vinyasa Yoga and Meditation

a) Tune in with a mantra of your choice, such as 3 *Oms.*[*] (2 minutes)

b) 5 Sun Salutations,[**] which in Sanskrit are called *Surya Namaskar.* (5 minutes)

c) Long Deep Breathing (page 277) (5 minutes)

d) Lie down on your back and completely relax with your arms extended down near the sides of your body with your palms face up. This is called corpse pose, or *savasana* in Sanskrit. (3 minutes)

e) End by chanting one long *Sat* followed by a short *Nam* on one breath.

SADHANA #3

Length of Time: approximately 30 minutes
Elements: Kundalini Yoga and Meditation

a) Tune in with *Ong Namo, Guru Dev Namo.* (2 minutes)

b) Surya Kriya (page 281) (26–30 minutes, including meditation at the end of the kriya)

c) End by chanting one long *Sat* followed by a short *Nam* on one breath.

---

[*] Visit tommyrosen.com to learn how to chant *om*.

[**] To learn and practice Sun Salutations, visit tommyrosen.com.

SADHANA #4

Length of Time: approximately 45 minutes
Elements: Kundalini Yoga and Meditation

a) Tune in with *Ong Namo, Guru Dev Namo.* (2 minutes)
b) The Basic Spinal Energizer Series (page 280) (30 minutes)
c) Savasana (5 minutes)
d) The Meditation to Remove Stress and Clear Past Emotions (page 282) (3–11 minutes)
e) End by chanting one long *Sat* followed by a short *Nam* on one breath.

SADHANA #5

Length of Time: approximately 60 minutes
Elements: Pranayama and Meditation

a) Tune in with *Ong Namo, Guru Dev Namo.* (2 minutes)
b) The Basic Breath Series (pages 281–282) (20 minutes)
c) The Nabhi Kriya for Prana-Apana (page 281) (30 minutes, including 5-minute meditation at end)
d) Savasana (5 minutes)
e) Sing "The Long Time Sun" song.* (2–4 minutes)

---

*   There are many versions of "The Long Time Sun." Two of my favorites are by Aykanna (aykanna.com) and Snatam Kaur (snatamkaur.com).

APPENDIX D:
IMPORTANT RESOURCES
FOR YOUR LIFE AND
RECOVERY

I wanted to provide you with the best ways of connecting with Recovery 2.0, me, and the Recovery 2.0 Conference presenters to date whose work is worth looking into. You will also find important recovery resources such as 12-Step fellowship contact information, alternative 12-Step approaches, and yoga resources. If you are looking for something that is not here and that you cannot find, please feel free to drop me an e-mail at info@recovery2point0.com.

CONNECTING WITH TOMMY ROSEN AND RECOVERY 2.0

My Website: tommyrosen.com

Recovery 2.0 Website: recovery2point0.com

Recovery 2.0 Retreats and Workshops: recovery2point0.com /retreats

Recovery 2.0 DVDs: The two DVDs in my Yoga, Addiction, Recovery series, *Strong Body, Calm Mind* and *Full Body Tune-Up,* are

available for purchase on my website at tommyrosen.com/yoga
/store.

Recovery 2.0 Power Hour on InTheRooms.com: Join me live
(often with guests) every Tuesday evening at 10 P.M. EST on
InTheRooms.com for an interactive hour of recovery and yoga
philosophy, sharing, and community.

YouTube: youtube.com/user/tommyrosen

Facebook:

- **Tommy Rosen:** facebook.com/tommyrosen31
- **Tommy Rosen Yoga:** facebook.com
/TommyRosenYoga
- **Recovery 2.0:** facebook.com/Recovery2point0

Twitter:

- **Tommy Rosen:** twitter.com/tommyrosen
- **Recovery2.0:** twitter.com/recovery2point0

RECOVERY 2.0 CONFERENCE FACULTY

The following list of names consists of all the people who have
presented their ideas at the Recovery 2.0 Conferences through
May 2014. These people are *all* doing extraordinary work in the
world. Their energies have gone toward the betterment of humanity, and I am grateful to each of them for presenting at Recovery
2.0. Look into their work and you will find a treasure trove of personal growth opportunities.

Dr. Bruce Alexander
Angeles Arrien
Beverly Berg
Gabrielle Bernstein
Sir Richard Branson
Yogi Cameron
David Crow
Krishna Das
Ram Dass
Anna David
Jackie Dumaine
John Dupuy
Daniel Frigo
Aruni Futuronsky
Sherry Gaba
Rolf Gates
Trudy Goodman
Chris Grosso
Elisa Hallerman
Christine Hassler
Kyczy Hawk
Tom Hill
Fred Holmquist
Jamie Huysman
Brenda Iliff
Akahdahmah Jackson
Sukhdev Jackson
Robert Jameson
Herbert Kaighan
Sat Dharam Kaur
Gurmukh Khalsa
Gurucharan Khalsa
Guruprem Khalsa
Guru Singh Khalsa
Mukta Kaur Khalsa
Elizabeth Kipp

Mastin Kipp
Christopher Kennedy Lawford
Durga Leela
Noah Levine
Dr. Marc Lewis
Karen Lindsay
Darren Littlejohn
Mark Anthony Lord
Rainbeau Mars
Dr. Gabor Maté
Jennifer McLean
Anand Mehrotra
Jerry Moe
Jamison Monroe
Nikki Myers
Nick Ortner
Lissa Rankin
Chelsea Roff
Buster Ross
Dr. Howard Samuels
Dr. Marv Seppala
Debra Silverman
Shivanter Singh
Scott Strode
Radhanath Swami
Ron Tannenbaum and Kenny
    Pomerantz
Ashley Turner
Jai Uttal
Julian Walker
Tim Walsh
Arnie Wexler
Greg Williams
Marianne Williamson
David Wolfe

12-STEP FELLOWSHIPS

You can find helpful information about the 12 Steps in Part II of this book. The 12-Step fellowships offer the most widespread solution for people seeking recovery from addiction. Here is the contact information for several of the primary ones. If you are looking for something you cannot find here, simply Google and you will find it.

The process is easy to follow: Find and attend a meeting. Connect with others who are overcoming or have overcome similar issues you are facing. Find a sponsor. Work through the 12 Steps. Live an extraordinary life.

Alcoholics Anonymous: aa.org

Narcotics Anonymous: na.org

Overeaters Anonymous: oa.org

Sex and Love Addicts Anonymous: slaafws.org

Al-Anon: (offering support for friends and families of people who struggle with addictions) al-anon.alateen.org

CoDependents Anonymous: (offering support for people who are seeking healthy relationships) coda.org

Adult Children of Alcoholics: (supporting people who grew up in alcoholic or otherwise dysfunctional homes) adultchildren.org

Gamblers Anonymous: gamblersanonymous.org

Debtors Anonymous: (Supporting people who habitually and addictively end up in debt) debtorsanonymous.org

ALTERNATIVE RECOVERY PROGRAMS

The Yoga of 12-Step Recovery (Y12SR) (y12sr.com) Nikki Myers' Yoga of 12-Step Recovery combines the practice of yoga with the

12 Steps. Y12SR offers an integrated approach to recovery, which includes universal 12-Step meetings (meaning all addictions are welcome in the same meeting) followed by a yoga practice. This format of meeting is catching on like wildfire. There are more than 100 Y12SR meetings that regularly meet across the U.S. I believe we will soon see Y12SR meetings everywhere across the country. Nikki offers 2 regular trainings—the Intensive and the Leadership Training—to teach people how to use the 12 Steps, yoga, and meditation together in the treatment of addictions of all kinds. This is an outstanding resource. If it calls to you, take advantage of it right away.

Refuge Recovery and Against the Stream (refugerecovery.org and againstthestream.org) Noah Levine's Refuge Recovery offers a nontheistic, Buddhist approach to Recovery. "Refuge Recovery is a community of people who are using the practices of mindfulness, compassion, forgiveness, and generosity to heal the pain and suffering that addiction has caused in our lives and the lives of our loved ones. The path of practice that we follow is called the Four Truths of Refuge Recovery."[1]

Noah offers something powerful and community-based that works and is growing. This is a much-needed resource for atheists and agnostics as well as anyone who simply prefers to follow the teachings of Buddha as their path of recovery. There are regular Refuge Recovery meetings in Los Angeles, which are very well attended by a growing community of people who are split 50-50 between people who also practice the 12-Steps and those whose recovery path is based solely on Buddhist practice and meditation. Also check out Against the Stream, which is the Buddhist teaching that Noah and other teachers are doing. Very powerful and uplifting.

SMART Recovery (smartrecovery.org) While I have no direct experience with SMART Recovery, I feel compelled to include it here because it offers a popular alternative to the 12-Step path. The fact that it stresses self-reliance and self-empowerment makes it markedly different from the 12-Step approach. I have heard good things, though, about their program, so in the spirit of "there is no one way," SMART Recovery appears to have provided a solution for some people.

InTheRooms (intherooms.com) InTheRooms (ITR) is an online social network for people in recovery as well as their families. I consider it to be one of the greatest uses of technology there is. As I am writing this, they have more than 307,000 members who share their experiences, strength, and hope with each other through live, interactive video meetings, personal profiles, direct messaging, and participation in a variety of recovery-related groups. I think it is important to get out to meetings and connect with people as much as you can, but I also see the immense value that ITR provides. If you are housebound, infirmed, sick, tired, nervous about connecting face-to-face, or enjoy having a meeting from home, ITR has you covered. Another amazing perk to online meetings is the ability to connect in real time with an international contingency of people in recovery from addiction. It is the coolest thing to "attend" an ITR meeting and hear from people from all over the world. Every Tuesday night at 10 P.M. EST, I host a live show/meeting on ITR called The Recovery 2.0 Power Hour. I have guests on my show from Recovery 2.0 Conferences, and we cover a variety of topics related to thriving in life as a recovering person. It is one of my most eagerly anticipated hours of the week, and I encourage you to come join us.

YOGA RESOURCES

Kundalini Yoga Resources

The Healthy, Happy, Holy Organization (3HO) (3ho.org) This nonprofit organization was set up by Yogi Bhajan to serve the worldwide Kundalini Yoga community. Among many other services they provide, each year they put on the Summer Solstice

Sadhana event in New Mexico and the Winter Solstice event in Florida.

The Kundalini Research Institute (KRI) (kundaliniresearch institute.org) This nonprofit focuses on training, accreditation, research, and publishing related to the science and technology of Kundalini Yoga.

The Library of Teachings (libraryofteachings.com) The Library of Teachings is a highly valuable, searchable archive of Yogi Bhajan's published lectures and kriyas.

Spirit Voyage (spiritvoyage.com) Spirit Voyage serves the worldwide Kundalini Yoga community by selling music, books, clothing, and accessories. Since music and mantra play such a major part in Kundalini Yoga, the role of Spirit Voyage cannot be overstated. Check them out.

Free Online Yoga Classes

Tommyrosen.com: Please visit my website to find a variety of recovery-specific yoga classes, meditations, and teachings. I am always adding more content to the site, so check in often. It is my intention to provide precisely what you need. If there is something you seek that is not there, drop me an e-mail through the website, and I'll do my best to add it.

YouTube.com: There is a lot of yoga online. Depending on what you are looking for, you can search and find almost anything on YouTube. Please check out and subscribe to my YouTube Channel: www.youtube.com/user/tommyrosen.

Online Yoga Subscription Services

Each of the following subscription services is doing a good job. They have different teachers, different nuances, and a different look and feel. My suggestion is to check out a free trial and see what and who speaks to you. The most important thing is to start a practice and build it over time. These services can help especially if you live in a place where you do not have access to well-trained, experienced teachers, if you prefer to practice at home sometimes, and/or if you are traveling.

MyYogaOnline.com/GaiamTV.com: These companies have merged and brought together two excellent libraries of yoga and wellness content with a wide variety of styles and excellent teachers to choose from. They both feature several videos of mine, including The Breakfast of Champions set, which is a lot of fun.

Yogaglo.com: Yogaglo offers access to a highly vetted group of yoga teachers whose content is available exclusively here. My wife, Kia Miller, has about 80 Kundalini Yoga classes on Yogaglo, making it an excellent resource. You will also find other outstanding teachers and a variety of classes all shot in the same sleek, beautiful style.

YogaVibes.com/Yoga Journal: YogaVibes recently merged with *Yoga Journal* and also offers a wonderful array of yoga classes of varying style and difficulty.

Yoga Media Resources

Yoga International Magazine: This is one of the most sophisticated and well-written magazines covering the history, ethics, practice, and lifestyle of yoga. Put out by the Himalayan Institute, this quarterly publication is packed with information and inspiration.

Yoga Journal: *Yoga Journal* has played a central role in the spread of yoga throughout the United States for nearly 40 years. Check out their tips and information about sequences and specific poses.

LA Yoga Magazine: While this is a Los Angeles–based publication, it is consistently so well done that I have to include it here. One of the goals of *LA Yoga* is to bridge the gap between physical yoga practice and the ancient art of living known in Sanskrit as *Ayurveda*. This sets it apart from other rags. Though its distribution is within the greater Los Angeles area, you can order *LA Yoga* to be mailed to your home, wherever it may be.

Mantra: Yoga and Health Magazine: This is a relatively new magazine that deserves mention because of the candid and powerful way it chronicles the lives of yogis across the world and the lifestyle that accompanies the pursuit of consciousness.

ENDNOTES

Chapter 1

1. United Nations Office for Drug Control and Crime Prevention, "Economic and Social Consequences of Drug Abuse and Illicit Trafficking." New York: UNODCCP, 1998, p. 3.

2. Excerpt from "Codependency," a talk given by Nikki Myers at Kripalu Center for Yoga & Health on May 29, 2014.

Chapter 2

1. Gretchen Cuda-Kroen, "Baby's Palate and Food Memories Shaped Before Birth," NPR (August 8, 2011): www.npr.org/2011/08/08/139033757/babys -palate-and-food-memories-shaped-before-birth.

2. "Gabor Maté: Why We're a Culture of Addicts," *Spirituality & Health:* spiritualityhealth.com/articles/gabor-mat%C3%A9-why-were-culture-addicts.

3. Peter Levine, Ph.D., "The Body as Healer: A Revisioning of Trauma and Anxiety." In Maxine Sheets-Johnstone, ed., *Giving the Body Its Due*. Albany, NY: State University of New York Press, 1992. www.traumahealing.com/ somatic-experiencing/reference-trauma-and-anxiety-giving-the-body-its -due.pdf.

Chapter 4

1. "Comes a Time" by Jerry Garcia and Robert Hunter. Copyright © 1976 Ice Nine Music Publishing Company, Inc. All rights reserved. Administered by Universal Music Corp. (ASCAP)

Chapter 5

1. *Alcoholics Anonymous: The Big Book,* 4th ed. Alcoholics Anonymous World Services, Inc., 2001.

Chapter 8

1. *Alcoholics Anonymous: The Big Book,* p. 45.

2. Ibid., p. 64.

3. Ibid., p. 65.

4. Ibid., pp. 83–84.

5. Ibid., p. 87.

6. Ibid.

7. Ibid., p. 88.

Chapter 15

1. B. K. S. Iyengar, *Light on The Yoga Sutras of Patanjali.* London: Thorsons, 2002.

Chapter 17

1. Excerpt from Anand Mehrotra interview at Recovery 2.0 Conference, September 2013.

2. Swami Rama, *The Art of Joyful Living.* Honesdale, PA: Himalayan Institute Press, 1989.

Chapter 18

1. David Wolfe, interview at Recovery 2.0 Conference, September 2013.

2. Raluca Schachter, "Shocking Statistics About Sugar Consumption: You Have to See It to Believe It," Guide2Health (October 25, 2012): www.guide2health .net/2012/10/shocking-statistics-about-sugar-consumption.

Conclusion

1. Excerpt from Dr. Martin Luther King, Jr.'s speech "A Christmas Sermon on Peace," 1967.

Appendix D

1. Refuge Recovery: www.againstthestream.org/community/buddhist-recovery.

ABOUT THE AUTHOR

Tommy Rosen is the founder and host of the Recovery 2.0: Beyond Addiction Online Conference Series and presents workshops annually at Esalen in Big Sur, California, and the Kripalu Center for Yoga & Health in Stockbridge, Massachusetts, as well as at many festivals and conferences. One of the pioneers in the burgeoning field of yoga and recovery, he holds advanced certifications in both Hatha and Kundalini Yoga and has 23 years of continuous recovery from acute drug addiction. Tommy and his wife, noted yoga instructor Kia Miller, live in Venice, California, where they teach yoga and grow organic vegetables in their backyard. Website: www.tommyrosen.com.

We hope you enjoyed this Hay House book. If you'd like to receive our online catalog featuring additional information on Hay House books and products, or if you'd like to find out more about the Hay Foundation, please contact:

Hay House, Inc., P.O. Box 5100, Carlsbad, CA 92018-5100
(760) 431-7695 or (800) 654-5126
(760) 431-6948 (fax) or (800) 650-5115 (fax)
www.hayhouse.com® • www.hayfoundation.org

◎ ◎ ◎

Published and distributed in Australia by:
Hay House Australia Pty. Ltd., 18/36 Ralph St., Alexandria NSW 2015
Phone: 612-9669-4299 • *Fax:* 612-9669-4144 • www.hayhouse.com.au

Published and distributed in the United Kingdom by:
Hay House UK, Ltd., Astley House, 33 Notting Hill Gate, London W11 3JQ
Phone: 44-20-3675-2450 • *Fax:* 44-20-3675-2451 • www.hayhouse.co.uk

Published and distributed in the Republic of South Africa by:
Hay House SA (Pty), Ltd., P.O. Box 990, Witkoppen 2068
Phone/Fax: 27-11-467-8904 • www.hayhouse.co.za

Published in India by: Hay House Publishers India,
Muskaan Complex, Plot No. 3, B-2, Vasant Kunj, New Delhi 110 070
Phone: 91-11-4176-1620 • *Fax:* 91-11-4176-1630 • www.hayhouse.co.in

Distributed in Canada by:
Raincoast Books, 2440 Viking Way, Richmond, B.C. V6V 1N2
Phone: 1-800-663-5714 • *Fax:* 1-800-565-3770 • www.raincoast.com

◎ ◎ ◎

Take Your Soul on a Vacation

Visit www.HealYourLife.com® to regroup, recharge, and reconnect with your own magnificence. Featuring blogs, mind-body-spirit news, and life-changing wisdom from Louise Hay and friends.

Visit www.HealYourLife.com today!